The LAND of FLICKERING LIGHTS

RESTORING AMERICA IN AN AGE OF BROKEN POLITICS

MICHAEL BENNET

Atlantic Monthly Press
New York

FIRST EDITION

Published simultaneously in Canada
Printed in the United States of America

First Grove Atlantic hardcover edition: June 2019

Library of Congress Cataloging-in-Publication data is available for this title.

ISBN 978-0-8021-4781-3
eISBN 978-0-8021-4782-0

Atlantic Monthly Press
an imprint of Grove Atlantic
154 West 14th Street
New York, NY 10011

Distributed by Publishers Group West

groveatlantic.com

19 20 21 22   10 9 8 7 6 5 4 3 2 1

For Susan, Caroline, Halina, and Anne,
with all my love

CONTENTS

PROLOGUE

On the thirty-fifth day of the longest government shutdown in American history, I rose on the Senate floor to protest. As much as against the shutdown itself, I lashed out against the inaction that has seized our government throughout the last decade. The vast majority of Americans elect representatives to Washington in the hope that their representatives will do something useful on their behalf. Of course, they know this work involves argument and even principled disagreement, but most Americans, along with most members of Congress, would expect this disagreement at some point to give way to the work of governing a nation. The last decade, however, has seen our politics break down, and the American people become increasingly disgusted with the inability of the two parties to collaborate in the country's best interest.

The five stories told in these pages are not ones parents would tell their children if they wanted them to be proud of America's federal government. Civics teachers will not turn to them for lessons on how our republic *ought* to work. These stories will not form the basis for a book about what John F. Kennedy called "the most admirable of human virtues—courage."

Bipartisan ineptitude, laziness, and an absence of vision gave loose rein to a small minority—mainly the Tea Party and, later, the Freedom Caucus, along with their wealthy backers—who turned American political processes against themselves. That small minority simultaneously demanded untenable policies and broke down public confidence in our government. After establishing one-party rule in 2016, that same minority set about making a new order that few Americans could imagine and none had asked for: a budget that spends money we do not have and expects our children to repay; a tax cut for the rich that widens economic inequality and steals opportunity from the vast majority of Americans; a foreign policy that drops our proud tradition of encouraging democracy and trade in order to start trade wars with our allies and play patsy to dictators; an approach to the environment that welcomes polluters and banishes the scientific community; a rush to fill seats in the federal courts, including the Supreme Court, with judges of partisan political orientation and often of questionable legal qualifications; an immigration policy that forces millions to live and work in a permanent, shadowy underclass while turning our border into an international symbol of nativist hostility.

From the country's unexpected beginnings in the eighteenth century, Americans built a nation on the high expectation that as a people we could govern ourselves better than any tyrant could govern us. These aspirations to self-government take many forms. They include our elections and the many offices in our three branches of government as well as our shared rights and obligations as citizens. They include our commitment to pluralism, democracy, and the rule of law. They include our most cherished beliefs: that we are created equal; that our rights to life, liberty, and the pursuit of happiness are inalienable; and that it is our collective obligation to seek a more perfect union. We have never fully realized these aspirations, and more than once we have betrayed them. They remain, however, the constellation that guides us to a better place. When we have lost our course, we searched them out. When we found them, we trued ourselves up to a better way. Our finest moments as a nation form a story of citizens who challenge themselves and their country to live up to the high expectations self-government requires.

If we imagine Americans whose political awareness began in 2010, the stories told here illustrate the only political conditions they know. For those in their twenties who may have missed out on a serious American history class, Washington politics look like those of a nation slouching toward despair, dysfunction, maybe even despotism. With every month that goes by, it becomes more difficult to remember an American government that functioned in any other way. As a people, we deserve to know that in the United States there once were—and still can be—better courses.

It is easy for the burden of present circumstance to convince us that we are in a dark hour. But we must also be honest enough to admit that as a nation we have faced challenges greater than this. We are not at our radios after the Pearl Harbor attack, on December 7, 1941, hoping that President Roosevelt might help us see our way through to the conclusion of yet another world war. We are not enslaved as human beings or enslaving other human beings. We are not now, as Native Americans have been, dispossessed of our homelands, subjected to serial broken promises, and only then offered the right to be citizens. We are not in the throes of civil war or torn apart by armed partisans and lynch mobs trying to roll back the progress of Reconstruction. Rather, we are, as we have been many times before, at political loggerheads and wondering, rightly, what we can do to emerge as a stronger union.

I think often about the words of James Baldwin, written deep in the crisis years of the American civil rights movement: "And here we are, at the center of the arc, trapped in the gaudiest, most valuable, and most improbable water wheel the world has ever seen. Everything now, we must assume, is in our hands; we have no right to assume otherwise."

Yes, everything now is in our hands.

—*MFB*
Denver, Colorado
January 2019

THE
ACCIDENTAL SENATOR

How I got into this—and why I stay.

I. "Disenthrall Ourselves"

It seems like a trick question: what does the Constitution of the United States of America have to say about politics? The answer is that it has nothing to say about politics, at least not in the sense we throw the word around today. The Constitution and its twenty-seven amendments contain 7,591 words. The word "politics" does not appear once.

The Constitution has a lot to say, however, about the purpose of the American republic and the responsibilities of its citizens. Look no further than the preamble. It reminds us that those who proposed and ratified the Constitution did so for specific reasons: "To form a more perfect Union, establish Justice, insure domestic Tranquility, provide for the common defence, promote the general Welfare, and secure the Blessings of Liberty to ourselves and our Posterity."

The Constitution is a document centrally concerned with accomplishing certain objectives and with the procedures we should follow to achieve them in a fair and orderly manner. It is not about a partisan game of capture the flag. It is not about spin. It is about *doing things*, which is something Americans have always seen as a national characteristic. We are a can-do people. Isn't that what we tell ourselves? The Constitution may not contain the word "politics," but it contains plenty of terms like "governing," "do business," "perform," and "provide for"—all of them having to do with accomplishing tasks that serve the public good. We commonly refer to the president as the chief executive—"executive" is another term found in the Constitution—but we tend to gloss over its meaning. Whatever else the president's duties are, a chief executive is a person who oversees, who manages. In his Farewell Address, George Washington emphasized the need to get things done. This, he believed, must be our North Star. The alternative was a civic culture that would spiral into excessive factionalism, which, in today's terms, means permanent partisan warfare fueled by narrow interests and big money.[1]

It is a commonplace now in America that political campaigns never end. The less frequently noted corollary to that observation is that governing never begins. We have forgotten how to actually run the country. We have forgotten that honest deliberation between people with different points of view leads to better decisions than rule by one person or one party. Decoupled from any desire to govern, our politics has lost its purpose.

At a moment like this—if you find yourself tilting toward one end of the ideological spectrum or the other—you would be

---

1 The original founders foresaw that keeping factionalism under control would be a central challenge. In "Federalist No. 10," James Madison defined "faction" as "a number of citizens, whether amounting to a majority or a minority of the whole, who are united and actuated by some common impulse of passion, or of interest, adverse to the rights of other citizens, or to the permanent and aggregate interests of the community." Sound familiar?

forgiven for thinking that the worst thing you could possibly do is let down your partisan guard. A sucker's bet if ever there was one. The other side will never join you in good faith. You'll be taken for a ride. Besides, there's no point in seeking agreement with the other side because its red-faced undemocratic faction will never allow you to reach one. As citizens, when we reach this point in our thinking, we reach the point of greatest vulnerability. To believe that we can counter the threat of some bad version of one-party rule only by replacing it with a preferred version of one-party rule is to be charmed out of the very pluralism we must protect: the idea that we draw strength from difference and wisdom from honest debate.

Is it naive to believe that at this moment in American history we can restore public trust in our republic? Is it naive to believe that elected officials can live up to the high expectations of that trust? Some may think so. But it's a pipe dream to believe we can move forward as a nation without devotion to the historic ideals that have offered us a path to address our problems in the past and can do so now.

In today's Washington, our politics have emptied themselves of imagination, integrity, and efficacy. Politics do little except generate more politics. Yet politics are beguiling. They are a strange force, simultaneously repulsive and seductive. Luring us with flattery and outrage, they flood our cable channels and social media feeds with opposing fronts of hyperbole—a never-ending series of melodramatic episodes with their penny-ante villains and heroes. We find ourselves spellbound by a face-off between mutually exclusive and untenable positions.

Under these circumstances, our first duty, as Abraham Lincoln advised, is to "disenthrall ourselves"—to snap the spell of dogmatic and useless commitments and remodel our politics for our uniquely stormy present. We should ask ourselves whether the repetition of last night's talking points on cable TV has any chance of educating our children, providing affordable health care to more Americans, securing our economic future, or defining America's role around the globe.

We need to remind ourselves that the real work of politics—in its best and highest sense—is not merely about disagreement. It is not about slaying the dragons of some demagogue's invention. It is about our families and our neighbors and the quality of their personal and civic lives. *Our families and our neighbors*: whether they are down the street, on the other side of the country, or yet to be born.

This book is partly about how we disenthrall ourselves and partly about our neighbors in the largest sense of that term. It is about where we went wrong and how we can become citizens again. This book is not a memoir. I couldn't bear to read such a thing, much less expect you to. But in the following few pages I share a little of my personal story just to give you a sense of where I came from and how I got here—not to the United States Senate, but to seeing things as I do.

II. Pioneers

In 2008, when my life took an unexpected turn, my immediate neighbors were the people of Denver, Colorado. I had lived in the city since 1997, and after a number of years in the private sector reorganizing distressed companies, in 2003 I became chief of staff to Denver's mayor, John Hickenlooper. Shortly thereafter the board of education selected me to become the superintendent of Denver's public schools, a job that brought me face-to-face with

America. Five years later, Barack Obama was elected president, and he soon nominated Ken Salazar, one of Colorado's senators, as secretary of the interior. This created a vacancy, and to my surprise Governor Bill Ritter appointed me to fill it. I had never run for office. Polls pegged my name recognition in Colorado at 3 percent. And my Rolodex—yes, I still used one of those—consisted of people I had met in business and education. My circle of neighbors was about to expand very quickly.

To say the least, I was not an obvious choice. A national political website greeted the news of my appointment with the encouraging headline: WTF?!! Colorado's Republican Party chairman derisively referred to me as "the accidental senator." He could not have been more right. I was not a native of Colorado; in fact, I was born in New Delhi, India, and grew up in Washington, DC.[2] None of this made for the kind of origin story that would carry much weight as I prepared to run for a full six-year term in 2010.

The truth is, though, that having an unusual background is not unusual for an American. When my second-grade class was asked to line up in order of whose family had arrived most recently and whose had been in America the longest, I turned out to be the answer to both questions. In their very different ways and for very different reasons both strands of my family were pioneering. My mom, Susanne Klejman, and her parents, John (once Jakób) and Halina, were Polish Jews who survived the Holocaust. They were split up during the Nazi invasion of Poland. My mom was sent out to a village in the countryside to live with a nurse, my grandmother

---

2 The only time my birthplace has been a political asset was when I traveled to India with my close friend in the Senate, Mark Warner, from Virginia. In every meeting, when introducing our delegation, he would point out that "in the history of our republic, out of more than twenty-three hundred senators who have served, only one has been born in New Delhi." A very reliable applause line in New Delhi, Calcutta, and Hyderabad. Less so in Colorado.

lived as a Catholic in a convent, and my grandfather hid, among other places, in the cellar of the best-known candy maker in Poland. My mom learned that her own mother, my Babcia, was still alive only when she arrived (along with thirteen nuns who then went on to a convent that had escaped destruction) at the cottage where my mom was hiding. My grandfather found them together after the war's end. The reunited family lived for two years in Warsaw, then emigrated to Stockholm and Mexico City before arriving in New York in 1950.

My mom, then twelve, was the only member of the family who could speak English. She enrolled herself in the New York City public schools, eventually graduating from Hunter College High School. The three of them spoke Polish at home, but my brother, my sister, and I never learned more than a word or two of it. I have traveled widely throughout Colorado and our country, and I have never met anyone with a stronger accent than my grandparents'. They knew how lucky they had been to survive the Holocaust, but that luck was colored by the memories of all and everyone they had lost. By contrast, the luck of being Americans filled them with pure joy. They never once let my siblings and me lose sight of how fortunate we are. And they saw to it that we received the best education they could afford. They knew the difference their education had made in their lives and wanted to make sure the next generation shared in that treasure. As the beneficiary of their commitment, I have learned many things, but one is that every American child deserves the same advantages.

I was born in New Delhi because my dad, Doug Bennet, motivated by Kennedy-era idealism, had taken a job as an assistant to the US ambassador to India, Chester Bowles, a former Connecticut governor who had worked in Franklin D. Roosevelt's administration.

My dad grew up in Hamburg, Connecticut, a little river town. His side of the family could trace its lineage all the way back to Edward Fuller, who had arrived with more than a hundred other religious refugees on the *Mayflower*, in 1620.[3]

In 1964, the year I was born, Bowles was serving as ambassador for a second time, and he had attracted a number of young Americans, like my parents, who were committed to helping India develop its economic, educational, and agricultural systems. Along with Bowles and many other Americans, they believed this was an important moment during the history of the Cold War when the United States and the Soviet Union were jockeying for influence among Asian nations—India, in particular. They believed they were on the front line of President John F. Kennedy's effort to counter Soviet influence. Today, India is one of our closest friends, but the relationship still carries the strain of Cold War international politics.

My parents' experience in India persuaded my dad to pursue public service as a career. That led us to Washington in 1968, the year the city erupted in anger and flames in response to the assassination of Martin Luther King Jr. My dad became a speechwriter for Vice President Hubert Humphrey and then the administrative assistant for a young senator from Missouri, Tom Eagleton. Throughout my childhood, he held a number of jobs with increasing responsibilities—ultimately taking him outside government, to the presidency of Wesleyan University. My mom was a librarian at my elementary school and made sure my siblings and I always had a good book. (She continues to make book recommendations to her

---

3 Edward and his wife, whose name is not known, died during the first winter in Plymouth, but a son, who followed them from England later, survived. The descendants apparently include Georgia O'Keeffe, Larry Bird, and Amelia Earhart. I am possible proof that their accomplishments are not genetic in origin. My jump shot is even worse than my painting.

grandchildren.) I had a strong sense that what my parents did for a living was virtuous and worthwhile. I still do.

Looking back, well aware of the traumatic events of the era and taking nostalgia into account, I find plenty of evidence that in certain respects Washington worked better then than it does now. Richard Nixon ended America's involvement in the Vietnam War—not as fast as he might have, and the fighting of course continued—and he forged a new relationship with China. When Nixon repeatedly broke the law in the scandal wrapped up in the word "Watergate," investigative journalists discovered and laid out the facts and Republican and Democratic senators enforced the rule of law. Ronald Reagan passed bipartisan tax reform, reached historic deals on Social Security with Democratic Speaker Tip O'Neill and on nuclear weapons with the Soviets, and in partnership with other nations took steps that ultimately shrank the hole in the ozone layer.

Reagan's election mattered to me mostly because it meant my father lost his job running the Agency for International Development, but it also represented a sea change in Washington. Ever since the days of Franklin Roosevelt, Democrats had almost always held majorities in the House and Senate. Until Reagan's presidency, there had not been a Republican majority in either chamber since 1955, a quarter century earlier. Now the Senate was Republican, while the House remained Democratic for both of Reagan's terms. The Senate would flip again in the middle of his second term. In his inaugural address, Reagan famously declaimed: "Government is not the solution to our problem; government is the problem."

I left for college in the middle of Reagan's first term. I would graduate in the middle of his second, just before he turned the White House over to his vice president, George H. W. Bush. This was a lively time at Wesleyan University, as we protested against what many of us saw as a right-wing domestic and foreign policy agenda. Although many of us worried about Reagan's overall direction—his cuts to domestic spending and increases to defense spending—there was not a sense that he was destroying our republic. He had said in that same first inaugural address: "Now, so there will be no misunderstanding, it's not my intention to do away with government. It is rather to make it work—work with us, not over us; to stand by our side, not ride on our back."

Reagan had a strong, conservative point of view. That did not stop him from passing major pieces of bipartisan legislation, including the Kemp-Roth tax cut in 1981 (carried by a voice vote in the Senate); the 1982 extension of the Voting Rights Act for another twenty-five years (passed in the Senate by a bipartisan vote of 85–8); the Tax Reform Act of 1986 (passed in the Senate by a vote of 97 3); and the Immigration Reform and Control Act of 1986 (passed by a vote of 69–30). When Reagan's administration flouted the rule of law, as during the Iran-Contra affair, the Congress, the courts, and the press provided oversight. Reagan himself appointed the Tower Commission—two Republicans and one Democrat—to look into the matter. It produced a scathing report.

Still, in retrospect, it was clear by the 1990s that something noxious was spreading through the political system. Richard Nixon's "Southern strategy" had deliberately (and successfully) relied on racially infected messages aimed at white voters. Politicians of many stripes found that religious and cultural issues could be usefully divisive—and instantly lucrative. The advent of dark money and new media placed more power in the hands of ideologues and blowhards—two qualities that often went together. Some people in leadership, notably Newt Gingrich, the Speaker of the House through much of the 1990s, openly encouraged a politics of division. The result: two government shutdowns and one presidential impeachment.

Shortly after college, with George H. W. Bush in the White House, I moved to Columbus to work for Ohio governor Richard Celeste. I traveled with the governor all over the state. Even though he had been the head of the Peace Corps, Celeste had a very low regard for Washington—not because Republicans were now in charge (although that aggravated him) but because he believed that Washington suffered from "a bicoastal bias" that favored the states bordering the Atlantic and Pacific at the expense of the middle of the country. Today, Dick Celeste is one of my constituents in Colorado, and his views have not changed.[4]

I concluded that I should go back to school and learn a profession, and since the last math class I took was precalculus in high school (I earned a grade of 70, on the retake), I applied to law school and was accepted at Yale. After graduating, I hustled down a path similar to that of many young lawyers. I clerked for a judge, spent nine months at a private firm in Washington, and finally landed a job with Jamie Gorelick, then President Bill Clinton's deputy attorney general of the United States. Her talented staff was led by a former federal prosecutor, Merrick Garland.

By now, I had met and fallen in love with Susan Daggett, an environmental lawyer who had grown up in Marianna, a small Arkansas town in the Mississippi delta. Neither of us had an interest in staying in Washington. We both thought it would be an adventure to begin our marriage in a new place, and we traveled

---

4 Dick himself also has not changed. When Sherrod Brown, one of my favorite people in the Senate, was thinking once about running for governor of Ohio, Dick said to him: "See that chair over there? You have to be willing to eat that chair if you want to become governor of Ohio." As every Election Day approaches, Dick calls with a list of chairs I know I should be eating but would rather not. And I eat them.

around the country, visiting potential cities. We spent a wonderful, although uncharacteristically rainy, weekend in Denver. We knew no one there, and it felt wide open. Susan and I applied for jobs, and, naturally, she was hired first, by the Rocky Mountain office of Earthjustice (formerly the Sierra Club Legal Defense Fund). She would later lead that operation.

I had concluded by then that if I stayed in the law, I would become the world's worst lawyer. Unlike Susan, I was not inspired by the practice of law, even though I had had the great fortune to work with some of the smartest lawyers and most decent human beings in Washington, both in private practice and at the Department of Justice. If I could not be satisfied under those circumstances, it seemed to me it was time for me to think about what else I could do.

I sent two letters to Denver, the first to John Hickenlooper, a Wesleyan alumnus who had lost his job as a geologist in Denver and gone on to start one of the first brewpubs between Chicago and California. The second was to Philip Anschutz, an entrepreneur with interests in railroads, telecommunications, and energy. Only one of them called me back, and the next thing I knew I was on my way to meet Phil Anschutz.

I was waiting in Phil's reception room when he and his lieutenant, Craig Slater, arrived. They were wearing clothes from that morning's dove hunt on Phil's ranch. I had shot a gun only once and never killed a bird. We had a conversation, and within fifteen minutes I knew Phil was sold. I think he liked the idea of having someone from a Democratic administration—it upset preconceived notions of his politics. Slater would be harder to convince, for good reason. I confessed to him that I had never read a balance sheet or an income statement. Trying to be kind, Craig said sometimes people

are just good at math, even if they have no formal business training. I referred him to my shabby high school mathematics record.

Over the coming weeks we traded calls. I had the sense Craig
was dodging me, hoping I would give up. My wedding drew closer.
The prospect of showing up in Marianna, Arkansas, to marry Susan
without a job was not what I might have wished. Just in time,
Anschutz agreed to hire me. I would have to take some business
classes at night, and learn the fundamentals of how companies make
payroll. If it didn't work out after six months, he and Slater would
provide a recommendation to a Denver law firm.

During my first week, I joined a meeting my colleagues were
having with a group of investment bankers from New York. As the
hour wore on, I began to realize that I had no idea what anybody
was talking about. It was like listening to a foreign language. It
occurred to me at that moment that there was a vast aspect of
American society that I knew nothing about.

Three or four nights a week I went to class to study business
valuations and accounting (a class everyone, including every liberal
arts major, should take). I was charged out-of-state tuition, steep
even then. I did my homework at the student union on the Auraria
campus in Denver and ate Taco Bell for dinner. In time, I began to
understand something about an entirely new language, one involving balance sheets, income statements, and risk assessment.

Just before my six-month deadline, Craig and Phil assigned me
to study Forcenergy, a small, independent oil-and-gas company with
assets in the Gulf of Mexico and Alaska. For months, investment
bankers had been coming by our office to peddle equity deals in
oil and gas, but commodity prices had fallen so low that a sizable
number of companies were facing bankruptcy. In many of these
companies, the equity was now worthless. Forcenergy was one.

We did not trade debt. Phil Anschutz was interested only in making long-term investments. In general, we looked for well-run companies with terrible balance sheets. And it was important to us that once a company was in bankruptcy, we were able to get it out as fast as we reasonably could. A company in a long bankruptcy can become a wasting asset. We started buying Forcenergy's debt when oil was $11 a barrel. By the time the court approved our plan of reorganization, oil was at $18. Thanks to commodity prices I did not control (and never would), I was off to a good start.

The last transaction I worked on with Anschutz involved the bankruptcies of three different movie theater companies: Regal Cinemas, United Artists, and Edwards. Their owners, mostly private equity and hedge funds, had borrowed catastrophic sums of money to build stadium-seating theaters, prematurely cannibalizing existing locations, on the theory that as a result attendance would grow. It didn't. Cash flow per screen plummeted, and the companies' debt began to trade at distressed levels. In the end, we saved the companies by restructuring the $3 billion of debt the prior owners had borrowed into a manageable $450 million. We created what was then the largest movie exhibition company in the world—Regal Entertainment Group—and also built a new digital advertising business. My daughters often bemoan my small role in the latter when we are sitting through twenty minutes of commercials before a movie starts. I assure them it was worse when all you could see were static slides of boring trivia questions and ads for the local muffler shop. They remain unpersuaded.

Years later, when I became superintendent of the Denver Public Schools, critics would say ominously that I was going to try to "run it like a business." I would remind them that I had made my living helping buy distressed companies and getting them back on their feet, saving jobs and investments, and that I knew private institutions could fail just as public ones sometimes did. The years at Anschutz were a crash course in why some institutions succeed and others don't. As my years at Denver Public Schools later would do, my experience in business gave me a new, more tangible understanding of our economy and our democracy.

III. "Let the Public Proctology Begin"

I would soon draw upon that understanding, because John Hickenlooper, who was by then a friendly acquaintance (and returning my calls), asked if I would help him in his campaign for mayor of Denver. Now a real estate investor, successful restaurateur, and philanthropist, John had waged a winning effort to keep the words "Mile High" in the name of the Broncos stadium. Out of the eight or so candidates running for mayor that year, our polls had him starting the race in last place. Naturally, I was happy to help out.

John began making headway by stressing that his business experience could help Denver's battered economy grow. By now I knew how to build and analyze spreadsheets. In just a couple of hours in my friend David Kenney's office, I was able to see that the city's revenue projections were way off and that Denver faced a budget deficit. John knew that this finding, which Denver's then mayor, Wellington Webb, usefully later confirmed, gave him a great additional issue for his campaign.

As the campaign progressed, John took the lead in a field split among veterans of the city's Democratic Party leadership. When he won, he asked me to be his chief of staff. I helped John recruit a great cabinet, balance the budget, and create a new system of police oversight. Two years later, Jerry Wartgow, superintendent of the Denver Public Schools, stepped down, and the independently elected school board appointed me to take his place.

Denver's schools suffered from many of the challenges afflicting urban districts around the country. Enrollment had been declining for years, we had too many schools for the kids who remained in the district, and our academic achievement was among the worst in the state. Over the next five years, with the backing of a courageous school board and teams of talented principals and teachers, we led a community-wide effort to improve the schools.

In the past decade and a half, Denver has become the fastest-growing urban school district in the country. Thousands of families have returned to the public schools and thousands more have moved into the city in part because the quality of the schools has improved so significantly. The overall number of high school graduates going to college every year has doubled, with the greatest growth in college enrollment occurring among students of color. With renewed confidence in their schools, Denver's voters have approved ballot measures that provide dedicated funding for pre-school education and college scholarship assistance for low-income families. Teacher salaries, still woefully inadequate, are now competitive in the Denver metro region, and the Denver Public Schools have the country's largest and most vibrant teacher-leadership program. A final area where Denver leads the nation, and for which I can take no credit, involves the implementation by my successor, Tom Boasberg, of an innovative apprenticeship program called CareerConnect, in which juniors and seniors work two days a week in paid apprenticeships in fast-growing areas of the economy (such as web design, health care, and high-tech manufacturing) and earn credits toward their high school diploma and community college during their three days a week at school. When they complete the program, they have earned their high school diploma and partial or full completion of an associate's degree, plus they have three years of valuable paid work experience building skills in a growing profession.

We have a long way to go to close the achievement gap in our school district, but thanks to students and their families, teachers and principals, and the people who work for them in Denver, we continue to make progress. This is where I was working when Governor Ritter approached me about filling the seat left vacant when Senator Ken Salazar became a cabinet secretary.

There was one intervening episode. One of my roommates at Yale Law School was John Belcaster. We spent those years cramming for tests, watching *Thirtysomething* (at least it wasn't *Alf*), eating dinners from Modern Apizza (established in 1934), and playing tabletop hockey and speed chess. Our third roommate, a theoretical math major who had grown up in Germany, Daniel Halberstam, almost always won (the chess—not the hockey).[5] After he graduated, John returned to Chicago and went to work for a civil rights law firm there. Davis, Miner, Barnhill & Galland was so small it had only two associates. One was John. And another was Barack Obama.

I had heard of Obama. I remembered reading about him in the *New York Times* when he became the first African American editor in chief of the *Harvard Law Review*. Now he was John's colleague, and I heard story after story: about a beautiful book—*Dreams from My Father*—that Barack had written and I had to read; about Barack's announcements that he was running for a seat in the state senate (improbable), and then for a seat in the US House of Representatives (impossible), and then for the US Senate (crazy). Now, he was running for president, making the announcement in Springfield, Abraham Lincoln's home.

---

5 One of my most memorable moments in law school was beating Daniel Halberstam at speed chess. It never happened again.

I was sitting at my superintendent's desk in Denver when the phone rang. Senator Obama was on the line, and he told me that Belcaster had passed along my number. By then, I had taken my measure of the candidate and had come to understand how meaningful his election could be to the children for whom I worked. Obama asked me to serve as an education adviser to his campaign. I said that I would. Throughout the course of the campaign, I participated several times in conference calls to try to refine candidate Obama's education policy. In those days, I spent most of my time in schools or traveling between them, and I found myself listening on my car radio to Rush Limbaugh, worrying every day about what damage he and people like him might do to Obama's candidacy.[6]

Just weeks after Obama's election, his transition team invited me to Chicago to interview for the job of education secretary. I knew the job would likely go to Arne Duncan, another school superintendent and a friend from Chicago, but still I went. After our meeting, the president-elect said, "I like what I've heard; let the public proctology begin"—by which he meant an FBI background check. My wife and I and our friends and neighbors came to understand what the vetting process entailed. It was indeed public proctology, though without anesthesia—and in the end the job went, unsurprisingly, to Arne. But the process revealed to me an important element of Obama's character. On the day Arne's appointment was announced, I was talking with one of my school board members when I received a call that I let go unanswered. Not long afterward, a reporter called asking me how I felt about Arne's appointment. I told him Arne would be great, and then I looked at my phone and realized that I

---

6 Among other insults, Limbaugh, while drawing pay from national consumer brands sponsoring his show, repeatedly played a racist song called "Barack the Magic Negro." Senator Obama received Secret Service protection nine months before Democrats cast their first votes, earlier than any previous presidential candidate.

had missed a call from the 312 area code. I listened to the message: "It's Barack, call me." I called him back—voice mail!—and left a message telling him he had made a great choice, offering my help to Arne, and saying there was no need to return the call. Fifteen minutes later, he returned the call anyway to explain why he had chosen Arne and not selected me. In a world in which most politicians do almost anything to avoid giving bad news, Obama had called me twice to deliver it himself.

Two or three days earlier, Bill Ritter had stopped by and explained that Colorado's own Senator Ken Salazar would be appointed interior secretary. The governor asked whether I would consider adding my name to the pool as a potential replacement. To this day, I really don't know why Ritter made such an unusual appointment. Appointing me to the vacancy did absolutely nothing to help him politically. I was relatively unknown in the state. No one, including myself, knew whether I had the skills required to win a statewide race, which I would have to launch immediately after the appointment. I did recall a moment from my tenure as superintendent that may have had some influence. After finishing his own Democratic Party meeting, the governor wandered into a town hall I was having at South High School. As often happened when we made changes, tempers were running hot. In this case, we were proposing to elevate the graduation requirements for students. The high school auditorium was filled to the rafters with concerned students, parents, and teachers. But, as I would do many nights during my time as superintendent, I invited every question and criticism that people had, and we parted with a better understanding about each other's points of view. Perhaps Governor Ritter thought that skill might come in handy. He would have been right. The worst Tea Party town hall I ever had was a

thousand times easier than the best meeting about a school closing I ever had.[7]

In truth, my toughest town halls have sometimes been in
places with strong Democratic majorities. There, after I've cast
a vote that has gone against the grain of the Democratic Party—
though very much in the interests, I'd argue, of the citizens of
Colorado—people are often taken aback that I have not toed the
party line. Usually, after I have had the chance to explain myself,
most people are satisfied that I represented Colorado fairly, even
if they still disagree. In the more conservative parts of the state,
on the other hand, town halls are filled with people whose news
comes largely from Fox and who sometimes are predisposed to
view me as a Bolshevik. By the time my town halls there are over,
people often ask me where I am getting my news and invite me
back to continue the conversation.

My town halls give me all the faith I need that our republic
will endure. I am fortunate to represent a complicated state that is
about a third Republican, a third Democratic, and a third Independent. But most people don't define themselves primarily by those
categories, and, after all those town halls, I believe there exists in
Colorado—and probably in many states—a broad consensus about
the policies our country should pursue to secure our children's
future and our place in the world.

In our time, much of the political drama plays out in continual
thirty-second TV spots slamming opposing candidates, eight-hun-
dred-word op-eds under a byline, talking heads on radio and TV,
countless tweets, and, in the end, millions of votes. Nevertheless, I

---

7 One of the reasons school closing meetings are so tough is that families are legitimately
aggrieved. They face the disruption of changing schools almost always because the school
district failed to deal with resource or academic issues forthrightly in the past.

believe we are at our best when we are face-to-face in a town hall meeting or discussions over dinner, obliged by proximity to acknowledge the humanity and citizenship we share. Maybe I am nostalgic. Too often, as on Facebook or Twitter or in the fevered, anonymous reaches of the internet, isolation affords us the lazy convenience of diminishing one another with impunity. My Facebook feed attracts plenty of vitriol soloists. I accept as a duty of elected office that I should receive input in this form. But we are not going to make a better future for our children out of this form of discourse. We should be embarrassed to think they will ever see this stuff.

Instead, we ought to take a page from the town halls, engaging each other as Americans—not as enemies whose battle lines have been drawn by politicians raising money, cable commentators chasing ratings, or billionaires and big-money influence outfits protecting their narrow interests. Too often over the last decade these actors have set our agenda. It is not an agenda that accurately assesses or addresses the challenges we face. It is an agenda that thrives on ceaseless conflict, without requiring any responsibility or sacrifice from the American people to achieve real results.

Americans have a lot more on their minds. We owe a debt to the generations of Americans who secured the republic and its prospects for us, and we have an obligation to provide at least as much to the next generation. Our responsibility requires us not to shade the truth but to face what Lincoln called "the unprecedentedly stern facts of our case." We are obliged to uphold enduring principles. And as we do, we must recognize that not every disagreement is one of principle and that out of disagreement we have the chance to fashion durable, imaginative, and unorthodox solutions.

The ties of citizenship are as demanding as they are precious. Citizenship is a bond of trust—trust that we will work out our differences and land on the side of generosity together, even as we know we will be sometimes disappointed with the outcomes as individuals. The necessary give-and-take of citizenship is enacted now—in the present. It is not some cloudy reservoir of memory from the past we can draw on whenever we like. It is not a resolve to behave better in some indeterminate future, like Augustine's famous prayer: "Lord, give me chastity, but not yet." The moment when we must act as citizens is *always* now: in the present.

Self-government is the only form of government that depends on virtue—on the goodwill of the people—to perpetuate itself. Montesquieu, the French political philosopher known and admired by many of our eighteenth-century founders, once observed that, in an autocracy, the king, the despot, or the political boss rules by coercion. Every act of omission by the state justifies and perpetuates the state. A "wise republic," on the other hand, where all citizens share in action through government, requires the people to take responsibility for their own freedom and prosperity. This means making decisions in common in the face of risk and uncertainty. I have always been stirred by the example of Ralph Carr, a former governor of Colorado, who alone among his peers stood in opposition to the internment of Japanese Americans during World War II. Taking responsibility also means placing trust in the goodwill we share with other citizens. We are not equally or perfectly virtuous, and we should not expect to be. Among us are people whose politics is aimed at stripping some citizens of their rights and opportunities, who despise pluralism, who succumb to fearful hatreds like racism, or who care for nothing but themselves. My own experience in politics tells me this: such people are small in number. Their presence means that the rest of us, most of us, whom Martin Luther King Jr. called "the great decent majority," must share an even deeper understanding of our patriotic obligation to our fellow Americans and our republic.

James McHenry, who represented Maryland at the Constitutional Convention, recorded in his notebook this story about Benjamin Franklin from the day after the meeting adjourned:

> A lady asked Dr. Franklin, "Well, Doctor, what have we got,
> a republic or a monarchy?"
> "A republic," replied the Doctor, "if you can keep it."

Too often, this story is told to dramatize the fragility of American democracy or to add color to a warning that as a country we are on the verge of losing something we should hold dear. It deserves to be understood in a more optimistic light—as a crystalline summation of every citizen's obligation to the republic. The "you" in this story isn't the woman who asks the question. The "you" is every one of us.

IV. Reclaiming Our Ideals

I arrived in the Senate in early 2009 at the depths of the Great Recession. Although I had little experience with partisan politics, my expectations of our governing institutions were high. I believed the election of a new president combined with the severity of the economic difficulties facing the country would produce a coherent political and policy response from Washington.

Over the past decade, my expectations have been dashed by our inability to get almost anything done for our country. Time and again I have wondered, and my constituents have often asked:

Why do the characters in our national political dramas so frequently take the path of least resistance? How is it that symbols become more important than outcomes? What caused our checks and balances to veer so far out of whack? Given the urgency to act on matters critical to this republic, and given the even graver urgency of the consequences of failing to act, what motivates Washington to accomplish so little?

To my mind, much of the cause must be laid at the feet of trivial, unprincipled partisanship masquerading as principled disagreement. The framers who drafted our Constitution knew that disagreement would be a defining characteristic of our republic. In Europe, no monarch cared what you thought. In America, no tyrant could tell you what to think. The Constitution the framers wrote established the most elegant mechanisms ever devised in human history—our three branches of government, our freedoms as citizens—to resolve a nation's political disputes and govern the country.

During my time in office, I have come to realize that our country is no longer using the mechanisms the framers provided in order to achieve results. We are using them to have disputes. We are damaging what generations have preserved and advanced—and what the next generations deserve to enjoy. The causes of our government's breakdown are poorly understood by the American people and even by their representatives in Congress. The election of Donald Trump, a reality TV star, is a symptom of this breakdown, not its essential cause. We arrived at this perilous American moment for many reasons, but they include specific episodes when Washington and our country failed to live up to obligations our best predecessors have fulfilled.

The purpose of this book is twofold. One purpose is to describe five moments when uncompromising factionalism in pursuit of ideological goals disabled both political parties and destroyed any bipartisan incentives to govern the American republic. Another purpose is to make an urgent case that to find our path forward Americans must reclaim the ideals of the founders and repair the damage already done. In doing so, we should reconceptualize the word "founder" itself. We should think of founders as those who constructed the ideas upon which our republic was built and which enable it to endure, thrive, and grow. The term encompasses the Americans who declared independence from England and the framers who drafted the Constitution. But it also should include all of those who, down the years, have expanded America's promise: for instance, Frederick Douglass, Elizabeth Cady Stanton, José Martí, Emma Lazarus, W. E. B. Du Bois, Martin Luther King Jr., Barbara Jordan, Cesar Chavez. Your list, your neighbor's list, the list of the senator across the hall—they all will vary. Combined, our lists make up America's honor roll, an assembly who put the republic before themselves and any narrow interest.

The first episode described in the book considers how the Senate has destroyed a long-standing custom of bipartisanship. The Senate's filibuster rule required sixty votes to act on presidential nominations and in so doing established a bipartisan equilibrium. Because it was rare for either party to control more than sixty seats, the rule forced a measure of bipartisan consensus. Although the Senate's patience with the rule had been straining for years, things took a turn for the worse in President Obama's second term, when Senate Republicans abused the filibuster to effectively freeze his nominees. This accelerated a cycle of preemptive retaliation, in which both parties tore down the written and unwritten rules of the Senate—a result that not only has degraded that institution but also threatens to infect the judicial branch with rank partisanship.

The second episode tracks the Republican Party's departure from its relatively honorable legacy on the environment to embrace an ideology of denial when it comes to threats to the global environment—culminating with President Trump's senseless commitment to pull out of the Paris Agreement on climate change. The episode explains this devolution by pointing to the way our campaign finance system has corrupted Congress. A series of Supreme Court cases opened the door to unlimited spending by so-called independent groups, allowing billionaire donors to cajole and threaten politicians at every level of government. This flood of money has created in Congress a corruption of inaction, stalling work not only on climate but also on a host of other issues.

The third episode chronicles how an insurgent faction of Republicans—first the Tea Party, later the Freedom Caucus—seized control of their party and ran their political playbook with no intention of compromise. Using the rhetoric of fiscal responsibility, they repeatedly blocked legislation to stabilize America's economy in a time of crisis while persistently refusing to make strategic investments that would improve opportunity for the next generation. At the movement's outset, and sometimes as it developed, its members claimed to revere the framers and American political institutions. And yet they were willing to break those very institutions to try to impose radical views that could never earn bipartisan support. They used government shutdowns and debt-ceiling showdowns to impose their highly divisive factional will. Instead of improving the fiscal condition of the government, they acted as fiscal hypocrites and made matters worse. They degraded the public's faith in our institutions and modeled a destructive hyperpartisanship that helped to cripple Washington.

The fourth episode examines the Obama administration's nuclear agreement with Iran and the failure of Republicans in the Senate to engage constructively with the president on matters of war and peace. In 2016, President Obama negotiated a multilateral arms control agreement with Iran to curtail its development of nuclear weapons. The vast majority of Republicans opposed the deal even before studying it. Instead, they lined up behind Senator Tom Cotton and signed a letter to Iranian religious hard-liners, undercutting President Obama's negotiating position. By 2017, the deal was clearly succeeding. Despite this fact—and the overwhelming view of US intelligence agencies and the international community—President Trump sacrificed our national security interests and withdrew from the agreement, capitulating to some of the Republican Party's largest donors.

The fifth and final episode considers one example of effective bipartisan legislating in the Senate—the work undertaken by the Senate's "Gang of Eight" several years ago to pass comprehensive immigration reform. This episode reminds us that the mechanisms of our republic may still be put to effective use. Within a short time frame, the Gang of Eight delivered a legislative package with a historic increase to border security, a massive overhaul of the nation's complicated visa processes, high-tech upgrades to our enforcement systems, the most progressive Dream Act ever written, and a pathway to citizenship for America's 11 million undocumented immigrants. The bill passed the Senate with sixty-eight votes but then met its death in the House, where the hyperfactionalism of a vocal minority on the right scared off the Republican leadership. That same factionalism—and that same stoking of unwarranted fears—sustained the rise of Donald Trump, who claimed falsely that our borders were out of control and in the speech announcing his candidacy slandered immigrants as "rapists" and "terrorists."

V. "What Is Wrong with You People?"

Each of these episodes demands the question: what has our government in Washington lately done to "secure the Blessings of Liberty to ourselves and our Posterity"—the central mission defined in the central document of our nation? We no longer have a good answer. The incredulity of the American people is entirely understandable. To borrow from what I hear in my town hall meetings: "What is wrong with you people?"

Let me briefly advance an argument that will run through this entire book. The state of our politics and the quality of life for ordinary citizens are not two separate things. The United States has had a social contract spelled out on parchment and engraved in our hearts and minds. It is that every person is endowed with inalienable rights, among them life, liberty, and the pursuit of happiness. A government of, by, and for the people secures those rights. I won't indulge in romanticism: the indelible sin of slavery blighted all of society and was recognized in the Constitution itself, and we will live with the consequences all our days. But the point is this: In a republic, the health of self-government and the health of society as a whole are not different things. They are bound together, inextricably. During the past several decades, we have seen much of our social contract—call it the American dream—erased. We used to tolerate some degree of stark income inequality because we were a land of opportunity where anyone could strike it rich (or at least live a middle-class life). Today, we have less economic mobility than most industrialized countries and our income inequality is higher than it has been in a century. Over the past fifty years, nine out of ten Americans have not seen their incomes rise. The vast majority of the benefits of economic growth have accrued to the wealthiest 10 percent of Americans. Far from ameliorating this economic inequality, our education system actually reinforces it.

In Colorado, and around the country, people who work a full week cannot afford housing, health care, higher education, and child care. In other words, in America today, most people cannot afford a middle-class life. If you are born poor, a person of color, or on the other side of the tracks, matters are much worse. Our politicians don't seem to care. Since 2001, according to the Institute on Taxation and Policy, Washington cut taxes by $5 trillion in the name of the middle class, but roughly two-thirds of the benefit has gone to the top 20 percent of Americans; the Trump tax cuts are even more skewed toward the top earners. At the same time, Washington spent $5.6 trillion on wars in Iraq and Afghanistan. Meanwhile, China's economy has quadrupled since 2001, tripled since 2004, and doubled since 2009, the year we entered the Great Recession. Imagine what our country would look like today if we had spent a fraction of that $10.6 trillion on our actual needs. Imagine what we might have accomplished if we had not been distracted by the five episodes of political shortsightedness (not to mention the foolishness, greed, and even cruelty) recounted in this book.

Meanwhile, our deficits and national debt have soared—largely because of those same tax cuts—and to deal with this, some voices now cynically cry for cuts to social programs for the poor and the elderly, cuts to health care, and cuts to loans for college students and to support for public schools. At the same time, globalization, which is a dynamic reality, has been pursued with great regard for Wall Street and little regard for the impact on working Americans. The real estate pages of the Mansion section of the *Wall Street Journal* and the House & Home section of the *Financial Times* display mouthwatering properties available to a transnational global elite—but the reality for tens of millions of Americans is the economic hollowing out of towns and cities. In some places, there is an abiding sense of hopelessness, cynicism, and abandonment. Far more people, most of them young, now die from opioid overdoses than in automobile accidents. For three years running—unlike in any other industrialized country in the world and not seen in the United States since before World War I—average life expectancy in the United States has fallen. The reasons: opioid addiction and suicides (half by guns).

It should not be surprising that these failures have eroded support for the idea of democracy itself, especially among younger Americans; barely a quarter of young Americans say it is "essential" to live in a democracy, and almost half of all Americans say they "never had" or "have lost" faith in US democracy. Lincoln told us that if the American government failed to meet citizens' basic expectations, we would lose "the strongest bulwark of any Government . . . the *attachment* of the people."

Washington's political dysfunction doesn't stay in Washington; it infects the rest of America. America's economic dysfunction doesn't stay in the rest of America; it paralyzes Washington. Nothing less than America's exercise in self-government is at stake.

To change course, we must embrace the imagination of our founders and those who improved upon their work. I have some ideas about how we might do that. But first it is useful to consider how Washington wasted the American people's time over the last decade—and served them ill in the process. Understanding this, we might hope to construct politics that will use the coming decade more productively than we used the past one. This new politics will require the American people and their elected leaders to hold higher expectations of one another as citizens. It will require us to build new constituencies in order to start undoing the damage done over the course of two generations—before two generations become three and four. Even better, we might aspire to enhance the rights, opportunities, and freedoms of our children and grandchildren.

POWER PLAY

Ignoring the Constitution,
ignoring a Supreme Court nominee,
and eviscerating the Senate as an institution.

I. "Less Than Zero"

The news came on Saturday, February 13, 2016, while I was attending a Jefferson-Jackson Day dinner in Colorado. It arrived in the form of a crawl on CNN: Supreme Court Justice Antonin Scalia had died suddenly at a hunting camp in Texas. At seventy-nine, Scalia was the third-oldest member of the Supreme Court. His death left the court split between four justices appointed by Democratic presidents and four appointed by Republican presidents. He died in a presidential election year, but with fully 342 days to go before the end of Barack Obama's second term.

Throughout our history, there has been little controversy about what should happen after a Supreme Court justice dies. Article II, Section 2, Clause 2 of the United States Constitution says that the president "shall nominate, and by and with the Advice and Consent of the Senate shall appoint . . . Judges of the Supreme Court." In practice, this has meant that when a vacancy arises the president nominates a replacement and the Senate approves or rejects the nominee by voting on his or her nomination.[1]

Before President Obama's last year in office, no Senate in history had ever refused to consider an elected president's nominee merely because the vacancy arose in an election year. Indeed, the Senate has confirmed seventeen Supreme Court nominees in election years since the nation's founding. It has rejected two. In only six instances in our history (election year or not) did the Senate deliberately ignore a president's nominee. In each case there were questions about the sitting president's legitimacy. In three of the cases, vice presidents had replaced presidents who died in office. The other three cases involved nominations made during the lame-duck session after a presidential election.[2]

It's fair to say that I disagreed with Antonin Scalia about almost everything. I also knew him to be a distinguished jurist with a sharp legal mind and a powerfully persuasive pen. He was a devout Catholic and a devoted family man. He had a winning sense of humor and had forged an improbably close friendship with Justice Ruth Bader Ginsburg, his polar opposite in so many ways. You could stand in opposition to Scalia on points of policy and principle while

---

1 According to Robin Bradley Kar and Jason Mazzone, writing in the *NYU Law Review*, since the founding of the country there have been 103 instances where "an elected President has faced an actual vacancy on the Supreme Court and began an appointment process prior to the election of a successor. In all 103 cases, the President was able to both nominate and appoint a replacement Justice, by and with the advice and consent of the Senate. This is true even of all eight such cases where the nomination process began during an election year."

2 Presidents Tyler, Fillmore, and Johnson assumed office following the death of their predecessors (Harrison, Taylor, and Lincoln respectively). Tyler and Fillmore each faced two Supreme Court vacancies and contemporaneous debate over their legitimacy as president. Nevertheless, the Senate allowed each to fill one of the two vacancies. Johnson's attempt to fill a vacancy was delayed as the Senate considered legislation that reorganized the court and ultimately eliminated the seat Johnson attempted to fill. Those instances occurred before the passage of the Twenty-Fifth Amendment, in 1967, clarifying the powers of a vice president who assumes the highest office.

agreeing that he was eminently qualified to serve on the Supreme Court and embodied extraordinary qualities as a human being and as an American. His unexpected death afflicted family and friends with a grievous loss. Most Americans, whatever their politics, likely received the news with shock and sadness.

But not all of them. A mere eleven minutes after the first press reports of Justice Scalia's death—and nearly forty minutes before official confirmation by Chief Justice John Roberts—Utah senator Mike Lee's communications director tweeted, "What is less than zero? The chances of Obama successfully appointing a Supreme Court Justice to replace Scalia?"

An hour after Roberts made his announcement, Senate Majority Leader Mitch McConnell, of Kentucky, declared: "The American people should have a voice in the selection of their next Supreme Court Justice. Therefore, this vacancy should not be filled until we have a new president." Soon after, the chairman of the Senate Judiciary Committee, Republican senator Charles Grassley, of Iowa, put out a statement: "The fact of the matter is that it's been standard practice over the last nearly 80 years that Supreme Court nominees are not nominated and confirmed during a presidential election year. Given the huge divide in the country, and the fact that this President, above all others, has made no bones about his goal to use the courts to circumvent Congress and push through his own agenda, it only makes sense that we defer to the American people who will elect a new president to select the next Supreme Court Justice."

Grassley failed to note that there had been *no vacancy* during an election year for eighty years. The last one had arisen eighty-four years earlier, when President Herbert Hoover nominated Benjamin Cardozo and the Senate confirmed him nine days later. It is worth noting that Grassley, a Republican, spoke very differently—and in this case accurately—when it came to judges nominated in 2008, at the end of President George W. Bush's term of office: "The reality is that the Senate has never stopped confirming judicial nominees during the last few months of a president's term."

Disregarding 230 years of custom and practice, members of the Senate, many of whom claimed to be—as Justice Scalia said he was—"constitutional originalists" or "textualists," began willfully ignoring the text of the Constitution in favor of something they falsely called "standard practice." McConnell and Grassley summarized their view of the constitutional requirements in the *Washington Post*: "It is today the American people, rather than a lame-duck president whose priorities and policies they just rejected in the most-recent national election, who should be afforded the opportunity to replace Justice Scalia." The reference here is not to anything in the nation's founding documents or to Obama's popularity and reelection but to the fact that the Republicans had picked up a few seats and taken control of the Senate.

McConnell and Grassley's argument led me to take the Senate floor with the actual words of the Constitution (in boldface) interwoven with their bogus ratonale (in plain text). It looked something like this:

> **he shall nominate,** It is today the American people, rather than a lame-duck president whose priorities **and by and with** policies they just rejected in **the advice and consent of the Senate, shall appoint** most-recent national election, who should be afforded the opportunity to replace **judges of the Supreme Court** Justice Scalia.

In the McConnell-Grassley version of the constitutional charge, only two words remained from the actual Constitution, a conjunction ("and") and a definite article ("the").[3]

Contrary to the impression McConnell and Grassley were attempting to create, the Senate, otherwise notorious for its glacial pace, has acted expeditiously when considering Supreme Court justices. Over the past forty years, it has come to a decision, on average, seventy days after the president's nomination.

There are good reasons not to delay. First is the unique nature of the responsibility. The framers of the Constitution lodged the obligation to advise and consent with the Senate. No one else, including the House of Representatives, can exercise it. Second, and crucial, is the essential importance of the Supreme Court's composition. No less an authority than Justice Scalia himself explained this well. Asked to recuse himself from a case involving Vice President Cheney on grounds of an apparent conflict of interest, Justice Scalia rejected the suggestion that he should "resolve any doubts in favor of recusal." He observed that such a standard might be appropriate if he were on a circuit court, where "my place would be taken by another judge, and the case would proceed normally. On the Supreme Court, however, the consequence is different: The Court proceeds with eight Justices, raising the possibility that, by reason of a tie vote, it will find itself unable to resolve the significant legal issue presented by the case." Scalia cited the Supreme Court's own

---

3 Moreover—and this is not a minor point—for all the cavalier use of the term "lame duck" by the Republicans, President Obama was not a lame-duck president. He would be a lame duck only in the period between the election, still nine months in the future, and the inauguration of a successor. The use of the term was an attempt to cast doubt on his constitutional legitimacy, something and the birther movement (later abetted by Donald Trump) had been doing since before Obama won election in 2008.

recusal policy to explain that "even one unnecessary recusal impairs the functioning of the Court."

It is easy to see why we would want a functional court, particularly in a presidential election year. Imagine, for example, a future court with an even number of justices confronted by facts similar to those of *Bush v. Gore*—the decision that gave the disputed 2000 election to George W. Bush—but with only eight justices on the bench. How long would the nation have to endure a constitutional crisis?

Mitch McConnell didn't care about any of this as he set out to establish a brand-new precedent. Just five days after Justice Scalia's death, the Judicial Crisis Network, financed by the Koch brothers, launched a multimillion-dollar "Let the People Decide" advertising campaign to keep the seat vacant. A new interpretation of the president's and Senate's constitutional responsibilities began to be pushed across the land. As events played out, one casualty would be norms and traditions that underlie the very essence of the Senate as an institution.

II. Pocketing a Treasure

Although the Republicans' theory of the case was novel, the fight over the Scalia vacancy was hardly the first partisan battle over judicial nominations. Earlier rounds, described by the *Washington Post*'s Helen Dewar as "political blood feuds, in which each side seeks to avenge the earlier assaults by the other side," had begun under President Ronald Reagan, with the defeat by the Democrats of Robert Bork's nomination to the Supreme Court. The battles escalated under President Bill Clinton when Republicans blocked votes on a record number of district court nominees. When George W. Bush won the presidency, Senate Democrats took it to another level by filibustering ten circuit court nominees during his first term.

After Bush won reelection and Republicans increased their clout in the Senate, Majority Leader Bill Frist, of Tennessee, vowed to retaliate. At a November 2004 meeting of the Federalist Society—an influential organization of conservative lawyers and jurists—he vowed: "One way or another, the filibuster of judicial nominees must end. This filibuster is nothing less than a formula for tyranny by the minority. The Senate cannot allow the filibuster of circuit court nominees to continue. Nor can we allow the filibuster to extend to potential Supreme Court nominees."

Frist, in 2005, became the first leader to threaten to use the "nuclear option." Making a change in the rules of the Senate had long required a two-thirds vote—a traditional means of making sure the rules had bipartisan support. Using the nuclear option meant allowing a rules change by means of a majority vote instead—making rules changes a partisan affair. Beginning in 1917, Senate rules required a two-thirds majority to affirm a decision to end debate on a judicial nomination and move to a final vote. In 1975, the Senate lowered the requirement to three-fifths, or sixty votes. It is uncommon for one party to hold sixty seats in the Senate, so nominations advanced only when there was support from at least a few members of the minority party. This rule had a moderating effect: judges were selected with an eye to making them somewhat acceptable to the other side of the aisle, and as a consequence all but a few nominations were confirmed by large bipartisan majority votes. Scrapping the sixty-vote threshold would make confirmations easier—and at the same time make them vastly more partisan.

The use of the so-called nuclear option to change the rules would threaten the balance of power in the Senate—indeed, would threaten the nature of the Senate—by allowing the majority to overcome the rights of the minority at any time it wished. That's the way it is in the House of Representatives, a more rambunctious and fickle body. The Senate is supposed to act with inclusive deliberation and to take the long view.

A group of senators—seven Democrats and seven Republicans— took it upon themselves to defuse the bomb. What started as hushed expressions of concern voiced between committee hearings turned into an urgent conversation on how to preserve the sixty-vote threshold. The Gang of Fourteen, as the group came to be known, reached a memorandum of understanding that each of its signatories would oppose the nuclear option and filibuster judicial nominees only in "extraordinary circumstances."[4] The 2005 agreement was technically unenforceable. The Gang relied on mutual trust; its members, as *CQ Weekly* noted, "did not want to serve in a chamber that essentially could look like a clone of the House." John McCain, a member of the Gang, explained, "This happened because there was a group of us that thought the institution and the very funda-mentals of the institution were at stake."

The agreement represented a rare moment of bipartisanship in a fractured Senate. Outside the chamber, there was less enthusi-asm for the deal. Many liberals expressed disappointment with an

---

4 The "Gang of . . ." formulation, which has been used on the Hill in other contexts besides this one, has an improbable origin: it comes from the term "Gang of Four," which referred to powerful Chinese Communists during the Cultural Revolution who were later charged with treason. The Gang of Fourteen consisted of Robert Byrd (D-WV), Lincoln Chafee (R-RI), Susan Collins (R-ME), Mike DeWine (R-OH), Lindsey Graham (R-SC), Daniel Inouye (D-HI), Mary Landrieu (D-LA), Joe Lieberman (D-CT), John McCain (R-AZ), Ben Nelson (D-NE).], Mark Pryor (D-AR), Ken Salazar (D-CO), Olympia Snowe (R-ME), and John Warner (R-VA).

agreement that moved forward Bush's "extremist nominees." Many conservatives, wanting to scrap the filibuster altogether, assailed the agreement as "an outrage" and "a complete bailout and betrayal" by the Gang's Republicans and predicted that conservative voters would punish the Republican Party.[5]

As it happened, in the following year, 2006, Democrats won control of the Senate, acquiring a slim 51–49 majority. After the Republican loss, Gang member Lindsey Graham, of South Carolina, who had himself won reelection, could not resist noting that the Democratic landslide proved the value of the Gang's work. He told a reporter, "If anything's certain now, it's that changing the rules would have been shortsighted. Conservatives having a say in judicial nominations would have been forever lost." During the final two years of Bush's term, the agreement held. A Senate controlled by Democrats confirmed sixty-eight judges nominated by President Bush.

All of this changed with the 2008 landslide election of Barack Obama and the emergence of Democratic majorities in both the House and the Senate. Obama hoped to move beyond the bitterness and gridlock of the past, but the leadership on the Hill had already laid plans to sabotage such efforts. Interviewed for a *Frontline* documentary, the journalist Robert Draper described a decision made on the night of Obama's inauguration at a dinner hosted by former House Speaker Newt Gingrich with top House Republicans and conservative power brokers: "So they decided that they needed to begin to fight Obama on everything. This meant unyielding opposition to every one of the Obama administration's legislative initiatives." As Mitch McConnell would later put it, "The single

---

5 John McCain, quoted in the *New York Times*, provided an astute analysis of the outrage among activist political groups: "Think of all the money they are going to lose."

most important thing we want to achieve is for President Obama to be a one-term president." The idea was to oppose Obama even when one agreed with him. Speaking later of the president's efforts to expand health care coverage for Americans, House Speaker John Boehner said, "We're going to do everything—and I mean every-thing we can do—to kill it, stop it, slow it down, whatever we can." With respect to judicial appointments, the Republicans adopted new obstructionist tactics—for instance, using certain senatorial prerogatives to place holds on particular nominees. They hoped to win the next election in 2012 and wanted to allow a Republican president to fill the judicial vacancies. As a result of these tactics, more vacancies existed at the end of President Obama's first term than at the beginning.

In the event, President Obama won reelection and Democrats retained their Senate majority, but their supporters were impatient with the lack of progress on judges during the first term. Some began to suggest that Majority Leader Harry Reid, of Nevada, resort to the nuclear option as the most efficient way to overcome Republican obstruction. Reid and McConnell reached an agreement to avoid a radical rules change in favor of temporary changes to speed up floor activity. "I'm not personally, at this stage, ready to get rid of the sixty-vote threshold," Reid told the *Washington Post*. "With the history of the Senate, we have to understand the Senate isn't and shouldn't be like the House."

The détente was short-lived. Within weeks, Republicans were filibustering President Obama's nomination of Chuck Hagel to be defense secretary. Until that point, the Senate had never in history filibustered a nomination for secretary of defense. This action sig-naled to Reid that Republicans would exercise no restraint. Hagel, after all, had served in the Senate—and was a Republican, no less.

Echoing the words of Bill Frist, Reid warned his colleagues: "I'm going to wait and build a case. If the Republicans in the Senate don't start approving some judges and don't start helping get some of these nominations done, then we're going to have to take more action."

Meanwhile, voters who had twice elected Barack Obama president were becoming enraged at the slow pace of judicial nominations and confirmations.[6] One of the new administration's priorities was filling three vacancies on the D.C. Circuit, the most powerful court in the country after the Supreme Court. The D.C. Circuit is the first court—and often the last—to review cases involving federal regulations and executive authority, including issues related to national security, environmental protection, campaign finance, and workers' rights. And it is frequently the launching pad for future Supreme Court justices.[7] President Obama simultaneously introduced three D.C. Circuit nominees in an elaborate Rose Garden ceremony. "These are incredibly accomplished lawyers by all accounts," he said. "There is no reason aside from politics for Republicans to block these individuals from getting an up or down vote."

Practicing tactics they would later use for the Supreme Court, Republicans immediately set themselves in opposition to the nominees and refused to give them an up or down vote. Even before

---

6 An example: "Even if the President is content to appoint moderate judges, it remains a mystery why the Administration is so far behind in its nomination of judges," Geoffrey Stone, who worked with Obama as dean of the University of Chicago Law School, told the *American Prospect*. "There is no excuse for the persistent failure to fill vacancies."

7 Every president since Harry Truman appointed at least one judge to the D.C. Circuit in his first term. That streak broke under Obama, when Republicans blocked his first nominee, Caitlin Halligan, for two and a half years, until the White House eventually withdrew her nomination. Obama's second nominee, Sri Srinivasan, who had worked in the solicitor general's office under both Bush and Obama, was originally nominated in June 2012 and then renominated in January 2013, ultimately waiting eleven months before unanimous confirmation.

Obama announced the nominations, Republicans had accused the president of "court-packing." In the words of Chuck Grassley, the highest-ranking Republican on the Judiciary Committee, "It's hard to imagine the rationale for nominating three judges at once for this court given the many vacant emergency seats across the country, unless your goal is to pack the court to advance a certain policy agenda."

Reid began counting votes to determine his caucus's support for resorting to the nuclear option. "I am not going to wait another month, another few weeks, another year, for Congress to take action on the things that we have been doing for almost 240 years," Reid said. This was not just about judges. Among the pending nominations were the heads of the Environmental Protection Agency, the National Labor Relations Board, the Department of Labor, and the Consumer Financial Protection Bureau—all nominees he knew would fail to reach sixty votes.

By then, a majority of the Democratic caucus had come to share Reid's frustration. Consensus emerged around a proposal to change the vote threshold to fifty-one only on executive-branch nominations, leaving the threshold at sixty votes for lifetime judicial appointments and all legislation. "The changes we are making are very, very minimal," Reid said. "What we're doing is saying, 'Look, American people, shouldn't President Obama have somebody working for him that he wants?' We're going to make this simple change."

As Republicans threatened "total war" if this limited version of the nuclear option went through, Reid and McConnell called an all-senators meeting in the Old Senate Chamber. The meeting place was significant. The room had housed the United States Senate and then the Supreme Court for much of the nineteenth century; had been torched by the British during the War of 1812;

and had served as the stage where Daniel Webster, Henry Clay, and John C. Calhoun had fought over slavery and struck precarious compromises to stave off secession and perpetuate the power of slave states in Congress.[8]

For more than three and a half hours on a humid summer night, I listened as nearly every senator voiced his or her opinion about whether and how the Senate should change its filibuster rules. Behind these closed doors, some of my colleagues expressed their misgivings that things had come to this. There were Republicans who supported filibusters against Obama's nominees and admitted that some of their opposition was unwarranted. There were Democrats who supported lowering the threshold yet expressed reservations about changing the rules in the middle of the game.

The genuine bipartisan debate in the Old Senate Chamber led to an overnight deal struck by Reid and McConnell that ended the immediate crisis. It included green-lighting the confirmations of Tom Perez as labor secretary, Gina McCarthy as EPA director, and five nominees to the National Labor Relations Board. The deal's limited scope made no broader commitments with respect to the use of the filibuster. "They are not sacrificing their right to filibuster, and we damn sure aren't giving up our right to change the rules if necessary, which I am confident it won't be," Reid said. "I am very encouraged about the discussion we've had over the last few days."

By the end of July 2013, the Senate had confirmed nearly one hundred executive nominees. But cooperation collapsed during the summer, weakened by a toxic August recess debate over health

---

8 It housed the Senate until 1860. Once the remodeling of the Capitol was nearing completion, it became the room where the Supreme Court met until 1935. The Old Senate Chamber is also where Senator Charles Sumner was brutally caned by an aggrieved member of the House in 1856. And it's where senators gathered in 1999 to negotiate and approve, 100–0, the procedures that would govern President Clinton's impeachment trial.

care and immigration reform that culminated in the Ted Cruz–led sixteen-day government shutdown over Obamacare. Cruz, of Texas, had come to the Senate with no real interest in legislating. He came for the platform it offered. And he immediately sought out ways to disrupt Senate business so that he could reap publicity and raise money online—and thereby build his stature and ultimately run for president. Carl Levin, of Michigan, whose office in the Russell Senate Office Building I now occupy, was adamant in arguing that the norms and procedures of the Senate have profound value and need nurturing and support—as well as bipartisan tending, because what goes around comes around. Cruz seems never to have given that idea a second thought or in all likelihood a first one. He chose to grind the Senate to smithereens to serve his own narrow political interests.[9]

Cruz's shutdown divided Republicans, and when the government reopened they were anxious for a display of party unity. A week after the shutdown came to an end, Senator John Cornyn, the Republican whip, wrote: "Republicans will always have internal debates, but—more importantly—we share a determination to reverse the destructive policies of the past five years." Republicans, Cornyn added, "should remain united in blocking Senate Majority Leader Harry Reid's attempt to pack the D.C. Circuit, which is America's second-most-influential judicial body."

---

9 In my imagination, an exchange between Levin and Cruz on the issue of norms and procedures would track the famous exchange between Thomas More and his son-in-law, William Roper, in Robert Bolt's *A Man for All Seasons*. Roper: So now you'd give the Devil benefit of law! More: Yes. What would you do? Cut a great road through the law to get after the Devil? Roper: I'd cut down every law in England to do that! More: Oh? And when the last law was down, and the Devil turned round on you—where would you hide, Roper, the laws all being flat? This country's planted thick with laws from coast to coast—man's laws, not God's—and if you cut them down—and you're just the man to do it—d'you really think you could stand upright in the winds that would blow then?

In November, Republicans blocked votes on all three D.C. Circuit nominees. An exasperated Harry Reid began to gauge, once again, whether he had the fifty-one votes he needed to invoke the nuclear option. Speaking of the Republicans, he observed, "They have done everything they can to deny the fact that Obama has been elected and then reelected. I have a right to change how I feel about things." Democrats believed that Republicans, by blocking qualified nominees, had violated the terms of the 2005 Gang of Fourteen deal. The Republicans were not citing any "extraordinary circumstances"; they simply objected to the president who nominated these men and women. Ted Cruz admitted as much, telling judicial nominees: "You find yourself in the midst of a broader battle, and a battle on issues, many of which are unconnected to your professional background and qualifications."

This time there would be no all-senators meeting in the Old Senate Chamber. And there would be no Gang of Fourteen to ride to the rescue. A majority of the Senate, fifty-five senators, were new to the institution, winners in wave elections of 2006, 2008, and 2010. Only five of the original Gang members remained in the Senate. The last generation to know the Senate as it had traditionally been had all but faded from the scene. In its place stood former House members accustomed to simple majority rule and outsiders who had come to Washington with the express purpose of blocking anything and everything the president pursued. This younger generation was eager to stop wasting the Senate's time and move quickly through our legislative priorities.

As Democrats gathered during our regular caucus lunches that November, the nuclear option dominated discussion. By then, Senate veterans like Patrick Leahy, Dianne Feinstein, and Barbara Boxer—initially reluctant to eliminate the sixty-vote threshold—had changed their minds, beaten down by unprecedented levels of partisanship. "You reach a point where your frustration just overwhelms and things have to change," said Senator Feinstein. "I think the level of frustration on the Democratic side has just reached the point where it's worth the risk." I was among the frustrated newer members who were seeking some way around McConnell's blockade. I was well aware of concerns that invoking the nuclear option might lead to chaos or a Senate without any rules at all. As chair of the Democratic Senatorial Campaign Committee (DSCC), I was also aware—agonizingly so—that I would forfeit my ability to do that job effectively if I voted against my party on this issue. In the end, I would support the rules change. I have since come to regret that vote more than any other I have cast.

The only consistent voice in opposition was Carl Levin's. Notwithstanding his over thirty years of service, I judged him to be the least cynical person in the United States Senate. Week after week, with his sleeves rolled up over his elbows and his glasses resting on the tip of his nose, Levin would say, "Don't do this." He reminded us that if we actually held the Republicans to the rules—making them hold the floor by means of a filibuster for a weekend or two—they'd think twice (because they wanted to get home). More important, Levin argued that changing the rules by a bare majority, instead of the sixty-seven votes required by the rules of the Senate, would mean that any majority could impose—or destroy—any rule it wanted at any time. In effect, such a rules change would mean there were no rules; any rule could vanish at the whim of a majority. He presciently observed that today's majority would be different from tomorrow's. "When the precedent is set that a majority can change the rules at will on judges," Levin said, "that precedent will be used to change the rules on consideration of legislation, and down the road, the hard-won protections and benefits for our people's health and welfare will be less secure."

Meanwhile, Mitch McConnell warily observed the scene as Democrats barreled toward the nuclear option. "Obviously, the majority in any given point in the history of the United States Senate could take the view that they want to change the rules with a simple majority," McConnell said in the midst of the debate. "So far majorities from both sides over the years have resisted the temptation to break the rules to change the rules. But we know full well that the majority could decide to change the rules if they so chose." McConnell understood that there were no longer the votes to block the nuclear option. Instead, a new understanding of the ways of the Senate was taking hold. Both sides now assumed that if we don't do it to them, they will do it to us. A cold war of preemptive retribution lay ahead.

And McConnell would be sure to exploit it. McConnell is patient, strategic, undistracted, impervious to give-and-take (except when he is taking everything)—and, in a political sense, ruthless. If Sean Hannity bad-mouths him, he doesn't care. If 80 percent of America hates him, he doesn't care. There is not a vote that is taken or a statement that he makes that isn't calibrated not only to win elections but also to achieve his strategic vision, which is very limited: cutting taxes and putting conservative judges on the bench.

Just before the Senate's Thanksgiving break, Harry Reid initiated the nuclear option, raising a point of order asserting that instead of requiring sixty affirmative votes, the Senate rules now required only fifty-one affirmative votes for all judicial offices other than the Supreme Court. The procedural mechanics behind the point of order were complicated; someone with a taste for medieval theology might enjoy them. Suffice it to say that the Senate parliamentarian refused to ignore the plain language of the Senate's rules, and the presiding officer refused to sustain Reid's point of order. Senator Reid then moved to appeal the ruling of the chair to the entire Senate, an appeal that would require only a majority to sustain.

Fifty-two senators, all Democrats, voted with Reid to over-turn the chair's decision; forty-eight voted against. Henceforward, the threshold vote for confirmations, not including those to the Supreme Court, was now a simple majority: "That is the ruling of the chair."

The language of the rule had not changed; the Senate rules still required that "three-fifths of the Senators duly chosen and sworn" must vote in the affirmative. But those words had lost their meaning. Debate would now end when fifty-one senators voted to end it.[10]

Even before the drama of the nuclear option vote, McCon-nell had prefigured the second act. He declared in a floor speech that the use of the nuclear option by the Democrats would have implications for the Supreme Court, even if the intention had been to make Supreme Court nominees an exception:

> They want to do it in such a way that President Obama's agenda gets enacted but that a future Republican President could not get his or her picks for the Supreme Court con-firmed by a Republican Senate using the same precedent our Democratic friends want to set. They want to have it both

---

10 I have always believed that Reid, who had a strong sense of right and wrong, had simply had enough. The first photograph visitors to Harry Reid's office would see was of a young African American boy, in the Oval Office, reaching out to touch President Obama's hair as if to see whether it was like his own. In the end, I think Reid finally decided to change the rules because he believed the stonewalling of Obama's nominees represented a particular kind of nullification, resembling the insistent and false claims that Obama was a Muslim or was not born in the United States.

ways. But this sort of gerrymandered vision of the nuclear option is wishful thinking . . . If the majority leader changes the rules for some judicial nominees, he is effectively changing them for all judicial nominees, including the Supreme Court.

He was correct in his assessment that Democrats wanted it both ways and equally correct that we couldn't have this. He put up no fight, daring Democrats to change the rules:

Let me say we are not interested in having a gun put to our head any longer. If you think this is in the best interests of the Senate and the American people to make advice and consent, in effect, mean nothing—obviously you can break the rules to change the rules to achieve that. But some of us have been around here long enough to know that the shoe is sometimes on the other foot . . . I say to my friends on the other side of the aisle, you will regret this, and you may regret it a lot sooner than you think.

We will never know whether Mitch McConnell, out of some supremely Machiavellian motivation, wanted Democrats to take this fatal step, but once it was taken we understood that at his first opportunity McConnell would extend the precedent we were setting to cover Supreme Court nominees. Senator Grassley said so the day before the vote:

If [Reid] changes the rules for some judicial nominees, he is effectively changing them for all judicial nominees, including the Supreme Court . . . I find it hard to believe members of the majority leader's caucus would actually believe they could change the rules on lower court nominees, and then turn around and filibuster a future Republican president's Supreme Court nominee.

McConnell knew that day that he was pocketing a treasure, something he could pull out and use to his advantage later.

In the event, after invoking the nuclear option, Democrats confirmed ninety-six judges—including the three nominees to the D.C. Circuit and eleven other circuit court judges. Less than a year later, Republicans won the midterms by a landslide majority and retook the Senate. Now it no longer mattered whether the confirmation threshold was sixty or fifty; the new majority leader, Mitch McConnell, would determine who would and who would not get a vote. In President Obama's last two years, the Republican-controlled Senate confirmed only twenty-two judges, the lowest total since the final two years of Harry Truman's presidency.[11] As a result, Obama's administration left open to his successor more than one hundred vacancies, a record number and almost sixty more than Obama had inherited from George Bush.

More surprising than the Republicans' midterm recapture of the Senate would be the 2016 election of Donald Trump as president of the United States. Needless to say, this possibility never informed the Democratic caucus's debate about whether to invoke the nuclear option back in 2013. Monday-morning quarterbacking of any kind deserves a skeptical view. Nevertheless, I suspect that if Carl Levin had been able to add to his argument, "Oh, by

---

11 By contrast, in the final two years of Bush's presidency, a Democratic-controlled Senate confirmed sixty-eight judicial nominees. Fully twenty-five of Obama's judicial nominations expired on the Senate floor after having been approved out of the Judiciary Committee with bipartisan support.

the way, Mitch McConnell will block Barack Obama from filling a vacancy on the Supreme Court and use the prospect of filling it with a conservative to help elect Donald Trump, the master of ceremonies on *The Apprentice*," there would not have been five votes to change the rules.

III. "Do Your Job"

Justice Scalia died two years after the nuclear option detonated. In this climate and perhaps hoping that cooler heads would prevail, President Obama nominated Merrick Garland, the chief judge of the D.C. Circuit, as his choice to fill the Supreme Court vacancy. I had known Merrick Garland for a quarter of a century. I worked for him fresh out of law school, when both of us served in the deputy attorney general's office at the Department of Justice. I never heard another lawyer—or anyone, for that matter—refer to Garland without the highest admiration. He set the standard for excellence.

By selecting Garland, President Obama signaled his willingness to work with Republicans to place a nonideologue on the court. In 2010, Senator Orrin Hatch, then the ranking member of the Senate Judiciary Committee, had described Garland as someone who would be a "consensus nominee" for the Supreme Court. In 1997, a Republican-majority Senate had confirmed Garland to the D.C. Circuit 76–23.[12] By picking someone of Garland's age—he was sixty-four—the president also signaled that he understood Republicans would object to a younger judge who might remain on the bench for half a century.

---

12 All twenty-three no votes were cast by Republicans. At the time, partisanship of this kind infuriated the Senate Judiciary Committee chair, Orrin Hatch, who lashed out at his colleagues, saying, "Playing politics with judges is unfair, and I am sick of it."

The president asked the Senate to fulfill its constitutional duty and "give him a fair hearing, and then an up or down vote." But only minutes later, Senator McConnell reaffirmed his blockade: "It is a president's constitutional right to nominate a Supreme Court justice, and it is the Senate's constitutional right to act as a check on a president and withhold its consent," he said. Orrin Hatch duly retracted his 2010 endorsement: "I think highly of Judge Garland. But his nomination doesn't in any way change current circumstances. I remain convinced that the best way for the Senate to do its job is to conduct the confirmation process after this toxic presidential election season is over."

Throughout 2016, McConnell simply refused to process the nomination. No Senate Judiciary Committee hearing. No public debate. No floor vote. Most Republicans refused even to a meet with Garland, as if such a courtesy were worse than sitting down with Kim Jong-un of North Korea (before doing so became fashionable).[13] "It isn't about the person. It's about the process. It's about the principle," Chuck Grassley said after the Garland nomination. "I think we've laid down a principle that's pretty sound . . . It should go over to a new president."

One Republican senator who objected to this lack of process learned the hard way who was now calling the shots in the Republican Party. Senator Jerry Moran, of Kansas, explained to a town hall gathering back home, as reported in a local newspaper: "I would rather have you complaining to me that I voted wrong on nominating somebody than I'm not doing my job. I can't imagine the president has or will nominate somebody that meets my criteria, but

---

13 Only two Republicans fully broke ranks and said the Senate should vote on Garland's nomination: Mark Kirk, of Illinois, who was running for reelection in a Democrat-heavy state; and Susan Collins, of Maine, who had been a member of the 2005 Gang of Fourteen.

I have my job to do. I think the process ought to go forward." The Kochs' Judicial Crisis Network soon weighed in. Carrie Severino, the network's chief counsel and policy director and a former law clerk for Justice Clarence Thomas, described the efforts under way since Moran's statement:

> We are in the process of putting the finishing touches on a robust, multifaceted TV, digital, and grass-roots campaign designed to remind Sen. Moran that he represents the people of Kansas and neither President Obama nor the Democratic Party. Obama is trying to deny voters in Kansas, and around the country, a voice in the direction of their Supreme Court and Sen. Moran should not play into his hands. He should stand with the Republican leadership and the American people.

The next day, Good Friday, the Washington-based Traditional Values Coalition, which has been designated an antigay hate group by the Southern Poverty Law Center, observed of Senator Moran: "At least Judas Iscariot had the common courtesy to wait until after supper to betray his friends."

As right-wing fury spread across the country, Senator Moran patiently reiterated that he was opposed to the president's nominee but that "he had a duty to ask tough questions and demand answers." Such a "thorough investigation would expose Judge Garland's record and judicial philosophy and disqualify him in the eyes of Kansans and Americans."

None of this appeased organizations that claimed to represent the base of the Republican Party, and the following week Senator Moran surrendered. His office explained that he had studied Judge Garland's record "and didn't need hearings to conclude that the nominee's judicial philosophy, disregard for Second Amendment rights, and sympathy for federal government bureaucracy" made Garland "unacceptable."

Democratic senators believed McConnell's refusal to hold a hearing stemmed from a worry that the American people might find Garland to be reasonable, experienced, and competent—a judge's judge. "Why are they afraid to meet with him? Why are they afraid to hold hearings?" asked Harry Reid during a photo op with Garland during his first visit to Capitol Hill. "Are they afraid the American people will watch these hearings and demand they do something more than they are demanding now?"

Buoyed by public opinion polls showing that more than two-thirds of voters believed Garland deserved a Senate Judiciary Committee hearing, Democrats were confident McConnell's strategy would backfire and Senate Republicans would suffer in the coming elections. We remonstrated with McConnell, wielding the slogan "Do Your Job." But McConnell knew he would suffer nothing politically. He would, in fact, galvanize the Republican base. As he would tell supporters at the annual Fancy Farm Picnic in Kentucky, "One of my proudest moments was when I looked Barack Obama in the eye and said, 'Mr. President, you will not fill this Supreme Court vacancy.'" Intuiting that the American people would see the Garland episode as just another example of Washington dysfunction and just another pox on both parties, the majority leader instead swung for the fences. He would make the Supreme Court vacancy a seminal issue in the 2016 presidential campaign—a seat he would hold open and a prize for the taking if a Republican won.

With Donald Trump emerging as the presumptive nominee, Republican Party officials had become nervous about their conservative religious base. Trump was twice divorced, had been credibly accused of sexual misconduct on multiple occasions, would be caught on the *Access Hollywood* tape making disgusting comments about women, and had no plausible record of supporting conservative Christian positions on issues such as abortion and homosexuality (rather the reverse). Republican Party chairman Reince Priebus suggested that the candidate could provide reassurance by releasing a list of his potential Supreme Court nominees—people who would find favor with the Federalist Society and the Heritage Foundation: "solid names that we can say, 'OK, this what this is about.' It's about a conservative Supreme Court for generations. So you take all this sort of gamesmanship out and say, 'What is this about?' This [is] about the future of this country. This is not a game."

Trump's campaign team wasted no time generating that list. A little over a week later, the campaign released the names of eleven judges, selected "based on constitutional principles, with input from highly respected conservatives and Republican Party leadership." No candidate for president in history had produced a list of potential nominees for the Supreme Court, and it galvanized the Republican Party. On the day Merrick Garland became history's longest-waiting Supreme Court nominee without a Senate confirmation vote, Trump delivered his acceptance speech at the Republican National Convention. There he pledged to replace Justice Scalia with a "person of similar views, principles, and judicial philosophy."

At a campaign rally one week later, Trump was more blunt. He knew he was despised by many in his own party, but he also knew that the prospect of filling the open seat would persuade many to hold their noses and cast a ballot in his favor: "If you really like Donald Trump, that's great, but if you don't, you have to vote for me anyway. You know why? Supreme Court judges. Sorry, sorry, sorry—you have no choice."

In the final stretch of the fall campaign, Trump doubled down by adding ten more names to his list, including Judge Neil Gorsuch and Senator Mike Lee. He stated that the list was "definitive" and that he would choose as a nominee only someone who was on it. Republicans coalesced around Trump's proposed names, and conservatives, in particular, replaced their misgivings about the Republican candidate with their hopes for a conservative court.[14]

Democrats, meanwhile, were anticipating a Clinton victory—as just about everyone was—and were already debating whether Hillary Clinton should replace Judge Garland with a younger, more liberal, nominee after her election. The head of one liberal advocacy group, the Progressive Change Campaign Committee, noted how grassroots energy had "plummeted" after Obama nominated Garland: he "was the most conservative possible Democratic nominee, and it makes no sense for that to be who Democrats offer the nation after winning a fresh mandate." Clinton may have sensed this tension in her party. Her only mention of the Supreme Court in her acceptance speech was a glancing line about the need to appoint "Supreme Court justices who will get money out of politics and expand voting rights, not restrict them."

Throughout the fall, Clinton said that she would not be bound by President Obama's nomination of Garland, although she would not object if the Senate approved him during the lame-duck session.

---

14 The updated list persuaded one Republican senator in particular to come off the fence. After nobly invoking principle and declining to endorse Trump at the summer's Republican convention—he instead urged delegates to vote their conscience—Ted Cruz formally announced his support of Trump via a Facebook post. He listed six reasons, beginning: "First, and most important, the Supreme Court." Cruz had apparently forgiven Trump for calling him "Lyin' Ted" and for insinuating that Cruz's father was involved in the assassination of John F. Kennedy.

Writing on election eve, the *New Yorker*'s Ryan Lizza explained the politics:

> There's plenty of uncertainty about the outcome of the election tomorrow, but if Hillary Clinton wins the White House and the Democrats take back the Senate, . . . Clinton will also have a big decision to make. Should she press for Garland's confirmation in the lame duck to avoid a confrontation over the Court in her first year? For the left, this would be a disappointment and would be taken as an early sign that Clinton's progressivism is negotiable. It could also be interpreted as rewarding Republican obstructionism.

Republicans, also considering the possibility of a President Clinton and a Democratic Senate, began floating the idea of leaving the vacancy open for four more years. On a campaign swing in Colorado—campaigning for my opponent—two weeks before the election, Ted Cruz suggested an indefinite GOP blockade by citing "long historical precedent for a Supreme Court with fewer justices."[15]

In the end, no one had to face any of these what-ifs. Shocking even his own campaign, Donald Trump won the presidency. An analysis by the Pew Research Center found that Trump had benefited from a 3 percent increase in support from evangelicals—a margin that by itself may have been enough to swing the election

---

15 Cruz's statement echoed one by Senator McCain, who had suggested earlier in the month that Republicans would be "united against any nominee" put forward by a President Clinton. McCain later walked that back, but conservative commentators justified the notion: "As a matter of constitutional law, the Senate is fully within its powers to let the Supreme Court die out, literally," wrote the Cato Institute scholar Ilya Shapiro. Comments like these make you wonder whether we should just be done with it; let feral cats overrun the Capitol, Supreme Court, and White House, as they did the ruins of Rome; and sell maps to the tourists who might happen by.

and one due in part to the prospect of preserving the Supreme Court vacancy for a conservative. According to CNN, exit polls showed that among the one-fifth of voters who said the Supreme Court was the most important issue in their decision, 56 percent voted for Trump.

IV. Nothing to Lose?

Eleven days after his inauguration, President Trump announced his choice for the Supreme Court. Neil Gorsuch, a Tenth Circuit judge, was fifty-one—young to take a lifetime seat. He was also among the most conservative and most qualified choices on Trump's list. He was the mirror image of the candidate some of Clinton's supporters had hoped she might select. And he was from Colorado.

From the moment the nomination was announced, there was no question that Judge Gorsuch would become Justice Gorsuch. The only question was whether McConnell would invoke the nuclear option in order to confirm him. And that question turned, in part, on whether Democrats would decide to filibuster.

Even before President Trump's official announcement, the call for retribution had begun. *Washington Post* columnist Paul Waldman laid out the case that many other liberals made: "Should they [Democrats] filibuster Donald Trump's first Supreme Court nomination? Yes they should. They should do it to make a statement about the unconscionable way in which Republicans held this seat open, and about their willingness to be strong in the face of Republican bullying. And they need to realize that in taking this step, they have absolutely nothing to lose."

Merrick Garland's mistreatment meant we lived in a land where an eye for an eye was the law. The seat had been Barack Obama's to fill, and Republicans had taken it from him. Ever since Democrats invoked the nuclear option in 2013, there was a sense that the Supreme Court would inevitably be next. So why not have that fight now, when Democratic voters demanded "resistance" and were engaged as never before, to demonstrate that Democrats in Congress were willing to take a stand? "This is the time to pull the trigger—when they have a real justification for it," Waldman wrote. "Their voters are watching."

In the early days of the Trump administration, the question whether to filibuster his Supreme Court nominee quickly became the defining test of whether Democrats had the will to resist. Having failed to force the Republicans to "do their job" and consider Merrick Garland, Democrats began pledging to use every tool to avenge Garland and hold open the "stolen seat." I shared that frustration and the desire to hold Republicans accountable for what they had done. But I questioned whether filibustering Judge Gorsuch was the right thing to do and strongly disagreed that we had nothing to lose.

Although extremely conservative, Gorsuch was indisputably qualified and had survived the hearings unscathed. If we obstructed them by filibustering, Republicans would successfully invoke the nuclear option without any political damage to themselves. Senator Lindsey Graham made the point plainly: "This man is as mainstream a judge as you'll ever find on the conservative side . . . If they filibuster this man, we'll have no other option but to change the rules because if we don't that means President Trump can never make a selection to the Supreme Court and I will not allow that to happen."

Moreover, Gorsuch would not change the balance of the court. Crudely, he represented a younger Scalia replacing an older Scalia and was therefore unlikely to produce an appreciable difference in the court's decisions. I was most worried about whether President

Trump might get the chance to fill another vacancy and, if so, who the nominee might be. The next one would likely replace Justice Kennedy or Justice Ginsburg, changing the balance of the court and threatening 5–4 votes overturning reproductive rights, affirmative action, same-sex marriage, and the Affordable Care Act.

If we had any choice about when to provoke a battle over the nuclear option, it seemed to me that the time to do it was when a change in the majority would threaten *Roe v. Wade*. My view in the moment was this: With such an important ruling at stake and with President Trump perhaps weighed down by lower approval ratings, we might at least have a chance to mobilize Americans (including even some Senate Republicans) to preserve the sixty-vote threshold. If we filibustered Gorsuch and, as was inevitable, failed, we would have no tools to withstand the next nominee. Donald Trump could nominate anyone he wanted, and Democrats would have no mechanism to stop it.

In the end, I also believed that the American people, on whose behalf, ostensibly, we were having these battles, had a lot to lose if the Senate turned the Supreme Court into an institution populated by judges placed there by purely partisan votes. For such a significant, lifetime appointment, every nominee should be required to merit bipartisan support. If not, then potential nominees would have no incentive to demonstrate moderation and fairness. They would audition for the part by adopting messaging crafted by the most extreme organizations on the left or right. Democratic politicians would insist that Democratic presidents appoint the most liberal candidates in the land; Republicans would insist that Republican presidents appoint conservatives. To me this created enormous risk that the Senate would infect the (lifetime-appointed) Supreme Court with our (hopefully temporary) rank partisanship.

On April 4, 2017, a dark cloud of inevitability hung over Washington. Using the same script Harry Reid had used in 2013, Mitch McConnell appealed the chair's ruling that "the precedent of November 21, 2013, did not apply to nominations to the Supreme Court; those nominations are considered under plain language of Rule Twenty-Two." Once again, the Senate voted along party lines, 52–48, to overrule the chair. "The decision of the Chair does not stand as the judgment of the Senate," Orrin Hatch, the presiding officer, said after the vote. Although the text of the rule still required a sixty-vote majority for the Supreme Court, a majority of the Senate established a precedent requiring only fifty-plus-one votes. Once again, words had lost their meaning, although at least now they were meaningless consistently.

The nuclear option once invoked, the Senate proceeded to confirm Neil Gorsuch by a vote of 54–45. I was among those who voted no, recognizing that we had entered into a new era of partisan decision-making. That Friday afternoon, after the final vote, I walked alone back to my office in the Russell Building. Directly across the Capital Plaza, I could see the Supreme Court about a quarter of a mile away. In all that sculptured and landscaped expanse, there was not a single American with a single sign who had been mobilized or inspired to celebrate or oppose what we had done.

I took the absence of citizens in this most significant public square to be an indication of how little they thought they could affect outcomes in Washington. This did not come as a complete surprise. Republican ad makers estimated that conservative groups outspent liberal groups on television ads by nearly 20 to 1. The anything-goes election-spending regime exacerbated by the decision of the Supreme Court in *Citizens United* was once more in evidence. The Judicial Crisis Network (JCN) pledged $10 million in pro-Gorsuch ads; in turn, JCN was supported by another non-profit, the Wellspring Group, whose war chest, according to the Center for Responsive Politics, came largely "from an $8.5 million contribution from a single anonymous donor." Consistent with the effect of the court's jurisprudence, that anonymous person was perfectly free to remain anonymous. We would never know who the donor was or what business, if any, he or she had before the court.

That same day, anticipating the next logical step in the descent of the Senate away from a framework that encouraged deliberation and even bipartisanship, I, along with sixty of my colleagues, signed a letter to Senators McConnell and Schumer expressing our support for preserving the filibuster for purposes of legislation. Even with this effort, most senators would readily acknowledge the tenuous condition of the legislative filibuster as a result of the decisions already made.

With complete control over what came up for consideration on the Senate floor, McConnell now set aside legislative priorities to focus solely on judicial confirmations. "Believe me, the next time the political winds shift, and the other guys are in the ascendancy" Democrats could roll back the Republican policy victories, he said. "But they won't change these judges for a generation."

Through the two years of the 115th Congress, McConnell pursued a relentless strategy to fill the many judicial vacancies President Trump had inherited thanks to Republican delaying tactics throughout the Obama presidency. By the end of Trump's first two years, the Senate had filled eighty-six of them, including two Supreme Court vacancies and thirty-one Circuit Court vacancies. By way of comparison, this was almost double the number of Circuit Court vacancies filled in the first two years of the Obama administration and just nine fewer than Obama appointed in his last six years. Donald Trump became the first president in history to take full advantage of the opportunity to fill every open seat by a simple majority vote.[16]

At a Rose Garden press conference in October 2017, Trump and McConnell stood side by side to celebrate their judicial success. "The judge story is an untold story; nobody wants to talk about it," Trump said. "But when you think about it, Mitch and I were saying, that has consequences forty years out, depending on the age of the judge—but forty years out." For his part, Majority Leader McConnell would later say, "The most important decision I've made in my political career was the decision not to do something; it was the decision not to fill the Supreme Court vacancy created by the death of Justice Scalia."

V. Winner Take All

The founders knew that "history does not repeat itself but it often rhymes." The remark is reputedly Mark Twain's, but it has a long ancestry. For this reason, the founders mined the politics of ancient Greece and Rome for lessons about the promise and the perils of self-government. They placed those lessons at the heart of the American political experiment. Since then, our system of government has endured because citizens and elected officials chose to uphold rules, written and unwritten, that help us resolve our differences without unleashing a cycle of partisan fury that could endanger the republic.

---

16 In August 2018, Jason Zengerle reported in the *New York Times*: "The White House refers to every new batch of judicial appointees Trump selects as 'waves'—in early June, it announced the 'Fifteenth Wave of Judicial Nominees'—as if they're soldiers landing on the beaches of Normandy."

The founders believed that while civility, compromise, and cooperation are not required by law, laws cannot pass without them. They recognized that while the majority may have the power to rule on its own, it should not trample over the minority. They knew that at some point partisanship must give way to patriotism.

Through our history, including moments far more difficult than our own, these principles have served as political guardrails, keeping us from veering off course into political dysfunction. But in recent years, we have begun tearing these guardrails down. And in doing so, we risk incurring the revenge of history by ignoring its lessons.

There is a tendency these days—and, in particular, in the Senate—to think our problems are unique and that the consequences of our actions are fleeting. Both thoughts are wrong.

Millennia ago—the tale is told by Thucydides—civil war consumed the ancient city of Corcyra. The majority party wished to remain in alliance with Athens, while the minority sought an alliance with Corinth. According to Thucydides, both sides, driven by their "lust for power arising from greed and ambition," spared "no means in their struggles for ascendancy." He goes on: "In their acts of vengeance they went to even greater lengths, not stopping at what justice or the good of the state demanded, but making the party caprice of the moment their only standard." As the civil war intensified, both sides struggled in vain to end it, because "there was neither promise to be depended upon, nor oath that could command respect; but all parties rather dwelling in their calculation upon the hopelessness of a permanent state of things, were more intent upon self-defense than capable of confidence." In the end, the Corcyrean civil war led to the dissolution of the city:

The Corcyreans butchered those fellow-citizens they regarded as enemies, charging them with putting down the democracy, but some also died because of personal hatred . . . Occasions for bringing in outsiders were readily found by those wishing to make any change in government . . . With public life confused to the critical point, human nature, always ready to act unjustly even in violation of laws, overthrew the laws themselves and gladly showed itself powerless over passion but stronger than justice and hostile to any kind of superiority.

The founders read Thucydides.[17] They knew that once factions sever the bonds of trust embodied in laws, norms, and traditions; once every disagreement becomes irreconcilable and we pursue the good of our party with complete disregard for the good of our country; and when we treat politics as a tribal war, distorting the obligations of elected officials and leaders, we lose the ability to do anything worthy of our roles. Indeed, we lose the ability to reason and even converse. Consider the similarity of the content of our social media feeds and cable television repartee to political attitudes during the Peloponnesian War, as described by Thucydides: "Reckless audacity came to be considered the courage of a loyal ally; prudent hesitation, specious cowardice; moderation was held to be a cloak for unmanliness; ability to see all sides of a question, inaptness to act on any." Once we consider our fellow citizens to be enemies, we invite the endless cycles of blame, escalation, and

---

17 Jefferson mentions him, for instance, in a letter to John Adams in 1812, in which he announces that he is, in effect, going off the grid: "I have given up newspapers in exchange for Tacitus & Thucydides, for Newton & Euclid; & I find myself much the happier."

retaliation that can destroy republican government. This mentality has damaged our ability to do anything of consequence, including tackling our debt or fixing our broken and cruel immigration system.

In the case of Supreme Court nominations, the two parties each did their part to tear up the incentives to reach bipartisan agreements. We are at real risk that lifetime appointments to the highest court, which touches every aspect of American life, will become just another partisan exercise. This episode reveals how hard it is for both sides to see beyond the partisan tactics of the moment. It shows that some lawmakers will never lack an excuse to break with custom or change the rules to their benefit. They may even argue, as some recently have done, that the damage is not so bad, that everything can continue as normal.

Consider the cost of the judicial nuclear fallout. Throughout the Gorsuch filibuster debate, McConnell justified the rules change by saying that he was "restoring the practice and custom of the Senate." By this, he meant the body was returning to an era when senators did not filibuster judicial nominees. McConnell's claim ignores an important part of the story, namely that for nearly all of our history, qualified judicial nominees, including Supreme Court nominees, routinely received the votes of a large, bipartisan majority; after 1970, it was not uncommon to see nominees supported by more than ninety votes.[18] In other words, though the filibuster was available to them, senators saw no need to resort to it, bound as they were by deference to a president's choices, and qualified and

---

18 When President Ronald Reagan nominated Antonin Scalia to the Supreme Court in 1986, the Senate understood his conservative judicial philosophy well. Nevertheless, it confirmed Scalia 98–0. That overwhelming vote reflected the Senate's understanding of its constitutional duty to confirm qualified nominees even when senators disagreed with a nominee's vision of the Constitution. Scalia himself recognized how modern politics had changed the confirmation process. In 2007, he observed, "I couldn't get sixty votes today."

mainstream as those choices generally were. For the foreseeable future, and perhaps forever, confirmation votes will now break on party lines, with the burden of confirmation resting entirely on the majority and with the minority relieved of any responsibility to advise and consent with respect to judicial nominees or any others. Time will tell what effect partisan confirmations will have on the American people's confidence in the judiciary and even in the rule of law, but it is unlikely to be good.

Just ten days before Justice Scalia's death, Chief Justice Roberts foreshadowed the confirmation fight ahead. He noted that the judicial confirmation process "is not functioning very well" and "is being used for something other than ensuring the qualifications of the nominees." Pointedly, he observed that Supreme Court justices "don't work as Democrats or Republicans . . . and I think it's a very unfortunate impression the public might get from the confirmation process." In our era, we have decided that this is the Senate's new custom and practice. Now and for the foreseeable future, judges will be chosen and approved primarily on the basis of their partisan credentials. The views of a president who appoints a judge will be more significant than the judge's judicial record, and every judgment will be seen as made by, say, a "Trump-appointed judge" or an "Obama-appointed judge."

Two years into the Trump administration, we have a better sense of what it meant to "go nuclear" on judges. The looming sense of a foregone conclusion lingered through the end of the 116th Congress. The Senate's approval of Brett Kavanaugh as a Supreme Court justice followed on the heels of a Punch and Judy version of the advise-and-consent process. The fight was set up by Beltway pros in advance. Even before Kavanaugh was nominated, Demand Justice, a progressive advocacy group, began collecting millions of dollars to turn up the partisan volume; meanwhile, the right-wing Judicial Crisis Network, which was still in business after the Merrick Garland fight, aired an attack ad using Senators Schumer, Feinstein, Warren, and Booker as convenient foils to generate opposition from its own reactionary base. One organization played Tybalt to the other's Mercutio, each spoiling for a fight someone else would have to settle.

This bellicose posturing might have played well on the coasts, but it did not build support for Democratic candidates in Indiana, Missouri, Montana, or North Dakota, states Democrats needed to hang on to if we were to take back the Senate. What it did instead was turn the incumbents into targets of their own party's progressive wing. But even if this rhetoric sounded tough on cable news, we lacked one thing McConnell had when he ran his campaign against Garland: the votes to win.

Not surprisingly, Democrats began to question whether their support of the nuclear option and of the filibuster of Justice Gorsuch was the right thing to do. Senator Chris Coons, who had expressed his misgivings in 2013 and again after President Trump's election and again in 2017, voiced them once more. Senator Amy Klobuchar expressed her doubts too, saying on *Meet the Press*: "I don't think we should've made that change, when we look back at it. But it happened because we were so frustrated, because President Obama wasn't able to get his nominees." Speaking in 2017 of the decision to use the nuclear option in 2013, Senator Schumer said, "I wish it hadn't happened."

By the time Christine Blasey Ford arrived to testify about Judge Kavanaugh's alleged sexual misconduct, the Senate Judiciary Committee was the worst possible forum on the planet to ascertain the background behind her allegations. As the confirmation hearings dragged on, the nominee diminished himself in full public view.

Kavanaugh replied to the allegations against him by uncorking a mix of indignation, self-pity, and even partisan rage. He went so far as to wonder whether the inquiry into his record was "revenge on behalf of the Clintons." Lindsey Graham came to Judge Kavanaugh's defense, blasting committee Democrats for turning the hearings into an unethical sham. His charges went unanswered.

When the hearings came to a close, whatever civic authority remained with the Senate Judiciary Committee was in tatters. Judge Kavanaugh was a nominee who under other circumstances— circumstances in which a nominee still required sixty votes—might have been withdrawn by reason of his temperament or his personal record. In this new world, his supporters came ready to win any fight. He was voted onto the Supreme Court of the United States by a mere two votes, the smallest margin for a nominee to the court since 1881.

All the while, Mitch McConnell pressed relentlessly to fill vacancies on the lower courts. These appointments don't rivet the country's attention the way the Kavanaugh hearings did; Majority Leader McConnell has made sure of that. He has used his post-nuclear leverage to cram as many Trump nominees through as the calendar permitted. And, no longer requiring sixty votes, the Senate has managed to seat a roster full of judges who otherwise wouldn't make the B-team cut.

The Senate confirmed Texas Supreme Court justice Don Willett, President Trump's nominee for the Fifth Circuit, 50–47. His record included writing a memo opposing a gubernatorial proclamation honoring the Texas Federation of Business and Professional Women. His reason? Their "talk of 'glass ceilings,' pay equity . . . the need to place kids in the care of rented strangers, sexual discrimination/harassment, and the need generally for better 'working conditions' for women (read: more government)."

The Senate confirmed the Kentucky lawyer John K. Bush, President Trump's nominee for the Sixth Circuit, 51–47 despite a past that included pseudonymously writing blog posts peddling conspiracies about Barack Obama and comparing abortion to slavery.

The Senate confirmed Wisconsin attorney Michael B. Brennan, President Trump's nominee for the Seventh Circuit, 49–46, despite Brennan's record of suggesting publicly that judges can ignore judicial precedents they deem "incorrect" and justifying denial of habeas corpus to enemy combatants who were once US citizens with the brutal ancient dictum, "In time of war, the laws are silent."

The Senate confirmed Nebraska attorney L. Steven Grasz, President Trump's Eighth Circuit nominee, 50–48, in spite of the fact that the American Bar Association (ABA) gave him a unanimous rating of "not qualified." The group rates judicial nominees based on their legal writings, professional reputation, and judicial temperament. It was the first time the Senate confirmed a nominee rated "not qualified."[19]

And as if one judge deemed unqualified by the ABA wasn't enough, the Senate also confirmed United States magistrate judge Charles Goodwin, President Trump's nominee for the US District Court in Western Oklahoma, by a vote of 52–42. The ABA questioned Goodwin's work ethic as judge magistrate, noting that his frequent absences until mid-afternoon were not compatible with the workload of a federal district court judge. Then, in December 2018, the Senate confirmed a third judge deemed "not qualified"— Jonathan Kobes, who joined Grasz on the Eighth Circuit.

---

19 The ABA has reviewed more than seventeen hundred federal judicial nominees since 1989. Before Grasz, it had only twice unanimously deemed judicial candidates unqualified, both of them nominees put forward by President George W. Bush. The nominations were withdrawn.

And what will happen in the future when vacancies arise on the Supreme Court but the party controlling the Senate majority is different from the president's party? What incentive is there for the majority to approve the president's nominee, especially if they can use the vacancy as a winning campaign issue? The probable result will be that no future Senate will confirm a president's Supreme Court nominee unless it is controlled by the president's political party. This can only result in a more polarized court. Which in turn will result in the American people's losing faith in the judgments rendered by our judicial system.

Our founders knew their history. But they could not guarantee that we would heed its lessons. They knew that unrestrained partisanship poses at least as great a threat to freedom as the size and power of government. They warned us to pay attention to that lesson. They built institutions to check the worst impulses of faction, to help us navigate profoundly consequential decisions—like confirmations for the Supreme Court—without tearing each other apart. But the founders also placed their faith in the willingness of elected officials to resist the passions of the moment and rise to defend our institutions and our traditions—especially in hard times. And they placed faith in the willingness of the public to compel elected leaders to do so. Today, with each escalating crisis, Washington's political leaders instead reinforce the fear that our present dysfunction is, as Thucydides said, "a permanent state of things"—and one more reason to write off the American experiment as a losing cause.

THE CORRUPTION
OF INACTION

*How "money politics," empowered by the Supreme Court,
has sapped our ability to do anything at all—such as
meet the threat of climate change.*

I. "That Good Old Global Warming"

On April 25, 2018, from a seat in a marbled chamber, I watched
and listened as French president Emmanuel Macron addressed a
joint session of Congress—the culmination of his three-day state
visit to the United States. These events are usually polite affairs.
Foreign leaders praise the values shared by "our two countries" and
Congress stands to applaud from time to time in routine affirma-
tion of mutual goodwill. Macron's visit had gone well. To symbolize
bilateral friendship, Macron and President Trump had together
planted an oak tree imported from France on the South Lawn of
the White House; few noted that the tree was soon dug up and
placed in quarantine—standard practice for life-forms from over-
seas, apparently, and not some new anti-immigration policy.

Macron's speech to Congress opened uneventfully, but as it
developed the French president became more forceful and more
frank about challenging issues. On the subject of climate change,
for instance, Macron warned about the danger of carbon emissions

and reminded the chamber that "there is no Planet B" for us to flee to. Democrats leaped from their seats to applaud this observation. From where I stood, on Planet A, I saw only one Republican senator, Susan Collins of Maine, standing to applaud. The other Republicans remained in their seats, stone-faced.

After the speech, Macron returned to Paris, where the United States in 2015 had helped lead the world toward a landmark accord—currently endorsed by 196 nations—to address climate change.[1] Now, under its new president, the United States had become the only country in the world to commit to withdraw from the agreement. The US government was also the only one officially questioning whether climate change was even happening. In Europe, in countries such as Germany, France, and the United Kingdom, parties on the left and right fight ferociously over many issues—but not over whether the planet is warming. Rather, they sometimes fight over which party can claim more credit for trying to address the problem. In the United States, an entire political party has embraced climate-change denial as political orthodoxy. How did this happen?

It's a question I began asking myself several years ago, when, for my sins, I was asked to chair the Democratic Senatorial Campaign Committee in advance of the 2014 midterm elections. The role of chair requires raising as much money as possible to win as many races as possible. It also requires understanding the dynamics of key races nationwide: the alchemy of candidates, conditions, and issues that decide elections—and, once the votes are counted, control of the Senate.

---

1 The goal of the Paris Agreement is to prevent an average global temperature rise beyond two degrees Celsius. Pursuant to the agreement, each signatory identified and committed to achieve its own national emissions target.

One lesson from that experience stands out above all others: not a single Democratic candidate for the Senate that year who was in a contested race faced a Republican opponent willing to argue unequivocally that climate change was real, that human activity was its chief cause, and that we needed to do something fast. Not in Louisiana, where salt water from a rising sea threatens to poison land all across the bayous. Not in North Carolina, where warming Atlantic waters are strengthening hurricanes and seem poised to swallow the Outer Banks. Not in Alaska, where temperatures are rising faster than anywhere else in America. Not even in my home state, Colorado, where continued warming has increased the severity of drought, diminished the snowpack, and fanned dangerous wildfires.

That year in every one of these states, Republicans who rejected the scientific consensus about climate change beat Democratic incumbents. Also celebrating on election night was Mitch McConnell, of Kentucky, who not only cruised to his sixth term in the Senate but also realized a lifelong ambition to be its Republican majority leader. (As I write these words, I am still awaiting his thank-you call.)

A few weeks after the election, I was home in Denver convalescing from a two-year purgatory spent cold-calling and annoying potential donors. I continued to ponder the political carnage Democratic senators had suffered.[2] My mind turned again to climate change.

Colorado's electorate is one-third Democratic, one-third Republican, and one-third Independent. Poll after poll shows that

---

2 Partly because so many Democrats were swept into office with President Obama in 2008, far more Democratic Senate seats were at stake in 2014. There were a total of thirty-six senatorial seats up for grabs in 2014. Republicans won twenty-four of the seats, a net change of nine, and took control of the Senate for the first time in eight years.

by a sizable percentage, Coloradans believe climate change is real. They also believe that human beings contribute to it, even if there is disagreement about what we should do to address the problem. In Colorado, the evidence of climate change is all around us. We see it in the Rocky Mountain wildflowers tricked by unseasonable warm air into an early bloom. We see it in the infestation of pine and spruce beetles that have destroyed our drought-stricken trees, turning entire valleys of green forest into expanses of dull and brittle gray. We see it in our crowded lodges and resorts as Coloradans cram a winter's worth of skiing into a shrinking season. We see it in the diminishing water used to grow our wheat, corn, and sorghum and to provide forage to our cattle.

Across the state, eight out of ten Coloradans are concerned enough about climate change that they support new policies to reduce carbon emissions, and nine out of ten support more investment in renewable energy. We have seen the promise of drawing energy from cleaner and more diverse sources. Compared with other states, Colorado ranks fourth in wind jobs; tenth in oil and gas jobs; and ninth in solar jobs. Our largest utility, Xcel Energy, has publicly committed to making a transition to 100 percent carbon-free electricity by 2050, while saving its customers money.[3] By protecting our iconic landscapes, farms, and ranches, we enjoy thriving agricultural, tourist, and recreation economies. Renewable energy now drives $9 billion of economic activity annually; our other outdoor industries account for $28 billion. Coloradans perceive climate change as a real threat but are confident we can transition our economy in ways that will foster growth and create

---

3 In December 2018, the utility tweeted: "#BREAKING: We're rolling out a #cleanenergy vision to serve all customers with #zerocarbon electricity by 2050 and cut carbon emissions 80% by 2030 company-wide—all while delivering affordable and reliable energy."

jobs. We share a responsibility to communities that have relied on coal for jobs—a responsibility to help them figure out how to manage these transitions in ways that benefit them. We know this commitment will not be easy to meet.

None of what I have reported is a universal view, but it is a widely shared view among Coloradans with a variety of political affiliations or no political affiliation at all. And it aligns with the universal view of scientists who have studied the question: human activity is warming our planet to an unsustainable level. In November 2018, a year when California suffered the deadliest and most destructive wildfires in the state's history, thirteen US federal agencies and more than three hundred scientists, other experts, and officials produced a study that not only confirmed that climate change was real and that human activity was responsible for it but also concluded that as a result of climate change America's economy could lose hundreds of billions of dollars annually by the end of the century. Some of the effects take their toll on our rural communities: climate change has already doubled the land burned by wildfires in the western United States and caused a severe reduction in stream flow in the Colorado River.

Republicans in Washington think very differently about all this. President Trump responded to his own government's report, which the administration tried to bury, by saying, "I don't believe it."[4] The gap between opinion on the right and established scientific fact is

4 To be fair, the president had more to say. As quoted in the *Washington Post*: "One of the problems that a lot of people like myself —we have very high levels of intelligence, but we're not necessarily such believers. You look at our air and our water, and it's right now at a record clean. But when you look at China and you look at parts of Asia and when you look at South America, and when you look at many other places in this world, including Russia, including—just many other places—the air is incredibly dirty. And when you're talking about an atmosphere, oceans are very small. And it blows over and it sails over. I mean, we take thousands of tons of garbage off our beaches all the time that comes over from Asia. It just flows right down the Pacific, it flows, and we say where does this come from. And it takes many people to start off with."

all the more baffling when we consider that not so long ago elected Republicans, including three Republican presidents, accepted climate science as correct, accepted climate change as a catastrophic threat, and accepted the responsibility of the US government to do something about it.

In the 1960s and '70s, a series of shocking environmental disasters had made it impossible to look the other way. From my childhood, I remember the image of flames shooting up from Cleveland's Cuyahoga River in 1969. I remember acid rain degrading the Appalachian soil and, in turn, devastating forest plant life and wildlife. Although I didn't live in Denver at the time, I recall headlines about the "brown cloud" obscuring the city's skyline and mountain views each winter as cool air from the Rocky Mountains trapped exhaust and other noxious gases at street level in a dingy haze. I also remember how scientists developed a powerful consensus that these were problems caused by human beings, demanding solutions created by human beings. In her 1962 book *Silent Spring*, Rachel Carson called on Americans to pay attention: "It is only within the moment of time represented by the twentieth century that one species—man—has acquired significant power to alter the nature of his world, and it is only within the past twenty-five years that this power has achieved such magnitude that it endangers the whole earth and its life." In 1970, President Nixon, a Republican, created the Environmental Protection Agency. That same year he signed the Clean Air Act. Two years later he signed the amended Clean Water Act.

Two larger environmental dangers soon came into focus, both with profound implications for the entire planet. First, evidence mounted that human activity was depleting the ozone layer—an invisible gaseous blanket that shields us from the sun's most harmful ultraviolet rays. It is essential for life on earth. Over the years, the

ozone layer had been thinned by the release of chlorofluorocar-
bons, which were widely used in refrigerators, air conditioners, and
aerosol spray cans. One looming consequence: potentially dramatic
spikes in skin cancer down the road. The chemical industry did all
it could to cast doubt on the science, but the reality became impossible to ignore when in 1985 a team of British scientists discovered
an actual hole in the ozone layer above the Antarctic.

Ronald Reagan, that great foe of regulation, is the unlikely
hero of this story. An avid outdoorsman and a survivor of skin
cancer, Reagan overcame objections from industry and his own
cabinet to champion the necessary protections, embodied in 1987
in the landmark Montreal Protocol, the first UN agreement to be
signed by all 197 countries. Deterioration of the ozone layer has
been halted and indeed reversed. By one estimate, the Montreal
Protocol will prevent an estimated 280 million cases of skin cancer
in America by the end of the century.

The second new danger identified during this period was climate change. For years, a growing number of scientists had warned
that a concentration of greenhouse gases in the atmosphere was
trapping the sun's heat and warming the planet through what
became known as the "greenhouse effect." In 1988, as a particularly
sultry June enveloped Washington, Colorado senator Tim Wirth
scheduled a hearing on climate change. Dr. James Hansen, then the
director of NASA's Goddard Institute for Space Studies, testified
that he was 99 percent confident that rising global temperatures
were the result not of a natural variation but of a buildup of carbon
dioxide in the atmosphere. Before Reagan left office, he supported
the formation of the United Nations Intergovernmental Panel on
Climate Change (IPCC), which was charged with reviewing available evidence and suggesting responses.

You might think that the election of President George H. W. Bush, an oilman from Texas, would have signaled the end of Washington's bipartisan concern about climate change. It didn't. During the campaign—at a stop in car-producing Michigan, no less—Bush declared:

> Those who think we are powerless to do anything about the greenhouse effect forget about the "White House effect"; as President, I intend to do something about it . . . We will talk about global warming, and we will act.

In 1989, President Bush sent his secretary of state, James Baker, to the UN's first annual meeting on climate change. Bush then offered a sweeping proposal to curb sulfur dioxide, the leading cause of acid rain, seeking caps well below the recommendations of his advisers. In 1990, Bush strengthened the Clean Air Act to bolster the fight against air pollution and ozone depletion. In 1992, his final year in office, Bush submitted the United Nations Framework Convention on Climate Change, the first-ever global treaty to reduce greenhouse gas emissions, to the Senate for ratification, and the treaty was indeed ratified through a two-thirds vote. The vote included ayes by Mitch McConnell and Trent Lott, neither of them known as a starry-eyed tree hugger.

There are many remarkable facts about this period, especially from today's perspective. For one, Washington actually functioned. Moreover, many Republicans—though not all by any means—endorsed sensible environmental protections and sometimes led the way. When some on the left proposed command-and-control regulation of industry, Republicans countered with ideas like cap-and-trade, a market-based approach that allows firms to buy and sell pollution credits (an idea that many Republicans now oppose and a classic example of how the political winds have shifted). The idea has been wildly successful over the years. President Reagan used it to curb leaded gasoline. President George H. W. Bush used it to slash ozone-depleting chemicals and sulfur dioxide emissions. Colorado built on changes like these to clear up the brown cloud in the 1990s; without them it would still be seen hovering over nationally televised Denver Broncos games.

When Bush's son George W. became president in 2001, the words "climate change" were still safe for Republicans to utter in public. Like his father, Bush promised to cap carbon dioxide and require power plants to reduce greenhouse gas emissions—again, on a campaign stop in Michigan. In 2008, Republican presidential candidate John McCain openly campaigned on his climate record. As a senator, McCain had introduced a version of cap-and-trade three separate times. He mentioned climate change in all three presidential debates with Barack Obama. Throughout this thirty-year period, the momentum in national politics, often pushed by Republicans, seemed to shift in favor of climate action. That was certainly true within Democratic politics, where climate change had emerged as a pillar of the party's agenda.

And yet, within just a few years, an outlook like McCain's was viewed with contempt in Republican circles. McCain's running mate, former Alaska governor Sarah Palin, had agreed during a 2008 campaign debate that "real changes are going on in our climate"—though not with the same conviction she brought to "drill, baby, drill"—but eight years later she would star in the far right documentary *Climate Hustle*, suggesting that climate change was "bogus" and wondering whether the federal government was exploiting the issue "to have more control over us, our homes, our businesses, our families, our lives." Her rhetoric, which in earlier times would have been dismissed as ranting from the paranoid fringe, had moved to the heart of the Republican Party.

In 2016, all of this culminated in the nomination and election of Donald J. Trump, who famously described climate change as a "hoax" perpetrated by the Chinese. The president has filled key cabinet positions—such as at the Environmental Protection Agency and the Department of the Interior—with some of America's top climate deniers. He has rolled back dozens of climate-change and other environmental regulations—rollbacks now being challenged in the courts—putting the health of our children at risk while at the same time leaving business owners unclear on whether to invest in pollution-reducing technologies. Trump has reversed the long-established tradition of conservation begun by Teddy Roosevelt, attempting to decrease the size of our national monuments and open up more land to oil-and-gas exploration. As noted, he has backed away from the global climate agreement negotiated by his predecessor. Afterward, during a cold snap, he tweeted, "Perhaps we could use a little bit of that good old Global Warming that our Country, but not other countries, was going to pay TRILLIONS OF DOLLARS to protect against. Bundle up!"[5]

II. Equating Money and Speech

The Republican shift from the environmental stewardship of Nixon, Reagan, both Bushes, and McCain to the anything-goes attitude of

---

5 On another occasion, in a moment reminiscent of *Back to the Future*, the president confused ozone depletion with climate change, complaining in one breath, "I want to use hair spray. They say, 'Don't use hair spray, it's bad for the ozone,'" and then declaring that when it comes to "the global warming . . . a lot of it's a hoax."

Palin and Trump is, to a significant degree, the work of the United States Supreme Court. The court has fundamentally misconceived the corrupting power of money in our politics and in so doing sanctioned a far more insidious form of corruption.

If President Nixon is directly responsible for much of modern environmental policy, he is indirectly responsible for much of the modern campaign finance system. The Watergate scandal involved allegations not only that Nixon obstructed justice but also that he accepted illicit campaign contributions. In response, Congress passed laws capping campaign contributions and campaign spending and required public disclosure of both. It also limited the amount of money that outside groups could spend on elections. Finally, it created the Federal Election Commission (FEC) to provide enforcement.

Almost immediately, corporations and other wealthy interests challenged the new regime as a violation of their rights under the First Amendment. This set off a prolonged legal fight stretching across three decades, beginning with the 1976 Supreme Court ruling in *Buckley v. Valeo* and ending (for the moment) with two rulings in 2010: the Supreme Court's decision in *Citizens United v. FEC* and the D.C. Circuit court's decision in *SpeechNOW v. FEC*.

In *Buckley*, the court grappled with two basic questions: What is the relationship between money and speech? And when can the government limit political spending to protect the integrity of our democratic system? On the first question, the court ruled that regulating spending for political speech required the same "exacting scrutiny" as regulating speech itself. Put simply, the court was effectively treating the spending of money the same way it treated speech. It left undecided the question of whether corporations enjoyed the same rights as people under the First Amendment.

On the second question, the court sought to define when it was acceptable to regulate money in politics. This answer was more complex and ultimately very consequential. The court's initial step was to define corruption narrowly. "To the extent that large contributions are given to secure a political *quid pro quo* from current and potential office holders," the court explained, the "integrity of our system of representative democracy is undermined." The court went on: "Of almost equal concern . . . is the impact of the appearance of corruption stemming from public awareness of the opportunities for abuse inherent in a regime of large individual financial contributions."

The idea behind this last point is that if someone directly contributes to my campaign (the apparent "quid") and I pass legislation consistent with that donor's interests (the apparent "quo"), and even if there is no actual corruption or corrupt intent, an *appearance* of corruption might arise that could cause Americans to lose faith in their democracy. This being so, the *Buckley* court found a "sufficiently important governmental interest" in the "prevention of corruption and the appearance of corruption." Accordingly, it upheld limits on what individuals could contribute to campaigns, along with disclosure requirements for those contributions.

But the court then made a damaging leap. Even as it upheld limits on individual contributions to political campaigns, it undid limits on political spending by outside groups. In the jargon of campaign finance, these are called "independent expenditures."

According to the court, "The absence of prearrangement and coordination of an expenditure with the candidate . . . alleviates the danger that expenditures will be given as a *quid pro quo* for improper commitments from the candidate." Put differently, the independence of outside groups meant there was insufficient concern about corruption or the appearance of corruption to justify restrictions on their political spending.

At the same time, the court distinguished between two categories of speech: express advocacy and issue advocacy. Express advocacy included political communication that explicitly supported or opposed a candidate. Issue advocacy, in the court's opinion, educated the public about general political issues. The court ruled that groups primarily engaged in express advocacy were subject to campaign finance laws, with all the attendant contribution limits and disclosure requirements. Groups primarily engaged in issue advocacy, however, faced no such restrictions.

In *Buckley* the court recognized the challenge of distinguishing between the two categories of advocacy and suggested that any advertising containing the phrase "vote for," "elect," "cast your ballot for," "support," "vote against," "defeat," or "reject" constituted express advocacy. In the years after *Buckley*, most lower courts interpreted the Supreme Court's holding to mean that advertisements without these "magic words" were not express advocacy and therefore could not face limits under our campaign finance system.

To Washington's ad makers, this was a distinction without a difference—preposterous to the point of irrelevance. As the former chair of the National Rifle Association's advocacy arm put it, "It is foolish to believe there is any practical difference between issue advocacy and advocacy of a political candidate. What separates issue advocacy and political advocacy is a line in the sand drawn on a windy day."

Consider the following example. If an outside group runs an ad saying: "Michael Bennet worships Stalin—vote against Michael Bennet in the election next Tuesday," then that would be a form of express advocacy, subject to campaign finance rules. But if the ad said: "Michael Bennet worships Stalin—contact Michael Bennet and tell him to stop supporting Communism," then that would be an issue ad and face no such rules.

In the twenty years following the *Buckley* decision, factions took full advantage of this loophole. In the 1996 elections, political parties, unions, and corporate-backed groups flooded the airwaves with $150 million worth of issue ads that to any ordinary human being were indistinguishable from campaign ads.

Thus, the National Abortion and Reproductive Rights Action League, a pro-choice group, ran ads excoriating Republican presidential candidate Bob Dole for his record on abortion:

> Now Bob Dole says he's tolerant on abortion? The real story is he's supporting a platform that would make abortion illegal . . . Take us back to back-alley abortions . . . Join us in opposing Bob Dole's extremist party platform. While we still have the choice.

On the other side, groups like Citizens for a Sound Economy lambasted President Clinton for opposing legislation to limit liability claims for defective medical products:

> My name is Peggy Philips. I was clinically dead twice. I had no pulse. And no blood flow to my brain. It was cardiac arrest. Doctors implanted a medical device that can shock my heart to keep me alive. My implant's special battery needs changing from time to time. But unfortunately, it may no longer be made because of the threat of frivolous product liability lawsuits. Congress passed product liability reform legislation.

Mr. President, won't you please sign this bill? I might not be lucky the third time around.

Ads like these were everywhere. Politicians took note. Congress tried to clean up after the court with the Bipartisan Campaign Reform Act of 2002, known more often as McCain-Feingold, after its sponsors: John McCain and Russell Feingold, a Democratic senator from Wisconsin. Among other reforms, the law tried to stem the tide of sham issue ads. Specifically, it barred corporations and unions from running ads that mentioned candidates by name within sixty days of a general election and within thirty days of a primary election. Unsurprisingly, McCain-Feingold came under immediate attack from both left and right, uniting unlikely bedfellows such as the National Rifle Association and the AFL-CIO in opposition. Among the critics was Senator Mitch McConnell, who became the face of a lawsuit challenging McCain-Feingold as unconstitutional under the First Amendment. In 2003, the Supreme Court disagreed, ruling 5–4 in *McConnell v. FEC* to uphold major provisions of the law. In its ruling, the court pointed to the "reams of disquieting evidence" showing how outside contributions and spending had "given rise to the appearance of undue influence." The new reforms, therefore, were a pragmatic and constitutional response to safeguard the integrity of our democracy.

In a few years, with two new justices on the bench, the court would come to a radically different conclusion. In 2008, the conservative nonprofit group Citizens United prepared to release a faux documentary titled *Hillary: The Movie*, which had been created to damage Hillary Clinton's presidential campaign. The group sought an injunction to prevent the FEC from blocking the film's distribution under McCain-Feingold. Once again, the case made it to the Supreme Court.

The 5–4 ruling in *Citizens United* released a depth charge into the currents of American politics. Essentially, the court upended the previous thirty years of precedent and doubled down on *Buckley*. Yes, the government had an interest in preventing the reality or the appearance of corruption; and yes, that interest justified limiting individual contributions to campaigns. But it could not justify restrictions on spending by outside groups.

The *Citizens United* court then went a step beyond *Buckley*. It declared that "political speech is indispensable to decision-making in a democracy, and this is no less true because the speech comes from a corporation rather than an individual." In other words, with respect to campaigns, corporations had the same rights under the First Amendment that "natural persons" have. Indeed, according to the majority opinion, the government had muffled "the voices that best represent the most significant segments of the economy"— that is, corporations—and placed "onerous restrictions" on corporate speech.

Not only had the court misunderstood American politics, but in its haste it also chose to decide the case with virtually no factual record to consider. Instead of remanding the case to a lower court, which would establish the facts, the *Citizens United* court simply imported the record from *McConnell v. FEC*, noting that "the *McConnell* record was 'over 100,000 pages' long, yet it 'does not have any direct examples of votes being exchanged for . . . expenditures' . . . This confirms *Buckley*'s reasoning that independent expenditures do not lead to, or create the appearance of, *quid pro quo* corruption." Once again the court defined its view of corruption narrowly, in this case as votes being traded for expenditures.

The Supreme Court reached one of its most pivotal decisions in a vacuum of evidence. In place of facts, it based its decision on a set of assumptions about money in politics that was utterly divorced from reality. For example, the court contended that "it is well known that the public begins to concentrate on elections only in the weeks immediately before they are held. There are short time frames in which speech can have an influence." That would certainly be news to voters in swing states and to candidates for federal office, who routinely campaign for two years before Election Day.

The court observed that even though outside groups "may have influence over or access to elected officials," such influence and access "will not cause the electorate to lose faith in this democracy." Moreover, the court went on, the fact that officials grant access or are influenced should not necessarily be taken to mean "that these officials are corrupt." Well, of course not—but there is still the issue of perception, which even *Buckley* recognized. And there is cause for alarm when someone like the former congressman Mick Mulvaney confesses that "if you were a lobbyist who never gave us money, I didn't talk to you. If you were a lobbyist who gave us money, I might talk to you." In December 2018, President Trump named Mulvaney as the acting White House chief of staff.

Where has all of this left us? Starting with *Buckley*, the court has in essence treated the spending of money as a form of speech. In *Citizens United*, the court wrote that "it is our law and our tradition that more speech, not less, is the governing rule." This line of reasoning leads to the inevitable conclusion that more money, not less, should be the governing rule in our democracy—and should in fact be welcomed. That is the opposite of what most voters believe.

I have yet to meet a single American who believes that the problem with our politics is that there is not enough money in it.[6]

Citizens United has taken America down a dangerous road. And it has become more dangerous still. After the Supreme Court struck down limits on what outside groups could spend, lower courts used the same logic to strike down limits on individual contributions to these groups. Money could now make its way unhindered into the coffers of two of the most corrosive entities in modern politics: dark-money groups and super PACs. Dark-money groups, officially considered "social welfare organizations" by the IRS, enjoy preferential tax treatment and do not have to disclose their donors. For this privileged status, they need only demonstrate that they are not "primarily" engaged in political activity.[7] By contrast, super PACs can legally spend and solicit an unlimited amount of money in our elections. Although super PACs, unlike some other dark-money vehicles, are required to disclose their donors, we know that few Americans will ever lay eyes on an FEC report. Most will see a flurry of ads that hide individual financiers behind Orwellian names like Colorado Rising or Protect Americans Now that give us no idea of their true agenda. These ads run all year, not just sixty days before an election. Far from clarifying the truth, our system of financing campaigns has become an exercise to obscure it.

---

6 In his dissent in *Citizens United*, Justice John Paul Stevens dismantled the majority's myopic view of corruption. "Corruption operates along a spectrum, and the majority's apparent belief that *quid pro quo* arrangements can be neatly demarcated from other improper influences does not accord with the theory or reality of politics," he wrote. "It certainly does not accord with the record Congress developed in passing BCRA [McCain-Feingold], a record that stands as a remarkable testament to the energy and ingenuity with which corporations, unions, lobbyists, and politicians may go about scratching each other's backs."

7 The FEC, through its rule making, has determined that "primarily" constitutes just over 50 percent, meaning that these phony "social welfare organizations" can spend nearly 50 percent of their money on politics without running afoul of the statute. The FEC must have been using an abridged dictionary when it issued its rules.

All of this goes beyond even *Citizens United*, in which eight of the nine justices at least seemed to agree that disclosure was not only constitutional but also essential. In another case decided that year, Justice Antonin Scalia captured this idea and the stakes perfectly:

> Requiring people to stand up in public for their political acts fosters civic courage, without which our democracy is doomed. For my part, I do not look forward to a society which ... campaigns anonymously and even exercises the direct democracy of initiative and referendum hidden from public scrutiny and protected from the accountability of criticism. This does not resemble the Home of the Brave.

Here is the problem: all of us share that home with Mitch McConnell. And as long as McConnell leads the Senate, the chance of strengthening disclosure is as likely as the majority leader's retiring to an ashram in Berkeley.[8]

If we lift our eyes from the legal arguments, the wreckage becomes clear. With no basis in fact, the Supreme Court in *Citizens United* imagined a world where the specter of McCain-Feingold was "chilling" the free speech of corporations. It then invoked this invented fear to justify unlimited donations and spending in our elections through largely unaccountable outside groups. Because of *Citizens United*, we now live in a world where an ordinary voter can make only a limited donation (a few thousand dollars) to a political candidate and must disclose it, while a billionaire casino owner in Las Vegas can contribute tens of millions to outside groups that can run ads without once mentioning the owner's name.

---

8 The only reason he might actually head to Berkeley would be if he thought he could get more judges as a result.

As if this were not bad enough, the court's rationale rests on the fiction that super PACs are independent. To pass the court's test for independence, there must be an "absence of prearrangement and coordination." In our campaign finance system, the FEC is responsible for making this determination, but it remains haplessly deadlocked and ineffective (as Congress designed it to be). It is common for a politician's senior staff to leave a campaign in order to run the associated super PAC, even as all involved continue to share the same media buyers, consultants, and fund-raisers. Politicians may attend fund-raisers for super PACs as "featured speakers," collect a small check for themselves, and, upon departing the event, leave behind a staff member to ask the crowd for unlimited donations.

Although super PACs cannot coordinate with campaigns, they can use publicly available information, such as a candidate's schedule, talking points, and even video, to mold into ads. People interested in the health of our political system should watch Ted Cruz on YouTube coaching his children to recite grace for the camera, soliciting compliments from his mother, and walking through cornfields for hours on end—all distributed by the Cruz campaign in 2016 to enable allied super PACs to download the clips and turn them into ads indistinguishable from anything his own campaign would produce. In 2016, the Republican presidential candidate Carly Fiorina created a Google calendar publicizing her schedule weeks in advance, allowing an associated super PAC, Carly for America, to rent venues, hire organizers, and register voters—effectively assuming core functions of the campaign.[9]

---

9 The FEC is hardly a stern watchdog. To avoid a violation of the rules, it required Fiorina's super PAC to change its official designation from Carly for America to CARLY for America, which technically removed Fiorina's name. "CARLY" officially stands for "Conservative, Authentic, Responsive, Leadership for You."

Increasingly, super PACs are becoming bolder, skirting even the modest disclosure requirements. It is now routine for them to drop millions in ads mere days before an election, knowing they will not have to disclose their donors until long after the voters' ballots have been cast. Some super PACs don't report their donors at all, in open violation of federal law.

As a politician, I have known only the system created by *Citizens United*. In 2010, during my first campaign for the Senate, super PACs and other outside groups spent $21 million in my race alone—more than in any other Senate race in the country. According to the Center for Responsive Politics, four years later, total outside spending on Senate campaigns climbed to $411 million—more than double the figure for the previous midterms. When I ran again in 2016, total outside spending on the Senate reached $571 billion, and the figure topped $1.4 billion for federal races nationwide.

Citizens United, quite simply, has warped the character of our political system: independent expenditures rose dramatically; super PACs proliferated; outside groups made up a larger share of all political advertising; and that advertising grew more frequent and more negative in tone.

The Supreme Court had agreed to hear *Citizens United* without a trial court's developing a factual record, out of concern that any delay would unconstitutionally restrain corporate speech. The flood of political spending after *Citizens United*, however, has not come mainly from corporations. (Generally, corporations have preferred to invest in lobbyists rather than super PACs as vehicles for political influence.) Instead, some of the wealthiest people on the planet have used super PACs to try to bend politics in their direction. The *New York Times* reported that in the 2016 election, a mere 158 families gave almost half of the early money to Republican and Democratic presidential candidates. Most of the $176 million in early contributions from these families went to super PACs.

During that cycle, Sheldon Adelson, a casino owner in Las Vegas, donated $78 million to super PACs. To any of us, this is a staggering amount of money. To him, it was trivial, given his net worth of tens of billions. The power of megadonors in this new environment has distorted the behavior of candidates in troubling ways. Candidates for public office routinely engage in an elaborate courtship with a handful of billionaires hoping they will bankroll a friendly super PAC (or, at the very least, spare them from millions in negative ads). In the 2018 election cycle, just 0.1 percent of all super PAC donors accounted for nearly 80 percent of all super PAC donations. Since *Citizens United,* just ten donors have given more than $1 billion to outside groups, with six of the ten supporting Democrats. Outside spending has warped behavior across the political spectrum.[10]

And it has corrupted Congress. This corruption looks nothing like the relatively benign image that worried the court in *Buckley.* That was low-dollar, quid pro quo corruption defined by palpable action—bad enough, to be sure. The corruption we actually face is a corruption of inaction; corruption that arises when billionaires threaten to spend unlimited sums if a politician strays from their wishes.[11]

---

10 Although it surely does not fall into the category of an explicit quid pro quo, President Trump's recent award of a Presidential Medal of Freedom—the nation's highest civilian honor—to Sheldon Adelson's wife, Miriam, a doctor and philanthropist, certainly raised eyebrows. (Trump has benefited from Sheldon Adelson's dark-money generosity.) Previous winners of the medal include the historian David McCullough, the astronaut Sally Ride, Justice Antonin Scalia, the architect Maya Lin, General Colin Powell (twice), and the novelist Toni Morrison.

11 The idea that power is as much about preventing things as it is about getting things done has a long heritage. Writing to John Adams in 1813, Thomas Jefferson recognized that "mischief may be done negatively as well as positively."

Quiet intimidation paralyzes Congress across vast areas of policy—from immigration to guns to taxes. It is difficult to detect because it is invisible. But, as with a black hole in space, we can see it through the gravitational force it exerts, pulling politicians away from hard choices we do not make; from tough votes we never take; from committee hearings we fail to hold; from bills we can't pass despite an urgent need; and from scientific facts we willfully ignore.

III. Out for Blood

On January 20, 2009, the day of his inauguration, President Obama stood before the country and promised to "roll back the specter of a warming planet." I imagine that among those listening to Obama, along with the 38 million other Americans who watched the ceremony, were Charles and David Koch, billionaire brothers and co-owners of Koch Industries, the nation's largest privately owned oil company. By some estimates, its refineries, pipelines, and chemical processors emit 300 million tons of carbon dioxide each year.

The Koch brothers have showered millions of dollars on advocacy groups and think tanks, all with the purpose of undermining environmental protections.[12] With a Koch Industries executive, they founded an entity called Citizens for a Sound Economy that labeled acid rain a hoax and fought regulations to reduce it. Later, as the Kochs extended their political reach, Citizens for a Sound Economy split itself into two new groups: FreedomWorks and Americans for Prosperity. In 2007, Americans for Prosperity took

---

12 The Koch family has long swum in the currents of the American far right. The father, Fred Koch, was a founding member of the John Birch Society. His son David ran on the Libertarian presidential ticket in 1980; its platform, described in press accounts, called for the abolition of Social Security, the FBI, the CIA, the IRS, the EPA, welfare, the postal service, and public schools—and the list goes on.

a page from Grover Norquist's "no tax" pledge by introducing a No Climate Tax Pledge for members of Congress to sign. Between 1997 and 2010, the Kochs gave some $48 million to groups that actively denied climate science or opposed climate action.[13]

Although the campaign created more doubt and less urgency about climate change, especially on the political right, it did not stop Republicans from nominating John McCain as their presidential candidate.[14] It did not stop Americans from electing Barack Obama in 2008. And it did not stop the House of Representatives from moving forward in the spring of 2009 on a cap-and-trade bill known as Waxman-Markey, to reduce greenhouse gas emissions. That spring the Tea Party emerged almost overnight as a new center of gravity in the Republican Party. Its origins were mostly spontaneous and driven by taxes, health care, and the national debt, but the Koch brothers immediately recognized the Tea Party as a useful vehicle for their anti-climate agenda. With donations to Tea Party candidates and causes, the Kochs stoked the movement's climate-denial potential and deployed its grassroots activists against elected Republicans who refused to toe the line.

As Waxman-Markey progressed in the House, Americans for Prosperity leveraged the Tea Party's national Tax Day rallies, handing out shirts and placards and framing the bill as "the largest excise tax in American history." The group dressed up staffers

13 This tactic revived a play from the tobacco industry, which had spent millions to discredit the emerging science that linked smoking to a range of diseases. Tim Phillips, the president of Americans for Prosperity, understood the stakes. "If we win the science argument, I think it's game, set, and match for them."

14 According to Gallup, in 2007, 61 percent of Americans agreed that global warming was caused by the "effects of pollution from human activities" while 35 percent attributed it to "natural changes in the environment." By 2010, those numbers were 50 and 46 percent, respectively. In 2008, 40 percent of Americans agreed that "global warming will pose a serious threat to you or your way of life." By 2010, that number fell to 32 percent.

as fake EPA "carbon cops" who threatened to ban barbecues and confiscate lawn mowers. It launched a "hot air tour," featuring a giant balloon, warning that cap-and-trade meant "lost jobs, higher taxes, less freedom." Although Waxman-Markey narrowly passed the House, the Koch-led campaign sharply politicized the climate debate. Confronted by this stifling political force, the Senate never took up the bill.

At this moment, the Supreme Court handed down its decision in *Citizens United.* The Tea Party was already out for blood. Now it gained the advantage of unlimited spending. I saw this firsthand in Colorado, where my opponent, Congressman Ken Buck, defeated former lieutenant governor Jane Norton in the Republican primary with backing from the Tea Party and from FreedomWorks. At a campaign event in Longmont, Buck stood next to Oklahoma senator Jim Inhofe, one of Washington's earliest and most vociferous climate deniers, and praised him for calling global warming "the greatest hoax that has been perpetrated."[15]

These dynamics played out across the country. As a member of the House Committee on Science, Space, and Technology, Robert Inglis, a Republican from South Carolina, had seen polar ice cores that conclusively demonstrated the spike in atmospheric carbon dioxide over the past century. For refusing to deny what science demonstrated, he lost to the Tea Party–backed candidate, Trey Gowdy, by forty-two points. Inglis knew why: he had "gone to Satan's side on climate change."

In Michigan, Congressman Fred Upton had long been considered a Republican moderate on the environment. At one time,

---

15 In 2015, after one of Washington's relatively uncommon snowstorms, Inhofe brought a snowball from outside onto the Senate floor in order to disprove, once and for all, the idea that climate change could possibly be real.

Upton's website avowed that "everything must be on the table as we seek to reduce carbon emissions." As *Mother Jones* discovered, after FreedomWorks launched a "down with Upton" petition, such language on the website mysteriously vanished.

In Arizona, John McCain faced the first serious primary challenge of his career. His opponent, J. D. Hayworth, was a television and radio personality turned congressman with strong Tea Party backing. As Waxman-Markey advanced in the House, McCain had begun drafting a parallel climate bill in the Senate. As pressure from the Tea Party mounted, McCain quietly backed away from his own initiative.

Having flexed their muscles in the 2010 Republican primaries, Koch-backed groups now set out to pummel Democrats in the general election. Americans for Prosperity and other groups hammered Democrats who had voted for Waxman-Markey, reviving their playbook pitting the environment against the economy. They targeted Democratic congressmen like Rick Boucher and Tom Perriello, who represented rural districts in central and southwest Virginia. One Americans for Prosperity ad excoriated Boucher for playing "a key role" in passing a cap-and-trade energy tax that "is expected to kill 56,000 Virginia coal and manufacturing jobs"—a highly improbable scenario, according to the independent fact-checking group PolitiFact. In November, both Perriello and Boucher lost their seats in an electoral rout of Democrats. Republicans picked up five Senate seats and took control of the House.[16]

---

16 Riding the wave were new members of Congress like Morgan Griffith, of Virginia. Griffith would serve on the House Committee on Energy and Commerce, where he has claimed that global warming was actually good for the Vikings. He has also wondered whether evidence of melting ice caps on Mars meant that human beings couldn't be responsible for melting ice caps here on earth.

I barely survived my own race, scraping out a narrow victory against Ken Buck. As I stood for my oath of office the following January, I was joined by new Republican senators like Marco Rubio, Rand Paul, Pat Toomey, and Mike Lee. All had prevailed in primary fights against establishment Republicans thanks to backing from the Tea Party and FreedomWorks. None had publicly embraced the science of climate change.

One week later, NASA issued a press release confirming that 2010 had tied for the warmest year on record.

IV. The Wrong Target

By the end of Barack Obama's first term, many environmentalists were expressing disappointment with his record. Although Obama had gone further than any predecessor to limit carbon emissions— regulating carbon emissions for vehicles and preparing to do the same for power plants—a comprehensive climate bill remained elusive.

For the tens of millions of Americans who believe we have a moral responsibility to act on climate change, this was an especially challenging moment. Faced with Republicans' denial on the one hand and diminishing opportunity to act on the other, they had no obvious path forward in Congress. President Obama's approach was to make what progress he could in the absence of legislation, through his executive authority. At home, he directed the government to set rules for fuel-efficiency standards for cars and light trucks, increase investment in renewable energy, and promote energy efficiency. Abroad, he pursued a comprehensive global treaty to set binding limits on carbon pollution. Although environmental groups cheered these steps, they hungered for a symbol that could energize the grass roots and build a powerful coalition to break Washington's paralysis.

In this context, America learned about the Keystone XL pipeline. In 2008, a company called TransCanada had proposed a pipeline system, known as Keystone, to transport heavy crude from the oil sands of Alberta to Gulf Coast refineries. The final phase, a twelve-hundred-mile pipeline from Alberta to Nebraska, was called Keystone XL. The controversy over the pipeline boiled down to whether we should allow the Alberta oil sands to move in a pipeline through US territory. Unlike the silky black crude of Texas or Saudi Arabia, oil sands are a thick, viscous mixture of sand, water, clay, and a heavy black oil called bitumen with a higher concentration of carbon dioxide.

In 2011, NASA's James Hansen wrote an open letter arguing that "exploitation of the tar sands would make it implausible to stabilize the climate and avoid disastrous global impacts." Hansen's words reached Bill McKibben, the environmental activist and founder of a grassroots group called 350.org. To McKibben, the pipeline proved irresistible. It offered a tangible manifestation of our fossil-fuel dependence and because it crossed an international border its fate lay with the State Department. Unlike stalled climate legislation, on which Congress needed to act, the fate of Keystone XL was entirely in President Obama's hands.

It is not generally the job of Congress to approve of any pipeline in America. Even so, Republicans on the Hill took it upon themselves to manufacture opportunities to weigh in and make more difficult the politics of the administration's decision-making process. Republicans relished training attention on Keystone XL. Reviving lines of attack that had devastated Democrats like Boucher and Perriello, Republicans falsely argued that by opposing the pipeline

Democrats opposed American jobs and infrastructure. The facts told a different story. According to the State Department in 2014, Keystone XL would create just thirty-five permanent jobs. It also represented less than a thousandth of America's 2.5 million miles of pipe. The most relevant finding in the State Department analysis was that regardless of whether the pipeline was built, the oil sands in Alberta would still be developed. The exploitation of the tar sands that Dr. Hansen warned against would occur anyway.[17] If the United States did not permit the pipeline, the oil would be transported by railcars, which were arguably worse than a pipeline in terms of environmental and safety consequences.

In order to wound vulnerable Democratic incumbents, Republicans seized the opportunity to bring resolutions to the Senate floor demanding that the State Department approve the pipeline. Democrats, sensing political jeopardy, took cover under alternative versions aimed at creating votes against the pipeline.[18] Among the mountain of pointless votes during my two terms in the Senate, the ones on Keystone XL stood out for their particular inanity. The pipeline would not have created thousands of permanent jobs; it would not have made America energy independent; and, because the oil sands would reach the market anyway by other means, it would make no substantial difference for our net carbon emissions.

Although Keystone was an effective and visceral symbol that activated the environmental movement, it had marginal effect on

---

17 According to the State Department, the pipeline would not result, as some alleged, in 29 million tons of incremental emissions annually since the oil would be developed whether or not the pipeline was built. Instead, the incremental emissions were 0.24 million tons in the first year (due to construction) and 1.44 million tons (due to operations) every year thereafter—an infinitesimally small fraction of global emissions and roughly 0.05 percent of Koch Industries' annual emissions.

18 Such bills are known as "side-side" amendments. Both parties commonly use them to obscure hard votes. They typically never pass.

climate. There might have been good reasons to defeat the pipeline. I often said, for example, that if the tar sands were in Colorado instead of Canada, I would chain myself to a fence to avoid the environmental degradation that would occur. Canada had made a different decision. I also am sympathetic to Oklahomans who might not want the pipeline to cross their territory. This, however, was not an issue before Congress. And as the State Department and Congressional Budget Office reports demonstrated, concern about climate change was not a sound reason to oppose the pipeline. I was keenly aware that I would soon be defending President Obama's Clean Power Plan on the basis of facts and science. I believed that opposing Keystone on the basis of climate change would destroy my credibility as I argued for the much more significant Clean Power Plan. It was not just my credibility; the credibility of the entire climate science movement was at stake. I have seldom felt this alone in my public life. I voted to build the pipeline when the issue came to the Senate floor several times over the next three years. I took no comfort or satisfaction in these votes and accepted the understandable beating from my allies in the environmental community.[19] Approving a single piece of infrastructure—one we had no business meddling with in the first place—was far from how I once imagined Congress spent its time. I would have much preferred that we debate and ultimately approve a comprehensive climate and energy bill.

It was not to be. Recognizing that Congress would prove unable to act, President Obama moved ahead in June 2013 by

---

19 There are some who argue that my decision on Keystone was a decision to support the oil-and-gas industry. An evaluation of my work in the Senate proves the contrary. I led the effort to prevent drilling in the Arctic National Wildlife Refuge. I have fought against the Trump administration's rollbacks of methane standards for the oil-and-gas industry and to protect pristine areas in Colorado and elsewhere from drilling.

issuing his own Climate Action Plan, a comprehensive policy to reduce America's carbon pollution. The following year, the EPA announced the Clean Power Plan, which laid down a deadline of the year 2030 for slashing carbon emissions from the electricity sector by 32 percent. Combined, these were among the biggest steps America had ever taken on climate change. Compared with the emissions associated with Keystone XL, President Obama's Clean Power Plan, when fully implemented, would be up to 247 times more consequential.

All of this nuance was lost in our political debate as the 2014 elections neared. As chair of the DSCC during that cycle, I saw debate over Keystone XL effectively hijack what should have been a real discussion about the country's challenges on energy and climate. As far as I could tell, the Republican energy policy amounted to little more than: approve Keystone XL, close the EPA, and deny climate change. In North Carolina, when a moderator asked all four Republican Senate candidates whether climate change was a "fact," three of them burst into laughter. (And the answer was no.)

On the Democratic side, Keystone XL had become the sole proxy for whether you cared about climate change. At a town hall in Frisco, Colorado, I faced a storm of questions about my support for Keystone XL from angry constituents. Not a single person asked me about the Clean Power Plan. I had to bring it up myself at the meeting's end. Later that day, I met with the national board of Earthjustice (my wife's former employer and an organization where we have many friends), which happened to be meeting in Grand County, Colorado. Someone asked whether I thought it was possible to enact a bipartisan version of the Clean Power Plan into law. I said that depended not just on Republicans but also on what Democrats could do. I wondered out loud whether Keystone could be traded as part of a deal or whether it had become such an ominous symbol of climate destruction that we could never explain to supporters why we would back a deal that contained it.

As the 2014 elections drew near, I spent almost all of my time dialing donors to keep pace with the tide of outside spending. With the floodgates open after *Citizens United*, Americans for Prosperity spent over $125 million nationwide during that cycle. Along with other groups, it ran ads flaying Democratic incumbents across the country on energy and jobs. In the end, Democrats lost nine seats, paving the way for Senator Mitch McConnell to take the reins as majority leader. In January 2015, McConnell scheduled our first vote of the year. It was not to tackle our national debt, then standing at $13 trillion. Nor was it to address a festering opioid crisis that would claim nearly forty-eight thousand American lives in 2017. It was to approve Keystone XL.

Ahead of the vote, friends from environmental groups, disappointed by my position regarding the pipeline, reached out to try to persuade me to vote no. They were willing to concede (if only for the purpose of indulging me) that Keystone's role was symbolic, but they pointed out that it had been a useful tool to organize grassroots activists. Keystone connected the abstract issue of climate change to the lives of many Americans and successfully activated the environmental movement.

For this reason, someone asked a member of my staff who had the misfortune of defending my position what I would have thought about the civil rights protesters who sat at the Woolworth lunch counters to defy segregation. I found this question clarifying. The young people knew that they would be beaten, literally, on national television for seeking to participate in what amounts to ordinary life—which had the effect of isolating segregationists from the overwhelming majority of Americans. They inspired white northerners, who up until that point had been largely content to look the other way, to embrace the civil rights movement.

While the Keystone XL campaign generated ferocious enthusiasm among the environmental community, it brought few, if any, who were not already predisposed to join the fight. Unlike the Woolworth protests, it was not designed to persuade a majority of Americans to care about climate change; it was designed to energize those who already cared about environmental issues but had been silent for years—a worthy cause that I support but one that was not comparable. I also doubt very much whether, in the designing of the pipeline campaign, consideration was given to how it might feed a false perception that Democrats were against high-quality construction jobs, against unions, against energy independence, and against building infrastructure in our rural communities, a point Republicans underscored with every Keystone vote. But that is what happened.

More broadly, the Keystone debate threatened to untether us from a politics rooted in facts, when our most powerful argument was that climate opponents ignored the science. That is a battle we have to win over the long haul, and it becomes harder if the other side can claim that climate proponents are playing fast and loose with the facts.

In the end President Obama rejected the permit to build Keystone XL, arguing that this strengthened his hand ahead of the landmark climate negotiations in Paris. In his statement, the president lamented the pipeline's "overinflated role in our political discourse" and described it as a "symbol too often used as a campaign cudgel by both parties." He also dismissed claims that the pipeline represented either a "silver bullet for the economy" or "the express lane to climate disaster." He offered nuance I had not heard on the Senate floor over the past two years.

Hailing President Obama's decision as a victory, 350.org blasted out a message to its supporters:

> This is a big win. President Obama's decision to reject Keystone XL because of its impact on the climate is nothing short of historic—and sets an important precedent that should send shock waves through the fossil fuel industry . . . We're looking to build on this victory, and show that if it's wrong to build Keystone XL because of its impact on our climate, *it's wrong to build any new fossil fuel infrastructure, period.*

A year later, Donald Trump was elected president of the United States.[20] He filled his cabinet with some of America's top climate deniers. He is attempting to cancel the Clean Power Plan and reverse higher fuel-efficiency standards. He opened our coasts and public lands to drilling, including the Arctic National Wildlife Refuge. He imposed tariffs on solar panels and sought to subsidize coal-fired power plants. In the first half of his first term, he has the worst environmental record of any modern president—and this at a time when relevant scientific data have never been more abundant. In political terms, our environment is in crisis.

---

20 After Trump's election, I met with the leader of a major labor union to help make sense of the result. He told me that although his members may not have tracked the nuances of the debate over Keystone XL, it left them with a clear impression: Republicans were for pipelines; Democrats were against them. As a consequence, most of his rank and file voted for Trump.

V. A Job for the 96 Percent

Like climate change itself, the damage of *Citizens United* is all around us. I saw it in the partisan applause to Emmanuel Macron's factual claim when he spoke before a joint session of Congress. But I've also seen it on debate stages where candidates stake out positions far outside the political mainstream; on my daily schedules, where whole afternoons are swallowed by ceaseless fund-raising; and in the abysmal approval rating of Congress, which ranks below support for root canals, traffic jams, and Communism.[21] Most important, I have seen it year after year on the Senate floor, where the priorities of the American people are met by relentless inaction.

Many forces contribute to this dysfunction, but the blame lies principally with our broken system of campaign finance. Consider the following: what if Congress passed a law requiring ordinary Americans to disclose their personal campaign contributions and also said they could donate only a certain small amount; allowed the wealthiest Americans to contribute an unlimited sum, anonymously, to organizations Congress deemed "independent"; allowed these same organizations to claim independence even when they were run by families and former staffers of members of Congress; permitted members to speak at fund-raisers for these organizations, so long as they left the scene before their staff asked the crowd for

---

21 I have nothing against dentists. I recently had an emergency root canal in Washington and am grateful to my dentist for his work. As for traffic, whenever I complain about it, my environmentalist wife responds, "We're not in traffic, we *are* traffic." As for comparative measures of congressional popularity, I once took a chart to the Senate floor to show where we ranked. Here are some actual data: the IRS had a 40 percent approval rating; Paris Hilton had 15 percent; Communism had 11 percent. The approval rating for Congress was 9 percent. Fidel Castro came in behind, at 5 percent. I expect that Castro's rating has improved since his death.

an unlimited donation; and then allowed these organizations to spend whatever they wanted whenever they wanted in our elections.

This is our existing campaign finance system, as designed by Congress and amended by the Supreme Court. The court has focused narrowly on preventing outsize direct contributions that may constitute corrupt quid pro quo arrangements between donors and politicians. Think of this as a corruption of action. But it lost sight of how big donors can drop giant money bombs on the other side of persnickety legal boundaries. As a result, the court has allowed a broader corruption of inaction to take hold: give me millions (or don't spend millions against me) and I'll keep something you dislike from happening. In a 2017 poll asking Americans to rank the sources of dysfunction in Washington, 96 percent blamed "money in politics." This was followed by the 94 percent of Americans who blamed "wealthy political donors." The American people see what the Supreme Court does not: that massive outside spending by a wealthy few, even without an explicit quid pro quo, corrupts their government and erodes their faith in our national political institutions.

To restore our government, we need to confirm justices who will broaden the court's dangerously narrow view of corruption, established in *Buckley* and elaborated to devastating effect in *Citizens United*. We need more justices in the mold of Sandra Day O'Connor—the last justice to have held an elective office—who have broad practical experience and know how politics actually works in the real world. But even with a pro-reform majority, the court will need a specific case to revisit its precedent with respect to campaign finance. Theoretically, the court itself may have opened the door. Toward the end of the majority opinion in *Citizens United*, the court observed that in the future:

> If elected officials succumb to improper influences from independent expenditures . . . we must give weight to attempts by Congress to seek to dispel either the appearance or the reality of these influences. The remedies enacted by law, however, must comply with the First Amendment, and it is our law and our tradition that more speech, not less, is the governing rule.

In other words, if circumstances change and new concerns about corruption arise, the court is prepared to review new campaign finance reforms. Of course, an irony of *Citizens United* is that by unleashing a flood of money in our politics the court has effectively disabled Congress with regard to enacting any such reforms.

There is no shortage of ideas about what reform could look like. They include banning members of Congress from becoming lobbyists, requiring political groups with anonymous donors to reveal their biggest supporters, and forcing outside groups to disclose who gives them money and where they spend it. After *Citizens United*, ideas like these survive more as lonely floor speeches than as meaningful priorities on the legislative calendar. A constitutional amendment, though it would be more effective, seems even more implausible. Our greatest hope lies in the vote. If those 96 percent of Americans made campaign finance a real priority in elections, they could soon have a Congress able to enact long-overdue reforms.

In the meantime, we must look to cities and states to pass campaign finance and disclosure laws to challenge the Supreme Court. For example, Colorado could pass a law that requires full and accurate disclosure of every political ad in our state, establishes limits on super PAC contributions and spending, and defines coordination rules to enforce meaningful independence. Communities from across the political spectrum have already begun to act. Purple states such as Arizona and Missouri have passed laws to publicly finance elections and limit campaign contributions in statewide elections. New York City provides a six-to-one match for all small donations if the benefiting candidate agrees to contribution and spending limits. Seattle provides $25 "democracy vouchers" for voters to contribute as they wish. When these laws prompt legal challenges, as they will, reformers will have an opportunity to develop evidence the Supreme Court never considered: that independent expenditures not only create an *appearance* of corruption but also lead to actual corruption—the corruption of inaction. Given the explosion of independent expenditures since *Citizens United*, the universe of potential evidence has only grown.[22] Citizens and advocacy groups can help by convening former members of Congress and their staffs to share examples of the specific bills abandoned, speeches shelved, positions disavowed, votes shifted, and facts rejected under the threat of massive outside spending.

We cannot wait for change in the courts, however, to address the threat of our changing climate. In 2016, Donald Trump successfully argued that reviving jobs and energy sources from the nineteenth century would make America great in the twenty-first. In doing so, he took a sledgehammer to more than a generation of progress on environmental and climate issues, threatening to wreck our global leadership and pull us into the past. His electoral success raises a mirror to the state of our politics around energy, jobs, and the environment. From one angle, we see the Republican Party forcibly dragged from the environmental stewardship

---

22 Justice Anthony Kennedy, the author of *Citizens United*, expected that in the "cyber age" unlimited corporate spending would be paired with immediate disclosure. In a 2015 interview, he admitted that disclosure was "not working the way it should."

of Nixon, George H. W. Bush, and John McCain to the taunting denial of Trump.[23] From another, we see millions of Americans hungry for better answers about lost jobs and the difficulties posed by a changing economy. Another tilt of the mirror and we see a Democratic Party that has yet to make a persuasive enough case to draw in (for instance) farmers and ranchers, union members, and the urban and rural poor who don't yet see how climate change is changing their lives.

More than any other issue, climate change requires policies that can endure across administrations, even generations. At a minimum, those policies should: adequately account for the costs of climate change without further burdening working families, dramatically accelerate our transition to renewable energy and zero-emission technologies, and prepare our communities for the dangers of climate change we can no longer avoid. Most important, whatever policy emerges has to survive changing political winds. To do that, we have to assemble an unusual—and powerful—coalition of Americans.

That coalition is hiding in plain sight. In the wake of *Citizens United*, the Kochs have effectively chained the Republican Party's position on climate change to their own. Instead of bemoaning this situation, we should seize it as an opportunity. Today, most Republican politicians find themselves locked into a position out of line with a majority of Americans in almost every single congressional

---

23 Teddy Roosevelt captured this vanishing Republican tradition in a 1910 speech: "I recognize the right and duty of this generation to develop and use the natural resources of our land; but I do not recognize the right to waste them, or to rob, by wasteful use, the generations that come after us. I ask nothing of the nation except that it so behave as each farmer here behaves with reference to his own children. That farmer is a poor creature who skins the land and leaves it worthless to his children. The farmer is a good farmer who, having enabled the land to support himself and to provide for the education of his children, leaves it to them a little better than he found it himself."

district. They find themselves at odds with leading American businesses such as Amazon, Target, and Nike; with a growing number of evangelicals and religious leaders; and with an overwhelming majority of voters under thirty. Republican politicians who deny climate science also occupy a political reality separate from the physical reality that increasingly confronts our outdoorsmen, farmers, and ranchers, who see the land changing with the climate. I am baffled by the newly elected Republicans in the Senate who refuse to acknowledge that the increase in the frequency of wildfires, droughts, hurricanes, and floods is affecting their constituents.

This should be an untenable position. But politically it isn't, because we have failed to construct any politics around climate that would be attractive to a broad enough cross section of voters. Americans are broadly supportive of wise environmental policies; we have repelled many of them by unwise political choices. Instead of galvanizing only those who already see climate as a priority, we have to reach those who have a direct stake in climate issues but may be turned off by our current debate. Climate must be a voting issue. Moral arguments will not be enough. We need to make a forceful case that emphasizes the business potential, high-paying jobs, and pocketbook savings that will come from climate action, along with the dire economic costs of inaction.[24]

The rewards of embracing a transition to clean energy are vast. One of the great ironies of efforts to address climate change is that in truth these are wise policies in their own right. I've long wondered whether many of those in opposition would have climbed

---

24 Unlike those who deny climate science, we can present actual numbers. Over the last decade, extreme weather events, which are made worse by climate change, have cost our country $350 billion. By the end of the century, climate change could result, each year, in $150 billion in lower labor productivity, $74 billion in coastal property damages, and $53 billion in agricultural losses.

aboard immediately but for the financial hazard to large donors and deep-pocketed special interests. Clean energy, renewable energy, and continually advancing energy technology—all these things would make sense even if the planet were not warming. When President Trump attacks America's climate policy, he draws from a deep well of smokestack-industry nostalgia and made-up facts; he conjures an America of years gone by, not comprehending the economy we now have and must sustain. Today, more than 3 million Americans work in the clean-energy economy. According to the Bureau of Labor Statistics, solar installers and wind-energy service technicians are the fastest- and second-fastest-growing job categories in the country. In Colorado, wind-energy jobs alone are expected to nearly double by 2020. The world is on track to have invested about $10 trillion in solar, wind, and zero-emission energy by 2040, more than all projected investment for fossil fuels. British Petroleum, which is not a coven of wishful thinkers, projects that renewable energy will be the fastest-growing energy source in the world over the next twenty years. The National Renewable Energy Laboratory, located in Golden, Colorado, found that renewable energy could comfortably provide 80 percent of US electricity by 2050. Put simply, there is no reason we should lose an argument about jobs and the economy to Donald Trump's empty promises, no matter how much of the wind in his bag is provided by the Kochs, the Tea Party, and the other forces making the spurious economic case for climate denial.

If America fully committed to a clean-energy transition, it would unleash a chain reaction of job creation: architects designing more efficient buildings, engineers developing energy-saving lightbulbs, contractors retrofitting an entire nation. At the same time, we could put Americans to work preparing for the dangers of climate change that we cannot avoid: raising bridges, reinforcing levees, strengthening dams, and helping homeowners, farmers, and ranchers prepare for the floods and droughts to come.

Although the rewards of a clean-energy regime are considerable, the transition will not be painless. America needs a plan to help those working in fossil fuels. Getting there will also take time and will involve the responsible production of natural gas as we scale up to cleaner renewable and zero-emission sources. Meanwhile, we cannot allow actors like the Koch brothers to stall the country's progress in order to serve their particular interests. Before coal, America's trains and ships ran on chopped wood. Before petroleum, America's families lit their homes with oil derived from whale blubber. Imagine if, in the nineteenth century, wealthy captains of dying industries had lavished storerooms of treasure (but for them, pocket change) on lawmakers to preserve an energy economy based on logs and whales.

I am starting to see cracks in the Koch brothers' influence. In the last six months, a few of my Republican colleagues have begun to talk about climate change. I attribute this to the increasing diversity of constituents coming into their offices urging them to address the issue. I have reached out to all groups to offer to work together and will continue to do so. That is the only way we are going to create a durable bipartisan solution to climate change. We are getting closer to a politics where we can have a bipartisan discussion in the Senate on how to address climate change—not whether we should address it at all.

Unlike millions of people across the globe, we have the benefit of a system built for change. The republic our founders fashioned is designed to evolve with the times.[25] In their own day, the founders would surely have struggled to imagine how our entire planet could be made to warm because of human activity—just as, I believe, they would have struggled to envision how our courts could have possibly come to take such a warped view of the First Amendment and money in politics. *Citizens United* is profoundly incongruous with our ideals and constitutional traditions. They would take comfort in knowing that the system they handed down was capable of meeting these challenges—but only if American citizens here on Planet A take action.

---

25 Contrary to politicians who claim to be "originalists," James Madison argued for a government that looked forward while retaining a regard for the past. He wrote in "Federalist No. 14," "Is it not the glory of the people of America, that, whilst they have paid a decent regard to the opinions of former times and other nations, they have not suffered a blind veneration for antiquity, for custom, or for names, to overrule the suggestions of their own good sense, the knowledge of their own situation, and the lessons of their own experience?"

GIVING AWAY
THE STORE

Ignoring the rise of inequality and the shrinkage of opportunity. Giving
tax cuts to the wealthy. Pretending there is no deficit.
How's that for a plan?

I. A White-Noise Rant

The episode was almost funny, like an outtake from *Saturday Night
Live*, but it was simultaneously disturbing. The time: November
2017. The place: a room in the Library of Congress, a Gilded Age
temple to books, learning, and democracy on Capitol Hill. The
venue had been set aside for a meeting between a number of Democratic senators and several members of the Trump administration.
The senators had been gathered by Joe Manchin, a Democrat from
West Virginia. The administration team was led by Gary Cohn, the
former Goldman Sachs executive who was then serving as director
of the National Economic Council. The ostensible purpose of the
meeting was to discuss President Trump's tax bill, which none of us
had yet seen—the Republican leadership had been working on it
with privileged lobbyists behind closed doors and would spring it
on all of us without hearings a few hours before a vote—and whose
bounty would fall overwhelmingly into the pockets of the wealthiest Americans. Democrats were hoping to make a few changes on

the margins as the bill hurtled toward its inevitable passage. I am not a cynical person, but a realist might describe the meeting as one where the administration pretended to listen and many of the senators pretended that they were being listened to.

At one point during the meeting Gary Cohn took a phone call, left the room, then returned and put his phone on speaker and placed it faceup on the table. The caller was President Trump, then in Japan. Presumably the purpose was to help make the case for his tax bill, but instead the president began reciting the itinerary of his state visit—as if reading from a travel agent's Enjoy Your Trip summary—and then did the same for his forthcoming visit to China. After ten minutes or so, Cohn tried to nudge the president back to the topic of the tax bill. Trump responded with many disjointed words—not a pitch to skeptics but more like a white-noise rant for a roomful of supporters. The main thrust of his argument was that his accountant had told him he was going to be "killed" by his own tax bill.[1] As the president's monologue went on, everyone in the room—senators, administration officials, staff members—began to ignore it. Conversations started between one person and another and then a third. Soon the din was at barroom level. No one was listening to the president. Trump never noticed; he was still talking. Finally Gary Cohn went over and picked up the phone, holding it in his hand. He did not know what to do. Administration officials looked at the senators with embarrassment. "See what we have to deal with?" their expressions seemed to say. Finally one senator made a suggestion, perhaps recalling how he'd dealt with a rambling

---

1 This was not true, by the way. As the business columnist James B. Stewart wrote at the time, "The proposals seem almost tailor-made to enrich the president and people like him." *Money* magazine characterized the bill as likely to produce a "monetary windfall" for the president. Estimates of the size of that windfall, which run into the tens of millions of dollars annually, are imprecise because the president has never released his tax returns.

uncle. He said to Cohn, "Just tell him he's breaking up and hang up the phone." Which is what Cohn eventually did.

Thus came to an end a colloquy at the highest levels between the executive and legislative branches of government on the most significant change to the American tax code for at least a generation. And as I left that meeting, I could not help but marvel at the distance—the practical and moral distance—between the way we conducted business at that meeting and the way my constituents in Colorado conduct their own affairs in schools and towns and counties and cities. Not to mention the distance between what the administration was proposing to do—filling the overflowing coffers of the wealthiest Americans while plunging the nation deeper into debt—and what ordinary citizens care about and need.[2]

Over nine years, I have held countless town hall meetings throughout Colorado. I almost never give a speech but instead begin every meeting by offering to address any questions or criticisms people may have. The Coloradans in attendance always have thoughts about a broad range of national concerns—the economy and our budget deficits, America's standing in the world, climate change, the Supreme Court, immigration—as well as issues that have particular resonance for Colorado, such as energy production (renewable or not), access to public lands, sage grouse, wildfires, and marijuana. If I had to boil it all down, the abiding concern that people express is that they are working hard but can't afford health care, housing, higher education, or early childhood education. They worry that they cannot save for the future and that their children will

---

2 Mayor John Hamilton of Bloomington, Indiana, captured this distance perfectly in a *Washington Post* op-ed essay titled "No City Would Ever Pass This Tax Bill." He wrote: "If I asked the city council to approve tripling our local debt to give hundreds of thousands of dollars per year to a few hundred of our most prosperous residents, they would ask what I was smoking. Preposterous, they would say."

have less opportunity than they did. It is obvious to them that the partisan show in Washington has nothing to do with what's on their minds. This knowledge rightly produces frustration and, sometimes, outrage. In 2016, with a shady real estate dealer and reality TV star as the Republican presidential nominee, many Americans decided they were angry enough to want to "blow it all up."

Washington was dysfunctional and incompetent before Donald Trump arrived. He has made matters much worse. All Americans now bear responsibility for setting things right. To appreciate what is required, it is critical to understand the economic challenges we have faced over decades and, more important, what they mean to our democratic republic, to every one of us no matter our economic standing, and to the next generation's political and economic prospects. Some will argue that we need a sustained period of shared prosperity before we dare try to reform our broken politics. Others say it's the other way around. I'll leave this chicken-and-egg question to the political scientists and commentators. My own view is that as Americans we have no choice but to try to accomplish both.

II. The Opportunity Deficit

Debates over debt and taxes sometimes seem to occur on an abstract level, as if they exist in a galaxy far away from the lives of ordinary people. And sometimes they occur—as the meeting at the Library of Congress demonstrated—in a way that resembles farce (because a farce is what it is). But these debates have real consequences for the lives of ordinary Americans.

Consider tax cuts for the wealthy. It's bad enough that we're enacting tax cuts we can't afford in order to put money in the pockets of people who don't need it. When spending and revenue are misaligned, the deficit gets out of hand and the national debt goes through the roof. In the eyes of some, that is in fact the plan: it sets the stage for a rollback of the essential functions of government that we can "no longer afford." This is what the slogan "Starve the beast" is all about: create a fiscal situation so frightening that the elimination of key programs seems like a prudent option. Often on the chopping block are programs that represent investments in the future—investments in education, infrastructure, and basic research and science. More recently, programs that help provide a minimally comfortable life for tens of millions of people have captured the attention of deficit scolds. I'm getting a little ahead of the story, but the most recent round of tax cuts for the wealthiest Americans, the tax cuts that President Trump was pushing for in his rambling-uncle phone call from Japan, have exploded the deficit to such a degree—upwards of $2 trillion—that the Senate majority leader, Mitch McConnell, has publicly pasted a target on Medicare, Medicaid, and Social Security.

The larger context here is the long-term erosion in the circumstances faced by 90 percent of all Americans. Wealth has always been distributed unequally in the United States, as it is throughout the world, but the distribution has not been this unequal since 1928, the year before the Depression began.[3] From the 1940s through the 1970s, the broad classes of poor and middle-class Americans held more than 60 percent of the country's wealth. The wealthiest Americans held roughly 40 percent. Today, as before

---

3 Economists use different methods to describe the phenomenon of economic inequality. Sometimes they compare income alone. But income tells only part of the story. It fails to capture other aspects of a person's (or household's) total economic picture, which often includes more, such as real estate and other property, taxes and transfers, savings, health and retirement benefits, and so on. Analysis of wealth rather than just income thus offers a more complete picture of economic security.

the Great Depression, the basic pattern of wealth distribution has flipped. Today, the top 10 percent of American households hold 80 percent of the wealth. Within that group, the top 0.1 percent (a mere 160,000 families) hold 22 percent of the wealth. That 22 percent is almost exactly the same amount of wealth held by the "bottom" 90 percent of American households—or nearly 290 million people.[4]

Money may not buy you happiness, but higher income and greater wealth bring obvious benefits, most of which start with the word "better": better housing in safer neighborhoods, better schools, better health care, better career options, larger savings and retirement accounts, a longer life, and greater opportunity for your children. The opposite is also true. The less money you have, the fewer benefits you enjoy. The Trump administration recently declared that "the war on poverty is largely over and a success." This is false. Tens of millions of Americans, including millions of children, live below the poverty line. Those just above it—poor working people and their families, along with a significant number of the elderly—are exposed to extraordinary levels of economic risk.

Historically, we have accepted these inequities confident that in America we have the right and ability to rise. When confronted by the hard facts of poverty or the growing challenges of middle-class families, we have consoled ourselves with the belief that Americans enjoy the opportunity to advance and thereby offer a better life to their children. We believe that the opportunity to improve our prospects in the long run offsets the short-term effects of poverty and economic inequality.

---

4 Research from many quarters is focused on this trend. The data here are from the economists Emmanuel Saez and Gabriel Zucman.

This link between mobility and economic opportunity has broken. In the United States, there is no better predictor of a child's future income then the current income of his or her parents.[5] An individual's fate is not inevitable, of course, but the association between parental income and children's income, at every level, is tight to the point of ruthlessness. For better or for ill, most Americans inherit from parents their own future economic circumstances as adults. If you're poor, your children likely will be poor too. If you're well-off, they're likely to be fine.

When a parent's present income predicts a child's future income so accurately, the only conclusion to be drawn is that there is little real economic mobility. Poor and middle-class Americans have a hard time climbing up. Wealthy Americans are the least likely to slide down. Real opportunity exists only when the possibility of upward mobility also exists. Take away mobility, and the American dream becomes meaningless—something between a nostalgic myth and a political lie. Take away mobility, and our society becomes profoundly unjust.

It was never as easy for Americans to move up the economic ladder as we told ourselves—never as easy to "turn over a new leaf" and rise, like Horatio Alger Jr.'s Ragged Dick, from shining shoes to a job in Mr. Rockwell's counting room. It has been harder still if you are a person of color and especially if you are an African

---

5 The philosopher and writer Matthew Stewart provides a vivid analogy. "Imagine yourself on the socioeconomic ladder with one end of a rubber band around your ankle and the other around your parents' rung. The strength of the rubber determines how hard it is for you to escape the rung on which you were born. If your parents are high on the ladder, the band will pull you up should you fall; if they are low, it will drag you down when you start to rise." Matthew Stewart, "The 9.9 Percent Is the New American Aristocracy," *Atlantic*, June 2018.

American male.[6] During the past forty years, economic mobility between generations has gone from being really hard to being much, much harder.

The combination of growing inequality of wealth and decreasing economic mobility defines the present era in America. A few years ago, Alan Krueger, the onetime chair of President Obama's Council of Economic Advisers, presented a "Great Gatsby Curve" to a gathering in Washington to illustrate the problem starkly.[7] The graph cross-references two factors. One is an index that captures the likelihood that a child will exceed the income of his or her parents. The other is an index that captures the degree of income inequality. Krueger took a set of relatively similar developed nations and compared them using both factors. The farther toward the right side of the graph a country lands, the greater its income inequality. The farther toward the top, the more probable it is that parental income determines a child's future income. So when we find the United States in the upper right-hand corner, Krueger is handing down two economic indictments: first, compared with the other countries in the set, we have a much greater gap between our richest and our poorest; and second, Americans are more likely to inherit their parents' economic circumstances. At the risk of writing something that my political opponents might use against me, if any country on the "Gatsby" chart

---

6 The literature on wealth and income inequality across races in the United States is also extensive. A 2018 analysis by Raj Chetty, Nathaniel Hendren, Maggie R. Jones, and Sonya R. Porter found that "black Americans have substantially lower rates of upward mobility and higher rates of downward mobility than whites, leading to large income disparities that persist through generations."

7 Krueger drew on research by the economist Miles Corak (see his 2012 paper, "Inequality from Generation to Generation: The United States in Comparison"). The nickname "Great Gatsby Curve" was not Corak's but came from the Obama White House, which issued a statement noting that "on the eve of the Great Recession, income inequality in the U.S. was as sharp as it had been at any period since the time of *The Great Gatsby*."

deserves the title "land of opportunity," it is Denmark or Finland, not the United States. Krueger sums up the relationship with troubling clarity: "Countries that have a high degree of inequality also tend to have less economic mobility across generations."

It is no coincidence that from the 1980s to the present, hourly compensation for Americans flattened, even as productivity steadily grew. There are many explanations for this trend, including global competition for labor, greater automation, less upward pressure on wages (caused by decreasing unionization of the workforce and decreasing real value of the minimum wage), rapidly rising health care costs, and the unequal distribution of earnings to people already at the top. The bottom line is that most people in America are not living reasonable middle-class lives. They cannot afford decent health care, housing, higher education, or early childhood education, to say nothing of saving for the future or taking a family vacation. That is why 60 percent of the American people have to borrow money to stay afloat. That is why the same number say they cannot afford an unexpected $500 expense. That is why (according to the Institute for Policy Studies) the median black family in 2013 had a net wealth of $1,700 and the median Latino family had a net wealth of $2,000—but the median white family had a net wealth of $116,800. (The statistics do not count certain basic belongings, such as a car and furniture.) It is a major reason we have become less mobile and more unequal. Income stagnation and growing inequality affect more than just individual lives. They drag down all Americans. As the prospects for the next generation's mobility decline, overall consumer spending for goods and services also declines and so does the size of the middle class. In his book *The Rise and Fall of American Growth*, the economist and historian Robert J. Gordon reaches the same conclusion. Surveying the long trends of the past century and a half and projecting into the future, he identifies inequality as the first of four forces—he calls them headwinds—that are likely to limit growth in the American economy in the decades ahead.[8]

These trends should trouble every American, and they should unite us to search for answers—even as we may disagree with one another about the best path forward. For if we treat the trends as inevitable, it is possible that for the first time in our history, as the economist Raj Chetty and his colleagues have shown, a majority of the next generation of Americans will earn lower incomes than their parents. That is where we are now headed. More than 90 percent of children born in 1940 went on to earn more than their parents. For children born in 1984, the figure is barely 50 percent. There is no doubt that a rising tide lifts all boats, but in America's economy today the yachts are being lifted far faster and far higher than the dinghies. And the American families in those dinghies are beset by a riptide of unequally distributed growth, lower mobility, stagnant wages, and rising costs.[9]

What about education as a means to address lack of economic mobility and rising inequality? Just as we want to believe consoling stories of upward mobility, so too we tell ourselves that one ingredient necessary for advancement is a good education. Frank Whitney, who serves as Ragged Dick's guide to a better life in Horatio Alger's fable, explains, "But, in order to succeed well, you must manage to get as good an education as you can. Until you

---

8 Gordon writes that "steadily rising [income] inequality over the past four decades is just one of the headwinds blowing at gale force to slow the growth rate of the American standard of living." He identifies these others: "education, demographics, and government debt" as well as "globalization, global warming, and environmental pollution."

9 To varying degrees, many western democracies find themselves under pressure from growing income inequality. The inability of elected officials to grapple with this phenomenon led the *Washington Post* recently to observe, of the annual economic forum, that "Davos is in decline as elites fail to tackle the globe's biggest problems."

do, you cannot get a position in an office or counting-room, even to run errands."

This is unquestionably true. Children from families in the bottom half of American earners who attain four years of college are likely to reach much higher levels of income. Census Bureau data tell us that a student from a household earning about $24,000 leaves college and enters the workforce able to earn between $45,600 and $74,800. Such students can buck the intergenerational trend. Unfortunately for our children and our country, the number of young people attaining the kind of degree that can change their economic trajectory is vanishingly small. The best predictor today of whether you are headed to college in the first place is—catch-22—your family's income.[10]

As the superintendent of the Denver Public Schools, I saw the way our students in poverty were often denied the cognitive and emotional building blocks required for academic success. Research bears these anecdotal observations out. Poverty is the primary factor generating gaps in measured academic performance between children from poor and wealthy families before they enter school. And once they start school, students living in poverty have fewer and lower-performing options for preschool and early childhood education. They are less likely to have a range of good academic choices and more likely to attend a school that struggles. They are more likely to be assigned to inexperienced or young and struggling teachers and to classes with lower-performing peers. To make

---

10 Let me stipulate that not every young person has to go to college. As noted, my old school district has been leading the way in creating modern apprenticeship offerings for our students. But the decision whether to pursue college or another path should be a young person's choice. It should not be the result of our systemic failure to educate children living in poverty. And, while I agree that not everyone should go to college, it's also true that I often hear that observation being made by parents about children other than their own.

matters worse, their parents have few resources to invest in closing the gap outside school—private tutors, test-prep services, enrichment experiences. For most children in poverty, school is a place where achievement gaps persist, even grow.

By age four, according to some estimates, a child born into poverty will have heard 30 million fewer words than her more affluent peers. When she reaches fourth grade, her chance of being a proficient reader is one in five. Her chance of earning a college degree is one in ten. These outcomes are terrible from the vantage point of the students and their families and from that of our country as a whole.

The economist Sean Reardon, along with his colleague Anna K. Chmielewski, has studied the relationship between overall income inequality and the achievement gap between students from the wealthiest and poorest households in twenty developed countries. Their research yields a result reminiscent of the "Great Gatsby Curve." The horizontal axis is the same measure for wealth inequality used by Krueger. The vertical axis captures the gap in average achievement between students from households with earnings in the lowest tenth and students from households in the highest tenth. Countries in the upper right-hand corner have both high income inequality and more academic distance between the most and least affluent students. Countries in the lower left-hand corner—such as Norway, Sweden, and even Slovenia—have the opposite characteristics: low income inequality and smaller income-achievement gaps. The United States does badly on both indices; our international peers are Portugal and Greece.

In America, educational outcomes are reinforcing economic inequality rather than liberating students and their families from it. In a different narrative, education would be the wind filling the sails of a generation—the way it did after World War II, when a national movement to improve high schools and the GI Bill, among other efforts, transformed the prospects of the baby boomers. In the narrative we are actually living, though, Robert Gordon counts education, along with rising inequality, among the headwinds we sail against.

It does not have to be this way. In Denver, I have seen signs of progress, even as stubborn achievement gaps remain. We must support efforts of educators, schools, and school systems serving our toughest neighborhoods to help students beat the odds. As superintendent, I came to understand directly what teachers and schools can add to the lives of our children and just how hard the work is. We should appreciate even more how much students themselves have done to beat the odds.

But we must also face the brutal facts that when one group of American children, with certainty, has access to high-quality preschool and the other, through no fault of its own, does not; when one group has access to high-quality K-12 schools and the other does not; when one group enjoys enrichment activities and tutoring and the advice of parents and coaches who themselves went to college and the other does not; when all this is true, then equal is not equal—and unequal is catastrophic for students holding the short end of the stick.

The fact that in our lifetimes economic opportunity has shrunk for nine out of ten Americans—especially the least fortunate—should shock us all into action.

III. From Surplus to Deficit

I am by nature an optimist, though many of the choices we have made during the past generation have sorely tested that outlook: the failure to invest in education, the merry pursuit of tax cuts for the wealthy, the utter disregard for the liabilities we have piled up for our children, and, on top of all that, the dishonesty with which these issues have been discussed.

In January 2009, when Colorado governor Bill Ritter appointed me to fill the Senate vacancy created by Ken Salazar's departure for the Department of the Interior, I thought that the kinds of deliberation I'd engage in at the federal level—particularly when it came to the budget and the economy—would be similar to what I'd long experienced in Colorado. I had seen more than my share of budgets, first in my work with Phil Anschutz and then in the public sector in the city of Denver and Denver Public Schools. When I was school superintendent, the Metro Organizations for People led an effort to take what then was a byzantine assemblage of budget formulas and transform it into a working tool that anyone could use and understand. The outcome of this reform, which we called a student based budget, was imperfect, but its transparency served the public better than its predecessor had and it is still in place today.

When I entered the Senate in early 2009, I imagined that our work might resemble my experience leading the schools. There was good reason. We were in the midst of the Great Recession, a moment of dangerous economic turmoil with no recent precedent. According to the Bureau of Labor Statistics, the economy had lost 4.3 million jobs the previous year; in the year to come, the number lost would nearly double. As the economy collapsed, so did tax revenues. At the same time, job losses triggered spikes in unemployment insurance, food stamps, and spending on federally funded health care for those who could no longer afford or get access to private insurance. The decline in revenue and the growth in costs sent deficits skyrocketing.

A new president, Barack Obama, and a new Congress faced the challenge of vanquishing the recession and mitigating its impact on millions of American families. Confronted by natural disaster, foreign attack, or any other national emergency, leaders in Washington would rightly be expected to resolve their political differences—and act decisively. Instead, when faced with an economic crisis of existential dimensions, Congress collapsed into bitter and counterproductive partisan warfare that left the American people deeply skeptical about their elected leaders' ability to tackle problems—and deeply suspicious of their leaders' motivations.

National crises aside, when it comes to the federal government's budget, the elected leaders of both parties—in their own individual ways and some more determinedly than others—have made a shambles of what should be a basic civic responsibility. What has passed for budget debate in Washington over the past decade has in fact been a bad serial novel. In each successive chapter, conflict escalates only to produce another sorry ending in which the leaders find yet another easy way out, further obscuring and enlarging a theft from the next generation of Americans. We are a long way from what we learned watching *Schoolhouse Rock!*

Let's start with two basic concepts: the deficit and the debt. The deficit is our annual budget shortfall; the debt is the accumulated burden of that shortfall. There have been only three or four times since World War II when the United States did not run a deficit, the most recent being in the late 1990s when Bill Clinton was president. In 2018, the US government spent more than $4.1 trillion and collected more than $3.3 trillion. The difference, around $780 billion, was our 2018 deficit. Looking forward, the debt and deficit are both projected to continue to rise—steeply—as a percentage of gross domestic product (GDP).

If we do not change course, our children will have less and less reason to thank us.

There is room for debate about the size that the nation's deficit should be, and the year-to-year number depends significantly on the state of the economy. In general, during financial crises or recessions, as the private sector falters, running larger deficits helps stave off economic implosion. Without government investment, capital remains idle and the economy is underproductive, unemployment deepens, and in the worst case the workforce experiences damage that outlasts the recession. So, in bad times, temporarily large deficits can make sense. But over the long run, when the economy is relatively healthy, deficits should be smaller. This stabilizes the debt and reassures lenders that they will be repaid, so they are willing to finance federal borrowing at reasonable rates if a major investment is warranted. As a rule of thumb, fiscal sustainability requires keeping annual deficits to just about 3 percent of our gross domestic product.

To understand federal government spending, think of it as falling into two buckets. The first is "mandatory" or "entitlement" spending. These are programs that grow as the number of eligible people increases, and they are not subject to the annual appropriations process. This category includes programs such as Medicare, Medicaid, and Social Security. The second bucket is "discretionary" spending, money that Congress allocates in the annual appropriations process. About half of discretionary spending is military and about half includes national investment in things like health research, transportation, education, agriculture, the national parks, NASA, law enforcement, and foreign relations. Since 1980, the Congressional Budget Office (CBO) reports, we have cut discretionary spending by 35 percent as a proportion of GDP. At the same time, according to the CBO, we have increased mandatory spending by 39 percent. We have cut revenue by about 4 percent.

When they persist, annual deficits and mounting debt act as a political head cold, robbing us of our imagination and ambition. At present, we are spending, as a share of the economy, a third less on investments in our future—on infrastructure, on education, and on basic research into and development of lifesaving cures or clean energy—than we were a generation ago. We don't have the decency to maintain the roads and bridges that our parents and grandparents had the wisdom to build for us, much less the foresight to build the high-speed broadband infrastructure or modern electrical grid our children and grandchildren will need to compete in the twenty-first century. As we fail to invest in the next generation of Americans, we also circumscribe their ability to invest in themselves and their children by sticking them with a debt obligation they did nothing to incur.

Given the country's current financial state, it's hard to believe that in June 1999, President Bill Clinton walked out to the White House Rose Garden to speak to the press about the nation's budget surplus. "We have now cut up Washington's credit card," he boasted. The economy was booming and national coffers were flush. Projections showed the government poised to run a surplus for the second year in a row, collecting about $100 billion more than it would spend. Americans had not seen a budget surplus since Richard Nixon's first year in office, and even then it was small, and a one-time-only experience. After twenty-nine years of budget deficits, we had reached a moment of unfamiliar opportunity. By the time Clinton left office, the Congressional Budget Office was projecting a surplus of nearly $5.6 trillion over the next decade. "The surplus is the hard-earned product of our fiscal discipline,"

Clinton announced. He tried to persuade Washington to use the surplus "to prepare for the great challenges facing our country—caring for our parents, caring for our children, freeing our nation from the shackles of debt so that we can have long-term sustained economic prosperity."

Clinton's press conference set off a debate unimaginable today. It is hard to conceive of politicians arguing over what to do with abundance. Clinton proposed investing the surplus in education and child care while shoring up Medicare and Social Security. His plan went even further, though, and pointed to a tantalizing goal: eliminating all $3.6 trillion of publicly held federal debt by 2015.

Congressional Republicans dutifully positioned themselves in opposition to Clinton. The former Republican staff director for the House Budget Committee (he had become a lobbyist) told the *New York Times* that Clinton's proposal was "doomed to fail from the beginning." Republicans raised questions about the CBO's numbers, then drafted legislation based on those same estimates as they called for a tax cut of $775 billion over ten years.

The two sides carried these positions into the 2000 presidential campaign. Early in the Republican presidential primary season, George W. Bush proposed a tax cut of nearly half a trillion dollars; John McCain offered a tax cut of about half that size, directing the remainder of the surplus to shoring up Medicare and Social Security and to reducing the national debt. As Election Day closed in, Bush expanded his proposal, calling for $1.3 trillion in tax cuts over ten years. Even the Democratic candidate, Al Gore, proposed some tax cuts.

By a few Florida votes (and an intervening 5–4 Supreme Court decision), Bush won the presidency. For the next eight years, the president and Congress repeatedly followed through on their vowed tax cuts. In June 2001, just after the dot-com bubble began to burst, Washington cut taxes by $1.35 trillion over ten years. Then, following the deadliest terrorist attack on our soil, on 9/11, we sent troops first to Afghanistan and afterward to Iraq, efforts that to date have cost Americans $5.6 trillion.[11] In 2003, three months after the invasion of Iraq, Washington passed another tax cut, estimated at the time to be $350 billion over ten years. Then, heading into his reelection campaign, Bush signed into law what he called "the greatest advance in health care coverage for America's seniors since the founding of Medicare," a prescription-drug benefit for seniors that costs hundreds of billions of dollars per year. We paid for none of President Bush's initiatives and instead borrowed all of it from our children.

By 2008, a subprime mortgage crisis, spurred by lax regulation, was upon us, destroying the brokerage houses Lehman Brothers and Bear Stearns, pushing the quasi-autonomous lending agencies Fannie Mae and Freddie Mac fully into the arms of the government, and leaving the country's largest financial institutions wobbling toward collapse. Housing values and stock prices plummeted, erasing almost $12 trillion of Americans' net worth—a larger percentage decline in wealth than occurred during the shock that precipitated the Great Depression. The market collapse, which saw the Dow drop 36 percent in three months, also devastated retirement savings. An elderly woman in Grand Junction, Colorado, captured the mood of my town halls when

---

11 The Bush administration encouraged the idea that the war in Iraq would cost nothing. Secretary of Defense Donald Rumsfeld promised that "the bulk of the funds for Iraq's reconstruction will come from Iraqis." His deputy, Paul Wolfowitz, assured Americans that "we're really dealing with a country that can finance its own reconstruction." One wonders if these two officials advised Donald Trump on getting Mexico to pay for his border wall.

she said her plan was to "die sooner" in order to preserve her standard of living.

To bring stability, President Bush and Congress passed the Troubled Asset Relief Program, known as TARP. Even though the funds were loans or investments that were to be at least partially repaid—and they ultimately were—the perceived price tag of $700 billion caused alarm among fiscal conservatives and those who believed it was the wrong way to stave off a looming economic crisis, even one that was now occurring worldwide. By the time President Bush left office, the United States had entered the Great Recession, the sharpest economic downturn since the Great Depression. All economic indicators pointed in the wrong direction: we were losing millions of jobs, federal revenue was plummeting, and unemployment-driven expenditures that protect our most vulnerable citizens were rising. The fiscal year 2009 deficit—fueled by tax cuts, the expense of two wars, and the unpaid-for expansion of Medicare benefits—rose to more than $1.4 trillion, almost 10 percent of GDP. Since the country's founding, the only time the deficit had been larger, as a percentage of GDP, was during World War II.

IV. Tea Party Rising

Unfortunately, people with no interest in making sound economic decisions—a minority of Republican lawmakers, primarily in the House of Representatives—suddenly got their hands on key levers of power.

The first steps by the government to deal with the financial crisis had been promising and necessary. In 2009, within six weeks of taking office and in the midst of a deepening recession, President Obama and the new Democratic Congress assembled a package of measures intended to boost the economy. In March, Obama intervened to save the American auto industry—and what turned out to be 1.5 million jobs—by providing bridge loans to General Motors and Chrysler. A month before, he required the nineteen largest banks in the United States to undergo stress tests of their balance sheets to reassure the American people of their capacity to withstand further economic disruption. The emergency measures culminated in the American Recovery and Reinvestment Act, which cost $831 billion, divided between new spending and tax cuts aimed at the middle class.[12] This was a necessary investment in our economy, and even though not all of the money was well spent it was a classic case of ramping up investment at a time of national need.

But all of this immediately became a lightning rod in a renewed debate about the nation's economic priorities, as Republicans rediscovered a commitment to fiscal probity now that there was no longer a Republican in the White House. To some, the emergency measures served as a symbol of out-of-control government spending. Reacting to the Obama administration's announcement of a program to help families refinance their mortgages and save their homes, the millionaire commodities trader and CNBC personality Rick Santelli took the floor of the Chicago Board of Trade and launched this tirade:

> This is America! How many of you people want to pay for
> your neighbor's mortgage that has an extra bathroom and

---

12 It may sound like Monday-morning quarterbacking, but I always believed it might have been useful for President Obama to have presented the Republicans with a package that contained much smaller tax cuts and then allowed them to work him up to a larger tax-cut package. That would have enabled Republicans to contribute something to the bill and might have given them a political incentive to support it. To this day, I have never met a person who was aware of receiving a tax cut from President Obama's stimulus bill.

can't pay their bills? . . . I'll tell you what, if you read our
Founding Fathers, people like Benjamin Franklin and Jefferson, what we're doing in this country now is making them
roll over in their graves.

He called for a "Chicago Tea Party in July" and asked the "silent
majority" to join him.

Whether Santelli's remarks lit the fuse or there was some other
cause, the so-called Tea Party movement quickly became an explo-
sive political force. Through the spring and especially on April
15—when federal taxes are due—hundreds of loosely organized
groups held meetings and rallies and protests. Over the summer,
the movement gathered grassroots strength as well as the backing
of powerful new patrons: conservative talk radio, Fox News, and the
invisible hand of the advocacy groups and paid operatives sponsored
by the Koch brothers.

By September, my town halls in Colorado were often dominated by Tea Party members with a new cause: defeating the Patient
Protection and Affordable Care Act, which was then being considered in Congress. Across the country (but it must be said not in my
Colorado town hall meetings), Tea Party members shouted down
elected officials in the name of an insurgent cause. In Washington, a
crowd of tens of thousands gathered outside the Capitol. The rally
was colorfully dotted with people costumed as George and Martha
Washington, Samuel Adams, and Paul Revere, or as blue-coated
soldiers from the Continental army, with a few in scary Barack
Obama masks to add a dash of menace. Reporters and photogra-
phers compiled a lively record of the signs demonstrators carried.
They gave voice to a grab bag of conservative causes:

What would Thomas Jefferson do?

You can't borrow to prosperity.

HONK . . . if you pay my neighbor's mortgage.

You lie!

Bailouts + Debt = fiscal child abuse

We will fire you!

Obamanomics: Chains you can believe in

Terrorists Won't Destroy America, Congress Will!

I want my country back![13]

Audience members and speakers alike conveyed a pervasive sense of outrage that, if not already lost, the United States as they knew it was in danger. The grassroots activists had no single message: the array of speakers included a car salesman, James Anderer, who blamed President Obama when Chrysler shuttered his dealership as it reorganized itself out of bankruptcy; coal miners objecting to cap-and-trade incentives to reduce carbon emissions, because the incentives would lead to the "final destruction of America"; and a rapper named Hi Caliber, who claimed to be "the nation's one and only conservative hip-hop artist." FreedomWorks, one of the Koch brothers' advocacy groups, was a main sponsor of the rally, which explains why the miners got so much slightly off-theme stage time. They were assisted by a bunch of other Beltway pros and pop-up contractors happy to grab their advocacy dollars. They brought

---

13 Though most signs presented civil if not subtle frustrations about government, many had a darker edge: "1984 Is Not an Instruction Manual!" "Obama . . . Commander and Thief." "The Zoo Has an African Lion and the White House Has a Lyin' African." And "Bury Obama Care with Kennedy," the reference being to the late senator from Massachusetts, Edward Kennedy, who had succumbed to brain cancer two weeks earlier and whose seat I had the honor of filling on the Senate health care committee.

along members of Congress, veteran campaigners, think tank talking heads, and backroom party power brokers like Congressman Dick Armey. The insiders stood on a simpler and more consistent platform. One of them, Indiana congressman Mike Pence, of Indiana—soon to be governor, now vice president—captured this focus: "We the people do not consent to runaway federal spending. We the people do not consent to the notion that we can borrow and spend and bail our way back to a growing America." Pence and his professional political colleagues had distilled the Tea Party's crazy quilt of grassroots causes into two basic demands: slash taxes and dismantle what they called "big government."

Beyond the rally, politicians affiliated with the Tea Party movement were gearing up for an Election Day reckoning with Washington Democrats more than a year later. More unusually, they also took aim at incumbent "conventional Republicans." Indeed, seated Republicans were among the first to fall during that election cycle. The insurgency thrived in the harder-to-find corridors of American politics—party primaries and especially the state conventions, notorious for arcane rules and low voter turnout. Many traditional Republicans were to lose their political lives in these arenas.

In May 2010, the Tea Party upstarts Mike Lee and Tim Bridgewater took Senator Bob Bennett out of his reelection bid on the first ballot of Utah's Republican convention. Bennett had led work on bipartisan health care legislation and had supported Bush's TARP, among other unforgivable crimes.[14] As spring turned to summer, Tea Party–backed newcomers for Senate seats bumped off establishment

14 Bennett lost even though he had the support of Utah senator Orrin Hatch and Republican national leaders like Newt Gingrich and Mitt Romney and even though he was preferred by more Utah voters than either of his opponents in polls preceding the convention. The convention upset was dramatic, with Tea Party members waving yellow Gadsden ("Don't tread on me") flags and shouting "He's gone!" when the vote tally was announced.

Republicans all across the country. In Kentucky, Rand Paul forced Jim Bunning out of the race even before the primaries began. In Delaware, Christine O'Donnell knocked out former governor Mike Castle. Nevada's Sharron Angle defeated a pack of other Republicans in the primary to earn a face-off against Senate Majority Leader Harry Reid. In Colorado, Ken Buck became my 2010 opponent by defeating a longtime state Republican leader, Jane Norton.

Although some proved better candidates than others, they shared the same roster of backers: the Club for Growth, the Tea Party Express, FreedomWorks, and eccentric diehards like South Carolina senator Jim DeMint and former Alaska governor Sarah Palin.[15] Their campaigns were unrefined and hard to predict, but Pence's two themes—dismantling big government and reducing the deficit—came through loud and clear. Ken Buck's remarks at the Colorado GOP Assembly, captured on YouTube, were typical:

> We have $100 trillion in unfunded liability, we have an out of control national debt, we have an annual deficit that is ridiculous, and what do we do? We bail out automobile companies, we bail out banks, we try to nationalize our health care system, and now they're talking about cap-and-trade. Folks, our country is financially bankrupt, and if we continue to push onto our children and grandchildren the debt, we are also morally bankrupt. I will fight in Washington, DC, for a balanced budget amendment, a constitutional balanced budget amendment.

---

15 Chosen for their willingness to recite a standard script of impossible and incompatible goals, the Tea Party candidates often proved undisciplined and problematic on the campaign trail. In Delaware, O'Donnell stumbled when she admitted that she had "dabbled into witchcraft" in high school. Angle got into trouble by maintaining that Islamic sharia law was in effect in American towns like Dearborn, Michigan.

On Election Day 2010, Republicans gained sixty-three members of the House—the largest swing since 1948—and won control of that chamber. They added six Senate seats. As the 112th Congress gathered in January 2011, we knew our political divisions would grow. We had no idea how wide these divisions would become, but the Tea Party rallies and campaign rhetoric foretold that many arguments would take place over the deficit, the debt, and the size of the government. We knew, too, that the Tea Party was happy to threaten shutdowns and defaults, as leverage in negotiating.

John Boehner, of Ohio, the new Speaker, tried to set a conciliatory tone when he took the gavel from Nancy Pelosi. He was a veteran lawmaker and understood that Congress could not govern by division. He made a number of pledges:

> We will dispense with the conventional wisdom that bigger bills are always better; that fast legislating is good legislating; that allowing additional amendments and open debate makes the legislative process "less efficient" than our forefathers intended . . . Legislators and the public will have three days to read bills before they come to a vote. Legislation will be more focused, properly scrutinized, and constitutionally sound.

Jim DeMint, of South Carolina, the de facto leader of the Tea Party senators, wanted none of this. "We need to have a shutdown at this point," he said, the day before Boehner's gentler remarks. "We're not going to increase our debt ceiling anymore. We're going to cut things necessary to stay within the current levels." Within weeks—and especially as temporary budget deals failed to produce the trillion-dollar cuts that Tea Party candidates had campaigned on—DeMint was joined by others.[16] Their ire seemed directed as much at members of their own caucus as at Democrats in Congress and the White House.

Americans can be forgiven for having only a foggy recollection of what happened over the next six years. The dreary cycle of shrill and tedious escalation and recrimination would be better forgotten if it had not had such an ill effect on the nation. As the weeks and months went by, a handful of members of Congress perfected the cynical craft of turning the legislative process against the government.[17] They saw every expiring budget as a moment to exact fiscal tribute both from political opponents (Democrats and the president) and from their own ostensible allies (other Republicans). The dozens of continuing resolutions we passed to keep the government running were as short as one day and as long as 188 days and set no national priorities. We had become the land of flickering lights, in which the standard of success was not what we were doing to benefit the next generation of Americans or to enhance our role in the world but instead whether we had kept government open for another few minutes. The dysfunction drove the approval rating of Congress

---

16 For instance, Senator John Cornyn, of Texas: "Our debt is $14 trillion and the deficit is $1.5 trillion and the public is looking for some adult leadership on these issues. I think the same old demagoguery is not going to win the day because in the end we are going to have to do something." And Senator Tom Coburn, of Oklahoma, a consistent voice for fiscal discipline: "We are spending trillions of dollars every year and nobody knows what we are doing. The executive branch doesn't know. The congressional branch doesn't know. Nobody knows."

17 In an interview with Ezra Klein about the political dynamics within the House Republican Conference, the journalist Robert Costa noted: "So there are thirty to forty true hard-liners But there's another group of maybe fifty to sixty members who are very much pressured by the hard-liners. So he [Speaker Boehner] may have the votes on paper. But he'd create chaos."

down and down—to about 9 percent the last time I looked—which served the hard-liners' antigovernment purposes well.[18]

No tactic better captures the behavior of the Tea Party affiliates in Congress than their stance against lifting the debt ceiling as leverage in budget negotiations. Only someone willing to break the government—and I mean that literally: only someone willing to do permanent damage to the United States—would ever make this threat credible. The posturing peaked in March 2011 when twenty-three Republican senators sent a letter to President Obama declaring their intention to weaponize the debt ceiling:

> Government spending is growing at an alarming rate, and the federal budget deficit has reached record levels. Congress will soon face a vote to increase the debt ceiling yet again, the fourth time in your Presidency and the 11th time in the last decade. Future generations will drown in a debt forced onto them by the inactions of Congresses and Administrations far before their time. The time to remedy these failures is now.

A decision to raise the debt ceiling is essentially administrative in nature. It grants the Department of the Treasury the authority to pay back debts resulting from prior, unpaid-for spending by Congress. Failing to lift the debt ceiling is no different from watching

---

18 This has been a deliberate strategy for some parts of the GOP since Newt Gingrich was Speaker of the House. The longtime Republican staffer Mike Lofgren wrote: "A couple of years ago, a Republican committee staff director told me candidly (and proudly) what the method was to all this obstruction and disruption. Should Republicans succeed in obstructing the Senate from doing its job, it would further lower Congress's generic favorability rating among the American people. By sabotaging the reputation of an institution of government, the party that is programmatically against government would come out the relative winner." In "Federalist No. 62," James Madison foresaw the effects of this antigovernment chicanery and wrote that it "poisons the blessing of liberty itself."

pay-per-view all month and then throwing the cable bill into the trash can when it arrives. What made the Tea Partiers' strategy so galling is that they pursued it in the name of fiscal prudence—a position no different from the pay-per-view customer's claim that by tearing up the bill he is living within his means. And just as surely as our deadbeat cable viewer would have to pay a premium to restore his service, so would a deadbeat Congress force the government to pay higher interest rates if the American credit rating was damaged.

For this reason, virtually every member of Congress knew the debt ceiling would have to be lifted in the end. Under circumstances like this, process managers hold the high cards, none more so than Mitch McConnell. As the 2012 presidential election loomed, McConnell was finally able to perform what Carl Hulse of the *New York Times* called "a legislative magic trick" to briefly resolve the problem. As a decision came down the wire, he worked with Harry Reid to construct a procedural path allowing President Obama to lift the debt ceiling unless Congress voted to disapprove. This permitted his Tea Party members to claim they had fought the good fight but also prevented the economic calamity that would result from a failed debt-ceiling vote.

All McConnell and Reid accomplished was to postpone the real decisions to a later day. Their deal conveniently set the deadline after the next presidential election, avoiding the inconvenient spectacle of Washington's failing to grapple with its finances as Americans went to the polls. The new deadline would be December 23, 2012. Members of Congress would have two days to come together on a deal before many of them missed Christmas.

This sort of scheduling is always intended to put leadership in the driver's seat and jam ordinary members with a precooked deal. This time, there was much at stake. The deficit-inducing Bush tax cuts from the decade before were set to expire. In addition, across-the-board discretionary spending cuts, known as the sequester, would take effect simultaneously. The sequester was the product of an earlier half-baked congressional measure that created a legislative vehicle so ugly and mindless that it would force the people's representatives to find a fiscal compromise. If nothing changed, it would go into effect. Taken together the expiring Bush tax cuts and looming sequester were called the "fiscal cliff."

The postponed deadline prompted the first downgrade of the sovereign debt of the United States in the country's history. Standard and Poor's took the view that the existing agreement fell short of what would be necessary "to stabilize the government's medium term debt dynamics." The ratings agency clearly believed that it was unlikely that delay would produce a better result.

> More broadly, the downgrade reflects our view that the effectiveness, stability, and predictability of American policymaking and political institutions have weakened . . . [W]e have changed our view of the difficulties in bridging the gulf between the political parties over fiscal policy, which makes us pessimistic about the capacity of Congress and the Administration to be able to leverage their agreement this week into a broader fiscal consolidation plan that stabilizes the government's debt dynamics any time soon.

The postponed crisis arrived on schedule. With the Election Day milestone crossed, President Obama reelected, and the fiscal cliff now visible on the horizon, the lame-duck Congress faced its deadline. Now adept at showdown tactics, in a short few weeks the Tea Party caucus generated rash demands, mounting threats, challenges to Boehner's leadership, and narrowing expectations that congealed into hard feelings and an impasse. There was no attempt at good faith negotiation.

Finally, with the clock running out, the White House and Mitch McConnell pulled another agreement out of their sleeves. This time it would make permanent almost all of George Bush's tax cuts. It made no effort to replace the sequester's arbitrary, automatic cuts with more thoughtful solutions. Instead, it proposed that if Congress and the administration could not reach agreement over the next sixty days, the sequester would automatically take effect. I was one of only eight senators to vote against the bill.

At the time, commentators hailed the deal as a major feat of bipartisan agreement. This is a baffling conclusion about a deal that then appeared and (even more so) now appears to be nothing short of total victory for Tea Party members and their allies.[19] Permanently extending the Bush tax cuts represented another huge loss in revenue. At the same time, the inevitable inability of the parties to reach agreement would mean that the mindless cuts to discretionary spending would begin (and without any member of Congress actually voting for them).

There is a grim coda to this story, proof that no matter how low we go, someone will find a way to go even lower. In March 2013, after it had still failed to act and with the sequester now in full effect, Congress voted to fund the government for an additional six months. This presented newly elected senator Ted Cruz with an opportunity he could not resist. For months, Republicans had failed to fulfill their promise to repeal the Affordable Care Act. Now, he

---

19 It is true that some of the Recovery Act's tax cuts were included in the fiscal cliff package. But they were much smaller than the permanently extended Bush tax cuts, and were extended only temporarily.

would seize on the tactics employed by his Tea Party comrades in the House. He rallied his troops by claiming that the threat of a government shutdown would force the Obama administration to defund the president's signature program.

Cruz shut the government down for sixteen days. Ultimately, he accomplished little other than to demonstrate that in lieu of becoming an effective legislator he could become a celebrity in his own reality TV show, raising awareness of and money for his campaign.[20] He also demonstrated that he was able to read *Green Eggs and Ham* and other writings as he occupied the Senate floor for hours on end. Even as the shutdown drove American confidence in the leadership of the Republican Party and Congress to new lows, Cruz boosted his own favorability rating with Republicans (according to the Pew Research Center) by eleven points and with his Tea Party base by twenty-seven points. He would ride the momentum he generated by shutting down the government to a first-place finish in the Republican Iowa caucus in 2016.

V. "I Alone Can Fix It"

I remember Ted Cruz's government shutdown vividly, for a lot of reasons. For one thing, I was there for some of it. His hypocrisy had a papier-mâché grandeur to it. One of the casualties of the shutdown was the World War II Memorial, which the National Park Service had to close until the government reopened. A number of Tea Party lawmakers were incensed. Senators Ted Cruz and Mike

---

20 Episodes like this one inspired me to introduce a bill requiring senators to report to the Senate floor when there is a shutdown and stay there until the government is reopened. When Coloradans hear about this bill, what they like best is the requirement that senators be arrested and taken to the floor if they refuse to attend. I am pleased that the cosponsor of this legislation is Cory Gardner, my Republican colleague from Colorado.

Lee, along with Sarah Palin, led a rally at the memorial to protest the closing. Cruz asked, "Why is the federal government spending money to erect barricades to keep veterans out of this memorial?"

But there is a more important reason why the shutdown is etched so vividly in my memory: it coincided with catastrophic flooding in Colorado—the kind of event that reminds you what responsible government can do for ordinary people.[21] In early September, Front Range towns from Fort Carson to Fort Collins received a year's worth of rain in a week, causing the most devastating floods in the last half century. Once rain-soaked mountain ground can accept no more water, the overflow obeys the laws of gravity, pouring into creeks, streams, and then rivers that carry water downhill, feeding into the South Platte and Arkansas Rivers. Rapids became torrents, and torrents became hurtling cascades—rolling boulders, stripping mountainsides, ripping trees out by their roots, tossing cars and trucks like toys, ramming bridges with silt and debris, and tearing canyon towns like Jamestown and Lyons to shreds. The mountain waters then poured east over the plains. More than twenty-eight thousand houses were damaged and eighteen hundred were destroyed. The state lost 486 miles of highway. Tens of thousands of people were displaced. Ten lives were claimed. Destruction tore across twenty-four Colorado counties, at a cost of $4 billion.

Even before the rains stopped and the water had receded, the resilience of our citizens, of their local elected leaders, and of

---

21 Six years later, the memory of this time would provoke me to respond to comments made by Senator Cruz on the Senate floor. As he pulled out his playbook to defend the Trump shutdown in the name of unpaid members of the Coast Guard, I suggested that he was crying "crocodile tears," since he had made the work of Colorado's first responders so much harder during his first shutdown. I remembered well his trip to the World War II Memorial and was inclined not to let him get away with it again.

our institutions was on display across Colorado. President Obama directed federal search-and-rescue services, supplies, logistical support, and manpower to Colorado and provided financial support to local governments and the people they represented. Neighbors, volunteers from around the state, and public servants joined together in community churches and schools to work with people from relief agencies, government experts, and strangers from across the country (and even from other countries). They were clear about their job: build things back better than they were before the rivers rose.

It occurred to me at the time that no state or local leaders confronted with a natural disaster could have governed as recklessly as we did in Washington in those same weeks. No mayor, city council member, or county manager could have walked a dog along the street, bought stamps at the post office, or faced fellow citizens at the grocery store without feeling embarrassment and shame for having shut the government down to score a political point in a quixotic charade. We should ask ourselves why we hold Congress to a lower standard.

And it would only get worse. After 2016, Republicans controlled the presidency and both houses of Congress. After years of deficit scolding, admonitions against overspending, and dire warnings about the economic fate of the Republic—after years of this, they now had a chance to lead the country toward the new era of fiscal restraint they had been demanding. To some degree, doing so might even have made sense. As President Obama turned over the keys, the economy had grown every year since 2009. The nation's deficit had fallen to $585 billion, roughly half of what Obama had inherited from George W. Bush and a third of what it had been at the depths of the Great Recession. Very little of that deficit reduction could be attributed to the destructive strategies the Tea Party had adopted. Most of it resulted from tax revenues generated by a growing economy. On its face, it might have been a good time for prudent legislators to conserve resources in the event that we were faced with another economic or foreign policy crisis.

Instead, after all the years of incessant obstruction of the country's business in the name of fiscal responsibility, the Republican Party nominated a candidate who promised to deliver "a giant, beautiful, massive" tax cut; pass "one of the largest increases in national defense spending in American history"; and "not touch Social Security, Medicare, or Medicaid." How would Donald Trump pull off this math-defying act? "I alone can fix it," he had claimed in his nomination speech. He would erase our debt in eight years by "vigorously eliminating waste, fraud, and abuse in the federal government, ending redundant government programs, and growing the economy," as well as by "renegotiating all of our [debt] deals."

What he actually did was cut taxes for the wealthiest Americans and explode our deficit. Throughout the first year of Donald Trump's presidency, Republican majorities in the House and Senate repeatedly tried and failed to repeal and replace the Affordable Care Act—a move whose main effect would be to deprive tens of millions of nonwealthy Americans of reliable health care, which many enjoyed for the first time in their lives. By the fall of the first year, the president and his congressional allies feared that both their base and their donors might abandon them because of their lack of legislative accomplishment. As Senator Mike Lee put it, "We haven't repealed Obamacare, so if we don't get tax reform done, we are in trouble. We might as well flip up our tent and go home." Representative Chris Collins (R-NY) explained, "My donors are basically saying, 'Get it done or don't ever call me again.'" Throughout President Trump's first autumn in office, Republicans frantically patched together a tax plan that could pass by the narrowest partisan majority.

Ronald Reagan's signature tax-reform legislation, enacted in 1986, had been a two-year effort that involved countless hearings in Washington and throughout the country and ultimately won broad bipartisan support. President Trump signed his tax plan only six weeks after its introduction in the House. Neither the Senate nor the House held a single hearing on the bill.[22] Its final text of 2,232 pages appeared at 10:30 on the night the Senate voted.[23]

Favored lobbyists had full access to the Republican staffers drafting the bill. The American people—and most of their representatives—had none. Democratic senators got that one briefing at the Library of Congress, where the president read from his Asian itinerary. The result of this rushed and sloppy process was a bill that will exacerbate, not ameliorate, the terrible income inequality America faces. The secretary of the treasury, Steven Mnuchin, had pledged repeatedly that any new tax bill would not result in a net tax cut for the wealthy—a pledge that came to be known as the Mnuchin rule. As Mnuchin stated: "Any reductions we have in upper-income taxes will be offset by less deductions"—that is, people in upper-income brackets would be able to take fewer deductions, increasing their taxable income—"so there will be no absolute tax cut for the upper class. There will be a big tax cut for the middle

---

22 The rush job of drafting and making changes to the bill generated a widely covered drama of consequential decisions done on the fly—handwritten adjustments made and lost; last-minute alterations on sticky notes—that endowed the Tea Party's rhetorical demands for legislative transparency with a lingering stench of hypocrisy.

23 It is an unfair comparison, but my old paperback edition of Constance Garnett's translation of *The Brothers Karamazov* is only 924 pages and it takes an undergraduate about three weeks to make it through that one. Unlike the tax bill, it is also well written.

class, but any tax cuts we have for the upper class will be offset by less deductions that pay for it." This was a charade. There was no big tax cut for the middle class; the wealthy got most of the money.[24] After President Trump signed the tax bill he told his well-heeled friends on his first night back in his gilded fortress at Mar-a-Lago: "You all just got a lot richer."[25]

The drafters of the tax cut bill made no effort to pay for it. Instead, they claimed that the tax cuts would pay for themselves by generating economic growth—exactly the argument George W. Bush had made as he converted Bill Clinton's $5.6 trillion projected surplus into a $1.2 trillion actual deficit. A more honest argument could be heard from Representative Mark Walker, Republican of North Carolina and at the time the chairman of the right-wing Republican Study Committee. He observed that concern about deficits is "a great talking point when you have an administration that's Democrat led. It's a little different now that Republicans have both houses and the administration."

At the time, the most credible estimates (other than those from Washington politicians who should know better) projected that the tax package would add at least $1.4 trillion to our deficit. However, even those estimates understated the damage. The true

---

24 Ironically, the most progressive aspect of the tax bill was its capping of the state and local tax (SALT) deduction at $10,000. Many Democrats continue to advocate for repealing this provision of the Republican tax plan. From the standpoint of parochial politics, this position is understandable. From the standpoint of America's middle class, it is not. Repealing the cap on SALT would cost the federal government $620 billion over a decade. More than half of the money would go to the top 1 percent of households, making more than $755,000. More than 80 percent of the benefit would go to the top 5 percent of households, making more than $319,000.

25 Trump's boast at his exclusive club was overheard by other guests, who in turn reported it to CBS News. Mar-a-Lago members pay a $200,000 initiation fee and annual dues of $14,000 for the privilege of sitting in that dining room.

cost of the tax cuts, according to the nonpartisan Committee for a Responsible Federal Budget, will likely be about $2.5 trillion over the first decade once budgeting gimmicks and interest costs are included. Combined with the spending laws President Trump has signed, the tax bill will create the largest deficit as a percentage of GDP that we've ever had outside periods of recession or war—a deficit brought to the country by a Republican House, a Republican Senate, and a Republican president. Unlike the deficit Barack Obama inherited at the depths of the Great Recession, this one has occurred at a moment when there is no good rationale; it is the very time we should be putting money aside for a future recession or conflict. Needless to say, and despite all evidence to the contrary, the Trump administration is already scheming to blame Democrats for his fiscal failure in advance of the 2020 election.

Those Tea Party ralliers in their tricorn hats seem awfully far away now, as do their original aims and impulses. But what the movement unwittingly brought about is staring us in the face.

VI. Shark Jaws

Sometimes, late at night, looking out the window at the well-tended and deceptively placid grounds of Lower Senate Park, I do some math. The exercise goes like this: what if, instead of blasting a hole in the budget, we had used that money for productive purposes? What could you do with that same sum of money? I'm not sure Steve Mnuchin and the president really need to pad their paychecks. But the rest of America could use some help.

Here are a few ideas for some onetime projects. We could have fixed our electricity infrastructure by investing in twenty-first-century generation, transmission, and distribution. That would have cost $177 billion. We could have repaired America's aging dams. That would have cost $45 billion. We could have cleared the backlog for bridge rehabilitation nationwide, $123 billion. We could have cleared the backlog for airport infrastructure, $100 billion. We could have funded maintenance at our national parks and land-management agencies, $19 billion. We could have maintained our tech lead over China for ten years, $50 billion. We could have laid broadband to provide high-speed internet to every rural community in America, $40 billion. We could have cleared Colorado's entire transportation-project backlog. That's just $9 billion. We could have eliminated the national backlog for the Rural Water Program, $2 billion. We could have done all of that—and that's just $565 billion.

So let's be more ambitious. What if we look at what we could have done differently with the full $5 trillion worth of tax cuts enacted in this millennium—most of which went to the wealthy—and some portion of the $5.6 trillion we spent in the Middle East. What else could we have done? We could have provided larger tax cuts for the middle class. We could have raised the salaries of teachers in this country by 50 percent. We could have provided early childhood education for every child in America. We could have made Social Security solvent for all time. We could have paid down some of our debt, instead of handing it to our children.

But we didn't do any of those things. Here is what we did instead: We failed to build significant infrastructure at historically low interest rates. We delayed our response to an opioid epidemic that takes more lives every year than automobile accidents. By governing with continuing resolutions, we even undermined our military preparedness. We have two thousand fewer air force pilots today than a decade ago because budget uncertainties have grounded training aircraft that have been scavenged for parts.[26] For the first time since John Glenn orbited the earth, we can't put an American into space on our own spacecraft; we need to ask the Russians for permission to ride on one of their rockets.

At the same time, we backed away to the outer limits of a democratic budget process and concentrated more power in Congress around its leaders. They in turn seized the opportunity and abandoned transparent legislative work in favor of self-serving showdown dramas. They replaced the daylight of a committee room with the closed doors of their offices. They turned their colleagues on the floor into hapless props who voted at the last minute according to the party line of the moment. And the more they emptied the process of meaningful debate and hard compromises, the more they enabled showboaters to transform what should be problem solving into campaign fund-raisers. With each repetition, Congress frittered away faith in the institutions of our republic.

All the while, we dug the country deeper into debt at the very moment when doing so made no sense. There's a chart I keep in a binder on my desk. It shows a simple correlation—the correlation between rising deficits and the unemployment rate. The two lines mostly move together, as they should: the government spends more to help people and collects less tax revenue when the economy slows. But the big exception comes at the end—the period to which we give the name Now. The two lines have parted ways, opening up like shark jaws. The deficit is moving up. Unemployment is moving down. This is the opposite of good government. It is a threat.

---

26 In September 2017, then secretary of defense James Mattis wrote to John McCain, chairman of the Senate Committee on Armed Services, explaining that budget uncertainties "obstruct our path to modernization, and continue to narrow the technical competitive advantage we presently maintain over our adversaries."

Meanwhile, the only thing the roughly 90 percent of Americans on the wrong side of the growing gaps of wealth and opportunity witnessed was an increase in the divide between themselves and their wealthiest fellow citizens. Creating opportunity and revitalizing mobility are a job for all of us—teachers, entrepreneurs, parents, everyone; they're not just a job for government. But government can make the task easier or harder. Thanks to the growing deficit, federal programs that make a real difference to poor and working-class Americans now precariously cling to existence. In late 2018, the majority leader, deigning to notice the deficit he helped to create, pointed the finger of blame at these very programs: *they're the problem*. It is hard to imagine how business as usual will result in greater upward mobility, a stronger middle class, or a reduction of inequality.

To choose a different direction we will have to elevate our expectations of our elected officials' real obligation to us. We will also have to expect of one another a more rigorous and productive engagement as citizens. We will have to call out our current politics for the con game that it is and replace it with something new. It is not enough to recognize fecklessness as a lost opportunity. We have to name it for what it is: a terrible theft from the next generation of Americans.

This is not, as we have come to believe, simply a fight between Democrats and Republicans. It is a fight between the future and the past.

VII. What Should We Do?

The American people are not prepared to accept that their children must settle for less. They are not prepared to accept that the rewards of a growing economy should accrue only to the wealthiest. There has been no growth in income for the poor and middle class in a generation, but Americans do not accept this as the new normal. Rather, the people I talk with at town halls express the view that Washington hasn't made much of an effort to turn things around. While working people scrimp and scrape, Washington can't even keep the government open long enough to have a civil conversation about what an effective economic strategy might be.

We need to put an end to a familiar but useless standoff. The Republicans are committed to cutting taxes for the few people who have benefited from economic growth in the United States— on the demonstrably false theory that the money will somehow trickle down to everyone else.[27] The Democrats are committed to protecting a set of social safety net programs. These programs are absolutely necessary, and they are as important to large portions of the Republican base as they are to large portions of the Democratic base. But many of them are not designed for the twenty-first century and have poor track records of generating upward mobility.

Instead of ducking our problems, we need to take action. Among the available ideas:

---

27 In a policy debate that cannot be held during a thirty-day legislative cramdown, we could have argued the pros and cons of whether it is better to tax work or reconsider the preferential treatment we currently afford gains on capital and massive transfers of intergenerational wealth. As Yascha Mounk argues in *The People vs. Democracy*, "it makes little sense to ask corporations that create a lot of jobs for a proportionally higher [payroll tax] contribution than corporations that create very few jobs." Consider a comparison: at this writing, Facebook's market capitalization is $431 billion and the company employs 25,105 people. By contrast, the market capitalization of General Motors is $54.49 billion, about an eighth of Facebook's, while it employs 180,000 people, seven times as many.

- Adopting regulatory, antitrust, and tax policies that encourage small business formation and investment in new ventures
- Investing massively in infrastructure improvements nationwide
- Adopting tax policies that help restore the dignity of work by better ensuring that workers can support themselves and their families[28]
- Strengthening our safety net for those who cannot support themselves while ensuring that citizens are able to return to gainful employment without losing assistance they may need
- Working to repatriate—to "onshore"—manufacturing and advanced manufacturing and their attendant (and critically important) supply chains back to the United States
- Leading a coalition of our allies in the Americas, Europe, Asia, and Africa to push back on China's mercantilist trade policies and level the playing field for the world, instead of pursuing potentially self-defeating tariffs that tax workers and consumers broadly throughout our economy
- Anticipating the world's transition to a fully digital economy, shaped by advanced artificial intelligence, with all its attendant implications for American jobs and wages
- Making college less expensive for everyone

---

28 Sherrod Brown's central campaign ad in 2018 was titled "Dignity," and in it Brown concluded with these words: "If you love this country you fight for the people that make it work." Sherrod was the only Democrat to win a statewide seat representing Ohio in Washington that year.

- Reinventing our high schools and community colleges to provide a pathway for young people who don't acquire a four-year college degree
- Vastly improving our lousy workforce-training programs and evaluating their success
- Ending our extended effort to roll back twentieth-century union victories, as we have done in states like Wisconsin, Florida, and Indiana, and entering into a new compact with organized workers that improves wages, benefits, and working conditions for twenty-first-century jobs
- Fixing our broken immigration system so that it better serves our economic needs (as we tried to do in the Senate in 2013)
- Ending mass incarceration and the stain it leaves on people attempting to find work
- Suggesting to the largest technology companies that have so disrupted our society, for good and ill, that instead of wondering out loud whether Silicon Valley ought to secede, they ought to use their extraordinary profits to invest in America's heartland
- Working with the private sector and regulators—and particularly Wall Street—to evolve away from the culture of "short termism" and earnings projections that is not a fundamental requirement of capitalism and has caused us to shift our focus from what matters

And one more idea: We should think about moving the headquarters of some federal agencies out of Washington and into the rest of the country. Dick Celeste has been saying this since I worked for him in Ohio in the late 1980s. I have long believed that the

Democratic National Committee should move somewhere like St. Louis or Kansas City to gain some useful perspective. At a stroke, decentralizing the federal bureaucracy would diminish the gravitational pull of Washington and plant seeds of growth throughout the country.

There is plenty we could be doing. As we summon the will not to be the first generation of Americans to bankrupt the next, we should be skeptical of politicians who spent trillions fighting wars in Iraq and Afghanistan and giving tax cuts to the wealthiest Americans—and who now say we have no money to invest in America. Perhaps we should send *them* the bill, instead.

NO PROPHETS
IN OUR TIME

*Sabotaging the Iran nuclear deal—and undercutting
the tradition of bipartisanship in foreign policy.*

I. The Common Good

When I was a child, the memory of World War II was very present
in my home. Although, as I have written, my grandparents cherished
their American citizenship and knew in their hearts how fortunate
they were to have it, I was always conscious of a deep and abiding
sadness as well—sorrow for what hatred and violence had erased
at a stroke. In truth, the horrors and dangers of the world and the
evil that people do to one another and to entire groups—whether
in the name of ideology or of religion or for purposes of material
gain—are never closed chapters. In small ways, every one of us
has witnessed examples in our personal lives and in the life of our
communities. As for the big ways: history offers a tragic record
of how the human moral sense can be upended—with lethal and
civilization-shattering consequences.

But history also demonstrates that there are counterforces.
It demonstrates that we can hold evil in check. But to do so we
must create durable institutions and agreements that represent at
least a small step away from what we dread. Sometimes this means

accepting a "lesser bad" as a weapon against an infinitely greater harm. This is a legitimate tool of visionary statecraft. There is no silver bullet for the world's most vexing and dangerous problems. There is no single button you can press to make them go away. These problems need to be treated as one might treat a chronic disease, with many clinical approaches and with coordinated tactics, chalking up moderate victories when one can while planning immediately for the next initiatives.

This is the context in which President Obama's decision to test carefully the possibility of a diplomatic solution to Iran's nuclear program must be viewed. The Iran deal, which was concluded in 2015, represented a shift from the maximalist philosophy—go in heavy and hard and seek to solve every problem completely and forever—that had informed much of our foreign policy since 9/11. After so many years of reacting to bad choices, the agreement sought to manage a dangerous situation, not go to war with it. The agreement, which curtailed Iran's nuclear program in exchange for an end to economic sanctions, was a case study in leverage. The United States drew on new alliances and multilateral diplomacy to address a serious potential threat to national security—while at the same time strengthening the global nuclear nonproliferation regime. It was a signal foreign policy achievement of the Obama administration.

President Trump has now withdrawn from the deal, and in so doing he has challenged basic assumptions about how America should lead in the world. Moreover, he withdrew from the deal in spite of ample evidence of its success, knowing he would have support from a significant segment of the Senate, one that had sought to undercut President Obama's efforts on Iran in a way that was at once unprecedented, insulting, and shortsighted. It is worth stepping back to understand how we got to this dangerous moment—to make sense of where we are and where we need to go.

II. Path to a Deal

In 2003, President George W. Bush ordered an invasion of Iraq based on the faulty assessment—perhaps a deliberately faulty assessment—that Iraq harbored weapons of mass destruction. Vice President Dick Cheney declared that "there is no doubt that Saddam Hussein now has weapons of mass destruction. There is no doubt he is amassing them to use against our friends, against our allies, against us." He predicted that US troops would be "greeted as liberators." Secretary of Defense Donald Rumsfeld maintained that the war would be inexpensive and would largely pay for itself. "Iraqi democracy will succeed," President Bush said. "And that success will send forth the news, from Damascus to Tehran, that freedom can be the future of every nation." The administration's optimism was one reason (among others) for the United States Senate's 77–23 vote to authorize the use of military force in Iraq. That authorization of force remains in place today, a decade and a half later.

On the day the Senate voted, Iraq was a majority Shia Arab state led by a Sunni strongman, Saddam Hussein. Its neighbor to the west was Syria, a majority Sunni Arab state led by an Alawite strongman. Its neighbor to the east was Iran, a Persian Shia state that exerted substantial influence in Syria. Just fifteen years earlier, Iraq and Iran had ended an inconclusive eight-year war that had resulted in more than a million casualties. By the time of the US invasion, Iraq and Iran had established an uneasy balance of power, one that held in check competing regional ambitions by a number of other nations. After the US invasion of Iraq, that balance became only a memory and new forces threatened to blow the region apart.

Iran was a clear beneficiary of the Iraq War. No longer constrained by Iraq's deposed Sunni dictator, over the next decade Iran exploited the chaos the war left in its wake and extended its lethal influence throughout the Middle East. It funded, equipped, and trained militias to fight coalition forces in the Iraqi theater as well as proxies throughout the region, from Hezbollah in Lebanon and Syria to Houthi rebels in Yemen. It exerted enormous influence—if not control—over many prominent Iraqi Shia political leaders. As it sowed violence and chaos, Iran continued to develop a nuclear program that had been of concern to the international community for many years.

The Bush administration was alarmed by Iran's progress, and in 2008 the United States, along with the United Kingdom, France, China, Russia, and Germany (a group that came to be called the P5+1),[1] as well as the European Union, proposed formal negotiations with Iran. As a precondition of negotiations and also to forestall additional sanctions, Iran would have to agree to suspend its uranium-enrichment program. Iran refused. "If the package includes suspension, it is not debatable at all," a government spokesperson said. Iran viewed its pursuit of a nuclear program as the prerogative of a sovereign country. Its president Mahmoud Ahmadinejad explained, "As long as this government is in power, it will not retreat one iota on the undeniable rights of the Iranian nation."

By late 2009, less than a year into President Obama's administration, the International Atomic Energy Agency (IAEA) had

---

1 "P5+1," meaning the five permanent members of the UN Security Council plus Germany. Germany, China, and Russia were among the nations that had significant trade relationships with Iran.

determined that Iran possessed roughly five thousand centrifuges—
devices used to "enrich," or manufacture, weapons-quality uranium.
This represented a substantial escalation in capability. In addition,
the country was stockpiling enriched uranium, violating UN Security Council resolutions. By the beginning of President Obama's
second term, the IAEA reported that Iran had increased the number of centrifuges to thirteen thousand and had built a potential
plutonium reactor at the industrial city of Arak.

Meanwhile, Congress passed sanctions bills with overwhelming
bipartisan support, reflecting its deep concern about Iran's nuclear
progress. The text of one of those bills in 2010 stated: "The serious
and urgent nature of the threat from Iran demands that the United
States work together with its allies to do everything possible . . . to
prevent Iran from acquiring a nuclear-weapons capability." In coming years, Congress aimed sanctions at Iran's central bank, at entities
around the globe supporting the Iranian oil economy, and at Iranian
shipbuilding and ports. None of these sanctions was designed to
produce regime change in Iran; the United States and its allies
simply sought to prevent Iran from becoming a nuclear power.

Iran continued to move ahead. Congress and President Obama
understood that sanctions had been ineffective largely because the
United States had never mobilized a vigorous multilateral coalition
that could mount a true economic blockade. As a result, our sanctions against Iran always "leaked." An effective sanctions regime
would require the cooperation of Russia, China, India, and Japan—
the largest consumers of Iranian oil. In addition, European banks
and industries would need to forgo opportunities to trade with a
lucrative partner. Diplomats dispatched by the Obama administration fanned out across the world, gaining support for a new sanctions
regime and shoring up its implementation. In the end, the United

States built a multilateral coalition to enforce sanctions effectively. The administration also persuaded Russia, China, India, and Japan to find substitutes for Iranian oil, at least for a while. The new sanctions began to slow Iran's economy.[2]

Partly as a result of economic dislocation, in June 2013 Hassan Rouhani was elected president of the Islamic Republic of Iran. Considered a moderate by Iranian standards, Rouhani had argued that Iran's economic situation could be improved through better integration with the West. As the chief negotiator for nuclear talks from 2003 to 2005, he was known in Iran as the "diplomat sheikh." In one campaign debate he observed, tellingly, that "it is good to have centrifuges running, provided people's lives and livelihoods are also running." He promised to work to lift the sanctions.

Three days after his inauguration Rouhani called for the resumption of nuclear negotiations with the international community: "We are ready—seriously and without wasting time—to engage in serious and substantive talks with the other sides. I am certain the concerns of the two sides would be removed through talks in a short period of time."

The Iranian president is an important political figure in his country, but his opinions and statements are not the last word. The final decision about Iranian foreign policy—particularly with respect to nuclear issues and the country's relationships with the West—is reserved for the supreme leader, who wields both religious and political authority. Iran's supreme leader was Ali Khamenei, a man deeply distrustful of the West and jealous of Iran's nuclear

---

2 Iran's crude oil exports fell from 2.5 billion barrels per day in 2011 to about 1.1 million barrels per day by mid-2013, starving the Iranian government of roughly $9 billion in revenue every quarter. The country's GDP shrank by as much as a fifth. Many Iranians lost their jobs or were working but unpaid or underpaid.

sovereignty. He controlled hard-line institutions such as the Islamic Revolutionary Guard Corps and the military and intended to keep Rouhani on a short leash. This internal dynamic was a reality that diplomats had to take into account: Iranians anxious for a deal could be pushed only so far.

Although the sanctions had dealt a serious blow to Iran's economy, they had not stopped its nuclear program. In fact, by August 2013 Iran had installed roughly nineteen thousand centrifuges and had produced enough enriched uranium to make ten nuclear bombs. American and Israeli intelligence agencies concluded that if it were so inclined Iran could break out to a bomb in as little as two or three months.

In September, President Obama called President Rouhani, establishing the highest-level contact between the United States and Iran in almost thirty-five years.[3] After the call, President Obama made a statement at the White House: "While there will surely be important obstacles to moving forward and success is by no means guaranteed, I believe we can reach a comprehensive solution." Rouhani's openness to some sort of deal was received in Iran by a mix of protesters, some cheering his diplomatic activity, others chanting, "Our people are awake and hate America!" and pelting his limousine with eggs and shoes.[4]

In November 2013, just months after President Obama's call to Rouhani, the P5+1 powers announced an interim agreement with

---

3 It was the first discussion between the heads of state of the United States and Iran since Jimmy Carter was president and Mohammad Reza Pahlavi ruled as the shah—in other words, since before the Iranian revolution.

4 A CNN report, citing producer Mohammed Tawfeeq, explained the significance of throwing shoes: "The act of throwing a shoe at someone or showing them your sole is 'incredibly offensive' in the Middle East, he said. 'The bottom line is, a shoe is dirt,' he said. 'Throwing a shoe on someone means throwing dirt on that person.'"

Iran on its nuclear program. Designed to allow negotiations to continue toward a comprehensive, longer-term solution, the agreement limited some of Iran's nuclear activities in exchange for a temporary easing of sanctions. Iran would be allowed access to some of its own frozen funds on a monthly basis provided that it abided by the terms of the interim deal. This arrangement—sanctions relief in exchange for nuclear limits—signaled to Congress that the president would rely on waiver authority granted to him in previous legislation to lift sanctions in any final deal.

President Obama used his 2015 State of the Union address to make his case:

> Our diplomacy is at work with respect to Iran, where, for the first time in a decade, we've halted the progress of its nuclear program and reduced its stockpile of nuclear material. Between now and this spring, we have a chance to negotiate a comprehensive agreement that prevents a nuclear-armed Iran, secures America and our allies—including Israel—while avoiding yet another Middle East conflict. There are no guarantees that negotiations will succeed, and I keep all options on the table to prevent a nuclear Iran.

At this sensitive time in diplomatic negotiations, the president asked Congress to refrain from passing additional sanctions.

III. The "Sheldon Primary"

Additional congressional sanctions turned out not to be the president's immediate challenge. Just one day after the State of the Union address, the American people—and their president—learned that

Speaker John Boehner and Majority Leader Mitch McConnell had secretly invited Israeli prime minister Benjamin Netanyahu to address a joint session of Congress about the prospective nuclear deal. They had invited him to come knowing that he would condemn the deal.

Speaker Boehner explained his actions by reminding the House Republican caucus: "You may have seen . . . the President warned us not to move ahead with sanctions on Iran, a state sponsor of terror. His exact message to us was, 'Hold your fire.' He expects us to stand idly by and do nothing while he cuts a bad deal with Iran. Two words: Hell no!" To defend his decision to invite Netanyahu, the Speaker referred to the need for a national discussion about looming security threats, which he said the president had "kind of papered over."

Six weeks later, senators and representatives filed onto the floor of the House for a joint session of Congress. On the same podium where President Obama had stood to deliver his State of the Union speech, the Israeli prime minister asserted that the proposed deal "doesn't block Iran's path to the bomb; it paves Iran's path *to* the bomb." He went on: "This deal won't be a farewell to arms. It would be a farewell to arms control. And the Middle East would soon be crisscrossed by nuclear trip wires. A region where small skirmishes can trigger big wars would turn into a nuclear tinderbox." And he warned pointedly: "Iran's regime is not merely a Jewish problem, any more than the Nazi regime was merely a Jewish problem. The 6 million Jews murdered by the Nazis were but a fraction of the 60 million people killed in World War II. So, too, Iran's regime poses a grave threat, not only to Israel, but also the peace of the entire world."

I sat on the House floor pondering the solemn trust and the accompanying pressure that Prime Minister Netanyahu carried to ensure Israel's survival. His burden is real and it is heavy. Nevertheless, I couldn't help imagining what Netanyahu's reaction would have been if President Obama had accepted an invitation from the opposition coalition to address the Knesset about Iran's nuclear program—without anyone letting Netanyahu know in advance.

A former Reagan foreign policy adviser, Robert Kagan, had ventured a similar concern. In a *Washington Post* op-ed, he asked:

> Is anyone thinking about the future? From now on, whenever the opposition party happens to control Congress—a common enough occurrence—it may call in a foreign leader to speak to a joint meeting of Congress against a President and his policies. Think of how this might have played out in the past. A Democratic-controlled Congress in the 1980s might, for instance, have called the Nobel Prize–winning Costa Rican President Óscar Arias Sánchez to denounce President Ronald Reagan's policies in Central America. A Democratic-controlled Congress in 2003 might have called French President Jacques Chirac to oppose President George W. Bush's impending war in Iraq.

Within a week of the prime minister's address, Tom Cotton, of Arkansas, who had been in the Senate for less than ninety days, circulated a letter during a Republican caucus lunch. Letters circulated at these lunches are typically light fare: corralling support for noncontroversial legislation, such as commissioning commemorative stamps and coins. Cotton's was different. He addressed it to the "Leaders of the Islamic Republic of Iran." Forty-six Republican senators signed the letter. Seven did not.[5] Susan Collins explained her refusal to sign: "It's more appropriate for members of the Senate to give advice to the president, to Secretary Kerry and to the negotiators . . . I don't think that the Ayatollah is going to be particularly convinced by a letter from members of the Senate."

In his letter, Cotton decided to give the mullahs a civics lesson:

> First, under our Constitution, while the President negotiates international agreements, Congress plays the significant role of ratifying them. In the case of a treaty, the Senate must ratify it by a two-thirds vote. A so-called congressional-executive agreement requires a majority vote in both the House and the Senate (which, because of procedural rules, effectively means a three-fifths vote in the Senate). Anything not approved by Congress is a mere executive agreement.
>
> President Obama will leave office in January 2017, while most of us will remain in office well beyond then—perhaps decades. What these two constitutional provisions mean is that we will consider any agreement regarding your nuclear-weapons program that is not approved by the Congress as nothing more than an executive agreement between President Obama and Ayatollah Khamenei.

To summarize: led by Cotton, nearly half of the United States Senate wrote to Iranian hard-liners in the midst of an arms control

---

5 These seven were Bob Corker, Jeff Flake, Susan Collins, Lamar Alexander, Lisa Murkowski, Dan Coats, and Thad Cochran.

negotiation in an attempt to undermine that negotiation.[6] There is no true analogue in American history, but here are some counterfactuals. Suppose forty-seven Republican senators had written to Stalin (or even Churchill) as Roosevelt steamed to Yalta to negotiate the close of World War II; or forty-seven Republicans had written to Fidel Castro as President John F. Kennedy took steps to defuse the Cuban Missile Crisis; or forty-seven Democratic senators had written to Soviet leader Mikhail Gorbachev as President George H. W. Bush negotiated the START arms control treaty.

For his part, President Obama observed, "I think it's somewhat ironic to see some members of Congress wanting to make common cause with the hard-liners in Iran. It's an unusual coalition."[7] The president knew well that political factions in Iran, primarily the Islamic Revolutionary Guard, were undermining any deal on the grounds that the United States would break its promises—an argument that the letter from the senators powerfully reinforced.

Normally, the president would have sole authority to negotiate an agreement such as the Iran deal. The Obama administration

6 Tom Cotton didn't stop there. He challenged Iranian foreign minister Mohammad Javad Zarif on Twitter to a debate about the US Constitution. On a single day, Cotton tweeted in four separate posts: "Hey @JZarif, I hear you called me out today. If you're so confident, let's debate the Constitution." "Here's offer: meet in DC, @JZarif, time of your choosing to debate Iran's record of tyranny, treachery, & terror." "I understand if you decline @JZarif after all, in your 20s, you hid in US during Iran-Iraq war while peasants & kids were marched to die." "Not badge of courage @JZarif, to hide in US while your country fought war to survive—but shows cowardly character still on display today." Zarif responded the next day: "Serious diplomacy, not macho personal smear, is what we need. Congrats on Ur new born. May U and Ur family enjoy him in peace. @SenTomCotton."

7 President Obama wasn't the only person who remarked on this irony. In "An Open Letter to 47 Republican Senators of the United States of America from Iran's Hard-Liners," the *Slate* writer William Saletan gets to the same point. Taking on the persona of the grateful hard-liners, he offers ironic praise: "We also very much admire the principal author of your letter, Sen. Tom Cotton of Arkansas. Sen. Cotton, like many of our young militiamen, served in combat in Iraq and believes that he is an instrument of God."

defended its constitutional authority. It explained that in the past, presidents of both parties had negotiated agreements resulting in robust changes to foreign policy without congressional approval. These included the Atlantic Charter, negotiated by President Roosevelt in 1941 (a joint declaration with Great Britain outlining common principles for the postwar international order); and the Shanghai Communiqué, negotiated by President Nixon in 1972 (a joint declaration with China that led to the normalization of relations). Moreover, unlike arms control treaties with Russia and the Soviet Union that had to be submitted for congressional approval, the Iran deal required no alteration in our own nuclear arsenal. Instead, the deal required Iran to alter its nuclear program in exchange for relief from broad economic sanctions. The administration pointed out that its authority to waive sanctions derived from language contained within the sanctions legislation itself.

Nevertheless, the substantive and political significance of the Iran nuclear agreement meant that many members of Congress, including me, wanted the chance to review it before the United States signed on the dotted line. Congress granted itself this opportunity in May 2015 by passing the Iran Nuclear Agreement Review Act, which permitted Congress to reject the agreement before the president could lift sanctions against Iran. President Obama signed it, making it law and subjecting his deal with Iran to congressional review.[8]

On July 14, 2015, the P5+1 powers announced the final terms of the nuclear deal with Iran. Formally called the Joint Comprehensive Plan of Action, it ran to more than one hundred fifty pages. Once Iran accepted and implemented certain restrictions

---

8 During the debate prior to the bill, Obama threatened to use his veto power to stop it, but the bill passed by such overwhelming bipartisan majorities in both chambers (98 to 1 in the Senate and 400 to 25 in the House) that it took that option away from him.

on its nuclear program and submitted to international monitoring and inspections to verify its actions, the United States, our allies, and the UN Security Council would lift sanctions on Iran's nuclear program.

The deal required Iran to affirm that it would never seek, develop, or acquire nuclear weapons, and that it would also agree to:

- Limit its uranium enrichment and other activities, including specific R&D activities, for the first eight years
- Limit the centrifuges at its Natanz plant to 5,060, compared with the 19,000 it currently possessed
- Reduce its proportion of uranium enrichment from 20 percent to 3.67 percent for fifteen years
- Reduce its uranium stockpile from ten thousand kilograms to three hundred kilograms for fifteen years
- Convert one of its enrichment facilities, known as the Fordow Fuel Enrichment Plant, into a nuclear, physics, and technology center, with no centrifuges operating
- Disable its plutonium reactor and rebuild a modernized heavy water reactor in Arak under international supervision to support peaceful nuclear research and production for medical purposes while rendering it impossible to produce plutonium for a nuclear weapon
- Refrain from building any additional heavy water reactors in Iran for fifteen years
- Ship out of the country all spent fuel
- Provisionally apply the Additional Protocol of the Nuclear Non-Proliferation Treaty, which ensures the International Atomic Energy Agency (IAEA) access to continuously

monitor Iran's nuclear supply chain as well as to seek access
to any undeclared suspicious location

- Allow the IAEA to monitor 24/7 the implementation of
these measures for their respective durations, as well as to
implement additional transparency measures

Those who understood its malign and dangerous role in the
region, as I did, had doubts about whether Iran would adhere to
the provisions of the nuclear deal and concerns about what might
happen when the deal ended. But the agreement addressed the
fundamentals of Iran's nuclear program, subjected Iran to the most
robust nuclear verification scheme ever negotiated, and earned support from virtually the entire international community, including
the United Kingdom, France, Germany, China, and Russia.

On its face, such an agreement might have seemed worthy of
serious consideration. Instead, the day the agreement was released,
Majority Leader McConnell set the tone for the Republican caucus,
all but charging the deal's negotiators with treason—"the Obama
administration approached these talks from a flawed perspective:
reaching the best deal acceptable to Iran, rather than actually
advancing our national goal of ending Iran's nuclear program."
Fifteen Republican senators issued statements, formally or in tweets,
opposing the deal the day it was announced—some before the text
had been submitted to Congress. In the days that followed, senators
raced one another to the floor, held press conferences, and stoked
social media accounts to exhibit their outrage.

"The deal shreds the legacy of arms control and nonproliferation that the United States has championed for decades—it will
spark a nuclear arms race in the Middle East that will be impossible

to contain," said Senator Jim Risch, of Idaho, who was the highest-ranking Republican on the Senate Foreign Relations Committee after the chairman. "This deal falls disastrously short of what the Obama Administration originally promised and gives the Iranian government what it desires."

Senator David Vitter, of Louisiana, also took to Twitter on July 14: "I think this #Iran agreement is a really, really bad deal for America, for Israel, and for freedom."

As soon as the deal was announced, Senator Ted Cruz released a long statement—so long that it had to have been written beforehand—condemning the agreement. He wrote: "This is a staggeringly bad deal. It is a fundamental betrayal of the security of the United States and of our closest allies, first and foremost Israel."

Presidential candidate Donald Trump was typically succinct: "The fact is, the US has incompetent leaders and even more incompetent negotiators. We must do better for America and the world. We have to Make America Great Again."

Some senators opposed the deal simply to punish President Obama or to preempt a foreign policy win for the administration. Others saw an opportunity to score points on the campaign trail. Opponents of the deal popped up an advocacy group called Citizens for a Nuclear Free Iran to teach Americans "about the dangers of the proposed Iran deal." The group promised to run a thirty-five-state ad campaign during the sixty-day review period—in the crosshairs were undecided Democrats. Prime Minister Netanyahu, as well as many other elected Israeli leaders, made their opposition widely known.

For Republicans with national ambitions, the fight over the Iran deal became a chance to court megadonor Sheldon Adelson, the Las Vegas casino magnate, multibillionaire, and avowed opponent of the nuclear agreement. In 2012, Adelson had contributed $93 million to support Republican candidates and causes.[9] To the crowd of Republican presidential hopefuls in 2016, Adelson's support was potentially decisive. Winning it meant outdoing competitors in parroting his views on the Middle East.

To get a sense of those views, consider Adelson's suggestion that we start negotiations by dropping a nuclear bomb in the Iranian desert:

> And then you say, "See! The next one is in the middle of Tehran. So, we mean business. You want to be wiped out? Go ahead and take a tough position and then continue with your nuclear development."[10]

Adelson also favored unilaterally moving the US embassy from Tel Aviv to Jerusalem before the conclusion of final status negotiations between Israel and the Palestinians—which now has come to pass under the Trump administration—and embraced the construction of Israeli settlements on the West Bank. Adelson's worldview seeped into Washington's debate about the nuclear agreement as

---

9 To any of us, this is an astounding sum. To Adelson, it is a trifling amount, given his net worth at the time: $34 billion. In 2012, I gave a floor speech comparing Adelson's campaign contributions with the average annual household income in Colorado—roughly $77,000. It was July when I made my remarks. Adelson had already given $35 million. If that typical household was to spend the same percentage of its annual income as this one casino owner in Las Vegas had by then spent of his, the sum would come to about $78. Many American families might skip one night at the movies if they knew that spending the amount they saved would have an impact like Adelson's.

10 Consider the gulf between Adelson's attitude and that of George Kennan, the architect of America's containment strategy in the Cold War. In 1951, Kennan said, "I think there is no more dangerous delusion, none that has done us a greater disservice in the past or that threatens to do us a greater disservice in the future, than the concept of total victory."

Republicans routinely solicited the casino magnate's advice on the proper conduct of US foreign policy. Over the course of this debate, a parade of Republican presidential hopefuls made the trek to Adelson's Venetian hotel in Las Vegas, tripping over one another to stake out ever more hawkish positions to win his endorsement. This became known, informally, as the "Sheldon primary." In effect, the gravitational force of a single donor pulled Republicans toward a position that practically speaking had no chance of achieving the same outcomes as the agreement, short of war. A debate over national security had been reduced to the cruder forms of partisan calculation.

Back in Washington, politicians of both parties understood the peril of crossing Adelson on this issue. Without the specter of Sheldon Adelson in the background, Tom Cotton's letter to the mullahs would never have received forty-six signatures. When Netanyahu addressed Congress in March 2015 about the Iranian nuclear program, Sheldon and his wife, Miriam, sat as guests in the House gallery. As Netanyahu spoke, Miriam's purple Hermès purse fell from the balcony, landing on a congressman. Fair warning!

IV. "A Proof of Our Strength"

As the most vulnerable Democratic incumbent up for election that year, in what is very much a swing state, I was acutely aware of the political realities influencing the Senate's consideration of the Iran deal. A cross section of Republican and Independent leaders in Colorado warned me that a vote for the Iran deal would demonstrate that I was the president's lackey, not an independent voice for my state. A vote of approval, they said, would ensure that opposition super PACs would descend on Colorado throughout the campaign. A vote against would keep them at bay.

As chair of the Democratic Senatorial Campaign Committee, I had seen national security become an Achilles' heel in the 2014 elections, with Democrats blamed for many vexing foreign challenges, including the proliferation of ISIS.[11] In my case, internal polling showed that the Iran deal was the only line of attack from which I would be unable to recover using response ads. In other words, a series of negative ads hitting me on my support for President Barack Hussein Obama's Iran nuclear deal—opponents for some reason always felt compelled to mention Obama's middle name—could be a fatal blow.

A no vote, on the other hand, would provide a vote against President Obama and seem to project "strength"—as certain voices on the right conceived of strength—on national security. It would also relieve me of responsibility if Iran conducted an attack on US interests during the course of the campaign.

By mid-August, a super PAC began to air ads in various states, including Colorado, urging members of Congress to vote against the agreement. Presented under the tagline "Veterans Against the Deal," the ads featured a retired staff sergeant describing how he had been injured by an Iranian bomb. The sergeant explained:

> Every politician who is involved in this will be held account-
> able. They will have blood on their hands. A vote for this deal

---

11 By the end of the 2014 election cycle, it almost seemed as though talk radio was claiming that ISIS fighters were infecting themselves with Ebola and then disguising themselves as unaccompanied minors from Central America making their way north to cross our border with Mexico.

means more money for Iranian terrorism. What do you think they're going to do when they get more money?

The ad concluded, "Call your senator. Tell them no deal with Iran. If you don't call, who will?"

I began placing a series of my own calls. Former senator Barack Obama—now the source of my political discomfort—once wrote that the best part about being in the Senate was that you could get your phone call returned from anyone in the world at least once. I have found that to be largely true and have used this privilege, in particular, to meet journalists and writers whose books matter to me. In the case of the Iran deal, so many people were anxious to voice their opinion that we could have filled the schedule without making any calls at all. Still, my office added numerous people to the schedule in an effort to seek a variety of perspectives and to examine more closely the technical details.

Meanwhile, President Obama made his case for the Iran deal in a speech at American University. He argued:

So this deal is not just the best choice among alternatives— this is the strongest non-proliferation agreement ever negotiated. And because this is such a strong deal, every nation in the world that has commented publicly, with the exception of the Israeli government, has expressed support. The United Nations Security Council has unanimously supported it. The majority of arms control and non-proliferation experts support it . . . I've had to make a lot of tough calls as President, but whether or not this deal is good for American security is not one of those calls. It's not even close.

As his speeches often are, this one was a logical and careful exposition of the merits of the agreement.[12] One by one, he addressed the arguments of the deal's opponents. But, in this case, he was overselling. For many of my Senate colleagues, just beginning to deliberate, this was indeed a close call or at least a very difficult one. Some were facing voters—not to mention organized interest groups—who believed that rejecting the deal was the call that was not close.

I myself had several contextual misgivings about the agreement even before studying its details. First, I thought it possible that administration officials had been too hungry for a deal, wanting to score a dramatic diplomatic win entering the last year of a presidency. Although I had no way really to know, it was not apparent to me that Iran ever believed we would walk away from an agreement. (In my days working for Phil Anschutz, we used to say that any deal worth doing would be one that the parties would have walked away from at least three times.) This made me wonder whether we had negotiated its terms as vigorously as we could, including, vitally, the length of some of the restrictions.

Second, some proponents of the deal asserted that we should approve it because it might strengthen President Rouhani and isolate hard-liners, leading Iran to moderate. This overestimated the upside. I had heard enough—from people with on-the-ground experience in the Middle East of Iran's dangerous behavior—to

---

12 President Obama crafted his remarks in order to reach multiple audiences: Congress, our international partners and allies, the press, and the American public. In June 2018, Donald Trump, on Twitter, demonstrated his own approach. (E.g., "Obama, Schumer and Pelosi did NOTHING about North Korea, and now weak on Crime, High Tax Schumer is telling me what to do at the Summit the Dems could never set up. Schumer failed with North Korea and Iran, we don't need his advice!" Or, "I am heading for Canada and the G-7 for talks that will mostly center on the long time unfair trade practiced against the United States. From there I go to Singapore and talks with North Korea on Denuclearization. Won't be talking about the Russian Witch Hunt Hoax for a while!")

conclude that in evaluating the deal, prudence required assuming that Iran would never moderate, would likely cheat, and would remain our committed adversary.

Third, even if the terms of the deal were acceptable, I wondered whether the United States had the attention span to enforce them. For Iran, this deal represented its most important piece of business. Its leadership, therefore, would focus on Iran's equities at every moment. The United States, on the other hand, had a vast array of other concerns, and popular support at home for any of them could be fickle. Many Americans could not distinguish between Iraq and Iran, Sunni and Shia. The Middle East was also very far away. Sheer distance might create political distortion that could distract us from securing our interests over the long term.[13]

The Iranian Americans I met who opposed the deal were particularly insistent that the United States had been outnegotiated. This seemed to have less to do with the substance of the agreement than with our differing worldviews. One person who had left Iran in 1979 after the fall of the shah told me that we in the West are always asking what time it is, while Iran is building the watch. Iranians think in centuries, he said, and we think in two-year election cycles.

Not surprisingly, as a general matter I discovered that people from the Middle East had a far more nuanced view of the situation than people—especially politicians—in the United States. Not that they disagreed among themselves about the merits of the deal any

---

13 More than two centuries ago, Alexis de Tocqueville captured the difficulty of conducting foreign policy in our democracy: "External policy requires almost none of the qualities that are proper to democracy, and demands, on the contrary, the development of almost all those it lacks . . . Only with difficulty can democracy coordinate the details of a great undertaking, fix on a design, and afterwards follow it with determination through obstacles. It is hardly capable of combining measures in secret and of patiently awaiting their result."

less than Americans did; if anything, they may have disagreed more heatedly. But they offered an informed, if sometimes self-interested, view. (In general, they also had a more sophisticated understanding of the United States than my colleagues and I had of their countries. They certainly did not need a civics lesson from Tom Cotton.)

Finally, I met a former high-ranking Israeli defense official who expressed ambivalence about the deal but concluded that it was the best of the available bad choices. During the course of our conversation, he observed, "There are no prophets in our time." As I reflected on the blazing partisan rhetoric in Washington—particularly from those who had objected before reading the deal—it occurred to me that this was a particularly useful observation: grounded in humility and informed by a recognition that diplomatic solutions come more often in small steps than in a thunderclap of revelation.

By the end of the summer, my review had included briefings from American defense, national security, and intelligence experts; international inspection and verification experts; regional experts; former Israeli military and intelligence officials; and the P5+1 ambassadors as well as Israel's ambassador to the United States. I had read countless pages of background material. Sheldon Adelson had called me twice.

And I had spoken with President Obama. Obama was not a schmoozer and arm-twister in the manner of Lyndon Johnson, to put it mildly, but if he thinks you're heading the wrong way—not so much politically as intellectually, on the merits—he can be effective in making you feel the force of that perception. On one occasion he invited the entire Democratic caucus to the White House to discuss the Iran deal. He had reasoned, compelling answers to each question and every criticism. His arguments did not eliminate the need for me to complete work with outside experts, or consider the perspectives of my constituents, few of whom were as convinced as the president. I concluded in August that the agreement presented the best available way to prevent Iran from obtaining a nuclear weapon, to protect our ally Israel, and to avoid another war in the Middle East.

Among other things, it did not seem plausible to me that new—particularly unilateral—sanctions would result in a better deal. Failure to conclude the deal on the table would exhaust our allies' patience and their willingness to sustain the multilateral sanctions that created leverage for the negotiators in the first place. The lifting of sanctions in the absence of a deal would send billions of dollars to Iran without any oversight of its nuclear program.

I retained deep concerns about what Iran's nuclear program could look like beyond the ten- or fifteen-year time horizon of some elements of the deal, but I also knew that shortsighted decisions had left us with an array of bad choices. Iran used the Iraq War—and the suppurating chaos that had infected the region ever since—to expand its sphere of influence across the Middle East and to bolster its proxies in Lebanon, Iraq, and Yemen.

During the pendency of the Iran debate, I never took issue with Coloradans who believed it was morally wrong to deal with Iran: "Don't shake this dirty hand," as one friend expressed it to me. Although I did not agree with where that sentiment led, I understood it to be a principled position. Supreme leader Ayatollah Ali Khamenei's statement that the "barbaric" Jewish state "has no cure but to be annihilated" would be sufficient for some to say no to any deal. However, it seemed to me that Iran's dangerous tendencies and ill intentions would only become more of a

threat if backed by nuclear weapons. I also believed that even as
we implemented the nuclear deal, we would have to do more to
counter Iran's conventional threat in the Middle East.

In September 2015, I put out a public statement to explain my
position. It made an additional point:

> We live in dangerous times. Our young men and women in the
> military—so many Coloradans, so many Americans—have been
> asked to sacrifice so much. None of us can have any doubt that
> if called upon again, our men and women in the Armed Forces
> would rise to any challenge, anywhere in the world. We honor
> their courage and spirit of sacrifice—and we demonstrate con-
> fidence in ourselves—by exhausting diplomatic options before
> we turn to military ones. This is not a sign of weakness but a
> proof of strength, and it will help us rally our allies to our side
> if ultimately we need to act militarily.

Later that month, Majority Leader McConnell attempted to
move a resolution of disapproval to the Senate floor pursuant to the
Iran Nuclear Agreement Review Act. A procedural vote failed, 58–42.
It fell below the sixty votes required to end debate. Four Democrats
joined all fifty-four Republicans to support moving to the resolution of disapproval. Maintaining the pressure, McConnell filed the
identical motion again immediately after it failed. Twice in the next
week, we took exactly the same vote with exactly the same result.

It is interesting to consider the dimensions of these votes. They
permitted individual members of Congress to signal their endorsement or rejection but allowed Congress as a whole to refrain from
upending the agreement—or provoking a constitutional crisis with
the Obama administration—unless the deal really was egregious. Only

then could both chambers pass a resolution of disapproval and over-come the administration's veto with supermajority votes. This balance may have favored the executive branch to the detriment of the legislative, but that tendency is not unknown or unwelcome in American diplomatic history.[14] The Senate engages in its share of theater by voting on symbolic measures designed to score political points; the two parties took shots at each other with measures on Keystone XL. But McConnell, smelling blood in the water, was aggressive in this case.

More prosaically, Senator McConnell seemed to have set the stage for Colorado's campaign season. Almost immediately, an ad appeared featuring children of various ethnicities counting down from ten in different languages, with the last child saying "one" as a nuclear flash, followed by a billowing mushroom cloud, eclipsed the screen. It concluded: "A nuclear Iran is a threat to the entire world. Senator Michael Bennet supports Obama's Iran deal and is jeopardizing our safety . . . Ask him why."

The ad's creator, who had previously run the Koch brothers' youth outreach program, explained its significance:

[Bennet] chose global chaos and terror over world peace, America and Israel's safety and security, and ignored the out-cry from his outraged constituents . . . We will never forget he voted to hold the American people hostage and sided with terrorists and madmen to silence the innocent people he rep-resents here in Colorado.

---

14 As a nation, we have long struggled to strike the right balance. In "Federalist No. 75," Alexander Hamilton writes: "The power of making treaties is, plainly, neither the one [passing laws] nor the other [executing laws once they are passed]. It relates neither to the execution of the subsisting laws, nor to the enaction of new ones." The framers ultimately landed on a novel compromise, granting the president the power to negotiate treaties and the Senate the role of offering advice and consent.

A cavalcade of Republicans then jumped into Colorado's Senate race, citing the Iran agreement as the primary reason to oppose me. Businessman and self-funder Jack Graham seeded his campaign with $1 million of his own money. The Iran nuclear agreement "was the tipping point," he said when asked why he was running. The National Republican Senatorial Committee recruited an Iraq combat veteran, Jon Keyser, into the race, in part as a result of my vote. Before he decided to run, Keyser traveled to Washington to attend the Republican Jewish Coalition's Presidential Forum. When he returned home to Colorado, he claimed to have secured $3 million in commitments of soft money to back his campaign. Unsurprisingly, his first ad accused President Obama and me of wanting to "give these guys nuclear weapons" (the guys being the Iranians).[15] After one debate, he told the press that he had been "taking the bark off of Michael Bennet" and that "Michael Bennet has failed Colorado on voting for Iran." For good measure, he added that I wanted "to close Guantánamo Bay with the president" and bring the remaining ninety prisoners held at the facility "right here to Colorado."

Darryl Glenn, an air force officer, won the Republican primary, and he beat the Iran deal drum right up to Election Day. In an October interview with *Breitbart News Daily*, he made it his first salvo, ahead of all other aspects of my record:

People are really angry about his support of the Iran nuclear deal. When you start thinking about the fact that he just

---

15 It went on to provide ample melodrama. The ad opened with a narrator highlighting Keyser's role as a military intelligence officer in Iraq, where he "conducted capture and kill missions to remove high-value targets in urban areas." A glaring Keyser continued: "For us, Baghdad was the roughest. We weren't fighting amateurs; we were fighting a vicious enemy armed by Iran. Now Obama wants to give these guys nuclear weapons and Michael Bennet, he was all for it. For me it's personal. You don't trust Iran and you can't trust Michael Bennet."

recently spoke to the *Denver Post*, and he thinks everything's fine. He's not up there talking about how absolutely unconscionable it is with the ransom payments that are going out there, and potentially here we are feeding the number one world sponsor of terror, that could potentially use those funds against our own men and women that wear the uniform.

Glenn, like my other opponents, knew that he could claim anything about an agreement negotiated by the Obama administration and Iran—and at least some of it would stick to me. He parroted talking points, including the misleading claim that by unfreezing Iranian assets we were paying the Iranians ransom. The Republicans had seen the same polling that showed that it would be difficult for my campaign to recover against a well-funded line of attack on the Iran deal.

In the end, I won reelection to the Senate. Whatever my failings, the people I represented in Colorado seemed not to believe that voting "to hold the American people hostage and side with terrorists and madmen" was among them.

V. Throwing a Fit

The outcome of the election in Colorado may have owed something to what Coloradans were now learning about the implementation of the Iran nuclear deal. Looking forward, the deal had seemed like a close call. In the rearview mirror, the results could be seen more clearly. By early 2016, Iran:

- Had shipped twelve tons of enriched uranium out of the country

- Had filled the core of the Arak plutonium reactor with concrete, rendering it inoperable
- Had allowed the IAEA access to the entire nuclear fuel cycle of uranium enrichment, including centrifuge production shops and uranium mines and mills
- Had decreased the number of its centrifuges from 19,000 to 6,104, limited to the most basic models
- Stood to receive far less than the $150 billion claimed by the deal's opponents during Congress's consideration, meaning that while Iran could still fund conventional mayhem in the region, its economy would not see the lift that some of its leadership (and some opponents of the deal) had predicted

Contrary to the claims made in ads run against me, the deal had put Iran further away from a nuclear weapon. In February 2016, James Clapper, the director of National Intelligence, testified before the Senate Armed Services Committee that Iran's breakout time to a nuclear bomb had increased from a couple of months before the deal to about a year. This difference provided the United States, Israel, and our allies time to coordinate and plan should Iran attempt to bolt toward a bomb. The inspections and verification regime would also give us much greater insight into the Iranian nuclear program—information that would make any future military option far more effective if we ever had to make that fateful choice.

Moreover, because our intelligence assessments, as well as those of international observers, had concluded that the deal was working, it was increasingly seen as a successful product of American global leadership. Success had not been preordained. President Obama had taken a calculated risk that it was worth testing whether multilateral diplomacy could deliver a viable alternative to military force. Now that the deal was holding and delivering its intended outcomes, it became increasingly regarded as an example of US leadership reinforcing a rules-based international system to address a serious security threat.

These were known facts by the time the 2016 presidential election rolled around. Nevertheless, candidate Donald Trump, who possessed no experience dealing with nuclear issues and was profoundly ignorant on questions of foreign policy, campaigned on the same arguments used by my opponents in Colorado.[16] He repeatedly labeled the Iran agreement "the worst deal that has ever been negotiated." He said, "Iran should write us a letter of thank you, just like the really stupid—the stupidest deal of all time, a deal that's going to give Iran absolutely nuclear weapons."

In March 2016, early in the race, Trump stood before a crowd of about twenty thousand members of the American Israel Public Affairs Committee, or AIPAC, in Washington's Verizon Center and said his "number one priority" was "to dismantle the disastrous deal with Iran." Speaking from a circular stage at the center of a basketball arena, he claimed he had "studied this issue in great detail. I would say, actually, greater by far than anybody else, believe me, oh, believe me." The reaction from the crowd of AIPAC activists, perhaps the planet's best-educated people on the deal, was uncertain laughter. In a related TV appearance, citing no evidence, Trump said: "I think it's going to lead to a nuclear holocaust."

---

16 When his ignorance on these matters was pointed out, he took refuge in ancestry, citing family heritage in the form of an uncle: "Look, having nuclear—my uncle was a great professor and scientist and engineer, Dr. John Trump at MIT; good genes, very good genes . . . Nuclear is powerful; my uncle explained that to me many, many years ago, the power and that was thirty-five years ago; he would explain the power of what's going to happen and he was right, who would have thought?" It might be worth pondering why someone who puts so much faith in the science of genetics remains skeptical about the science of climate change.

By 2017, with Donald Trump now president, the State Department's assessment was that Iran was complying with its obligations. Ambassadors from France, Germany, the UK, and the EU met with Congress and also expressed their strong view that Iran had complied. The IAEA, whose inspectors continued their work, confirmed the same.

Congress had required the president to certify every three months that Iran was complying with its commitments. It had drafted the certification requirement for a president acting in good faith. That oversight structure lost its meaning in a Trump presidency. Despite the known facts, the assessment of our intelligence agencies, and the opinions of our allies and multiple international authorities, and against the counsel of his own advisers, the new president, according to an administration official quoted in the *Washington Post*, "threw a fit" when asked to certify Iran's compliance with the nuclear deal.[17]

The second time he had a chance, President Trump refused to certify, claiming that the agreement was not in the national security interest of the United States. He kicked the issue to Congress, saying, "I am directing my administration to work closely with Congress and our allies to address the deal's many serious flaws . . . In the event we are not able to reach a solution working with Congress and our allies, then the agreement will be terminated." To America's allies, he said, "I hereby call on key European countries to join with the United States in fixing significant flaws in the deal, countering Iranian aggression,

---

17 The *Post*'s article cites a source "familiar with the meeting." It was clear then and is clearer now, however, that some of his cabinet members strongly disagreed with him. Trump's then secretary of state, Rex Tillerson, had criticisms of the deal but advocated for its continuation, noting that the United States was working with the other signatory parties, "our European allies in particular, to ensure we are fully enforcing all aspects of that agreement." Tillerson was eventually forced out of the Trump cabinet.

and supporting the Iranian people. If other nations fail to act during this time, I will terminate our deal with Iran."

In Washington, people often make elaborate promises with no intention of keeping them—something President Trump has often done. In the case of the Iran agreement, he behaved differently but even more destructively: keeping a promise even when the facts proved he should break it.

President Trump's decision to withdraw from the deal, announced on May 8, 2018, was an act of national self-sabotage. While we were right to make a critical—even skeptical—examination of the deal when it was first presented to Congress, the decision to scuttle it even though it was working and even though there was no alternative in place was like abandoning a lifeboat at sea because we wanted a better one, even with no better one in sight. Further, blowing up the Iran deal isolates our country from our closest allies while diminishing the credibility of America's intention to abide by the agreements we negotiate. It drives a wedge in the transatlantic alliance—a community of interests and values we forged from the ashes of World War II. This outcome represents a gift to Russia and China, which benefit from a divided West. President Putin and President Xi wasted no time presenting themselves as defenders of the rules-based world order Trump had just abandoned.

Many of my Republican colleagues have defended President Trump's decision by saying that the deal was flawed. Let's think about that for a moment. All deals that are the product of tough negotiation between parties with divergent interests are going to be imperfect representations of the parties' maximalist positions. Indeed, in this respect, the Iran deal has shortcomings; we didn't get everything we and our partners would want (and neither did Iran get what it wanted). And, while I have no reason to believe that American negotiators did anything but use their leverage and expertise to press for as much as possible (the domestic politics surrounding the deal created a powerful incentive to do so), we might even grant that we didn't get every last thing that we could have gotten in the deal. But even if we grant both these points, it does not then follow that we should tear up the deal we had. President Macron of France had even offered to build on the foundation of the deal by seeking additional concessions from Iran. President Trump refused. The deal was working, and President Trump now owns the consequences of abandoning it. My fear is that all of us, and particularly our women and men in uniform, will pay for his recklessness.

One of the grave consequences is the precedent President Trump has set for any future nuclear negotiations. As we now know, even the Trump administration sees the value of a potential settlement with North Korea. Any negotiation will occur in the shadow of his abandonment of the Iran deal. Knowing that the United States withdrew when Iran had complied with its terms ought to make Kim Jong-un skeptical about whether any deal he struck with the United States would be honored.

In addition, President Trump has the challenge of negotiating a better agreement with North Korea than the Iranian deal he ripped up. This will not be without its challenges. Until recently, President Trump has proved so eager to tie up a deal with North Korea that he has trumpeted Kim Jong-un's commitment to denuclearize—a promise that North Korea has broken repeatedly in the past and has not actually made in the present. There is no timeline for denuclearization and no provision for an international inspections and verification program—the kind of program Obama had carefully put in place to constrain Iran.

Intelligence assessments indicate that North Korea's nuclear program is continuing. Up to the moment when the negotiations predictably fell apart in Hanoi, the president seemed to care only for the good opinion of his new best friend. "Cross my heart" was the extent of his verification regime.[18]

For its part, Iran will be liberated to build a bomb in secret if it chooses to do so. This will ensure that Iran is in the driver's seat to decide whether to test our resolve to go to war. The regime will be free to creep toward a line that may leave us no choice but to attack its nuclear capabilities. As we knew before the nuclear deal was negotiated, military action would, at best, set Iran's nuclear program back by several years. At worst, it would drag the United States into a protracted war in the Middle East—something our allies may very well let us fight alone.

Finally, we must be mindful of the dangers that President Trump's decision poses to American leadership of the international order. Taken together with his decision to pull out of the Paris Agreement and his even more mercurial decision to bring American troops home from Syria, his withdrawal from the Iran deal endangers an international agreement that the United States took the lead in negotiating, after also taking the lead in building an international sanctions regime. Given this casual disregard for our own international commitments, we should worry about whether

---

18 We don't even know what the agreement entails, much less whether Kim promised "no backsies." Following his June 2018 meeting with the North Korean dictator, the president tweeted triumphantly: "Before taking office people were assuming that we were going to War with North Korea. President Obama said that North Korea was our biggest and most dangerous problem. No longer—sleep well tonight!" The North Korean leader's own post-summit remarks are studiously ambiguous. At a meeting in September with South Korean president Moon Jae-in, Kim said that his country would permanently dismantle its nuclear production facilities but refused to acknowledge commitments that North Korea would give up its nuclear weapons or missiles. American intelligence agencies have determined that North Korea's network of ballistic missile bases is still active.

Trump's decision undermines America's ability to lead in the future. Will other nations go along with our sanctions policies? Will the major powers defer to us to lead important diplomatic initiatives? Will other nations trust us to keep our word?

VI. The Value of Values

The Iran nuclear agreement challenged the Senate to consider how to recalibrate our strategy toward one aspect of the turmoil in the Middle East. The insertion of domestic partisanship into the debate denied the American people the chance to consider fully the implications of the deal as well as broader questions relating to America's role in the world. Throughout the Cold War, we were able to sustain decades of bipartisan consensus about how to fight Communist expansionism, even if different administrations of different parties pursued different policies and priorities. We badly need a similar bipartisan consensus to deal with the even more complicated world of today. In losing this opportunity on Iran, we postponed any attempt to develop a bipartisan consensus about America's foreign policy in the twenty-first century.

The United States lost a fundamental organizing principle when the Soviet Union collapsed. The Cold War was not just a fight against the Soviets; it was a fight against tyranny. They were the builders of the Berlin Wall; the erectors of barbed wire fences and secret prisons; the invaders of Hungary and Czechoslovakia; the snoopers into people's everyday lives; the grandstand of medaled gray men atop Lenin's mausoleum watching tanks roll by during May Day parades. The United States was the champion of liberty and opportunity; architect of the Lend-Lease Act, which built the military strength of other nations in their struggle against fascism; sponsor of the Marshall Plan, which helped reconstruct a devastated postwar world; advocate of free expression, human rights, and democracy; underwriter of health, infrastructure, and agricultural projects across the developing world; principal sponsor of international law and the network of institutions anchored in the United Nations. If World War I had taught Americans that they were unavoidably part of the larger world, World War II taught us that we would have to lead it. The strategic objective was remarkably constant, and at its center was the idea that the citizens of the United States would benefit from a system of global politics governed by rules grounded in human dignity and freedom.

For Americans of my generation, the Cold War defined our foreign policy, for good and for ill. It also defined us as a people and defined who we were not. It gave us purpose, unified us, and made us deliberate about our role in the world. In important ways, it also constrained our actions—limiting to some extent our behavior abroad and disciplining our politics at home. In the fight against Communism, we made more than our fair share of egregious mistakes: among them, the witch hunts that come under the name McCarthyism; our ignominious penchant for supporting "loyal" dictators in developing nations; and the Vietnam War, which divided us as a people as well as greatly diminished our esteem among the world's nations. Nevertheless, our foreign policy in those days and the values that underlay it strengthened our republic at home and advanced US interests abroad.

The fall of the Berlin Wall disoriented us. Could America continue to lead the world without the moral and political organizing principle of an ideological foe? One answer was to reject the question; the triumph over Soviet Communism meant that the liberal order had been endowed with its own momentum. There were those who believed our political project was done; the trajectory of the world was set: we just had to be ready to watch democracy spread. That naive optimism ended when Osama bin Laden orchestrated his plot to fly planes into the World Trade Center and the Pentagon. If the 1990s were characterized by a relatively benign incoherence, the first decade of the 2000s was characterized by a single-minded focus on responding to the pain, shock, and tragedy of 9/11. Since then, we have been fighting not a Cold War against a single rival superpower but a perpetual global war on terror that finds enemies everywhere and has led to catastrophic decisions. A perpetual war on terror has terrorized us.[19]

Americans' ambivalence about our engagement in the world made us susceptible to the disjointed bluster of Donald Trump's foreign policy in the first place. On the one hand, he decried (after supporting) the Iraq War and President Bush's instinct to "nation build" or export democracy. On the other, he has overseen one of the largest increases in defense spending since Ronald Reagan's buildup in the 1980s—rivaled only by President George W. Bush's buildup at the height of his administration's response to the September 11, 2001, attacks. He has deployed additional troops to Afghanistan and escalated all of our military engagements in the Middle East— before abruptly changing his mind just before Christmas 2018 and deciding to pull US forces out of Syria (where they were assisting Kurdish forces in the fight against ISIS) and letting it be known

---

19 Since 9/11, we have fought the longest wars in the country's history. If we are in Afghanistan in 2021, a not unlikely possibility, we will have been there for a fifth of a century. No American high school senior will know a time in his or her life when the United States was not waging this war. In the post-9/11 conflicts, according to cautious estimates, we have spent roughly $5.6 trillion. We have lost nearly seven thousand American lives.

that he would likely cut the US presence in Afghanistan by half. The sudden announcement prompted the resignation of Defense Secretary James Mattis—the first resignation in history by a defense secretary over a matter of policy. Meanwhile, Trump has leveled threats of nuclear "fire and fury," and of "CONSEQUENCES THE LIKES OF WHICH FEW THROUGHOUT HISTORY HAVE EVER SUFFERED BEFORE." He has blurred our doctrine for the use of nuclear force, asked the Department of Defense to develop low-yield tactical nuclear weapons for use on the battlefield, and suggested that Japan should think about developing its own nuclear capability. All of this undermines global nuclear nonproliferation.

In his inaugural address, President Trump promised to "eradicate completely" extremist Islamic terrorism "from the face of the earth." The next day, he visited the CIA and explained:

> We don't win anymore. The old expression, "to the victor belong the spoils"—you remember. I always used to say, keep the oil. I wasn't a fan of Iraq. I didn't want to go into Iraq. But I will tell you, when we were in, we got out wrong. And I always said, in addition to that, keep the oil . . . So we should have kept the oil. But okay. Maybe you'll have another chance. But the fact is, should have kept the oil.

Never in our history has "winning" meant the plunder of another country's natural resources and certainly never in a case where our invasion of another country was wrong. President Trump's view is egregiously at odds with international law and with Harry Truman's instinct to rebuild Japan and Germany. It is a recipe for endless conflict. And, like so many of his foreign policy pronouncements, it threatens to unhinge or rearrange traditional alliances. As David Hendrickson, a foreign-affairs specialist and historian at Colorado College, points out, Trump's proposed oil grab in Iraq is the only policy that would ensure unification of Shia, Sunni, and Kurdish interests in that region.

President Trump's foreign policy efforts also represent a significant departure from our highest aspirations: the rule of law, democratic freedoms, and human rights.[20] Trump has praised President Rodrigo Duterte of the Philippines, whose official drug policies include the execution of suspected offenders without a trial; applauded China's President Xi Jinping for constitutionally paving the way for an unlimited term as head of state; apparently taken advice from Turkey's Recep Tayyip Erdoğan, hardly a human rights paragon, about our involvement in the Syrian civil war; and congratulated Russian president Vladimir Putin on winning his own rigged election. He has tried to ban immigrants from certain Islamic countries and looked for every excuse to avoid taking refugees during the worst global refugee crisis since World War II.

He has withdrawn the United States from important multilateral diplomatic efforts. He has questioned the value of NATO in the wake of Russia's attack on our elections and its invasion of Crimea. He has threatened to cut by almost half our funding for the United

---

20 The importance of these values—and of the US role in sustaining them, though our own record is imperfect—was underscored by Václav Havel, the president of a newly free Czechoslovakia, in a speech to a joint session of Congress in 1990: "As long as people are people, democracy, in the full sense of the word, will always be no more than an ideal. One may approach it as one would the horizon in ways that may be better or worse, but it can never be fully attained. In this sense, you, too, are merely approaching democracy. You have thousands of problems of all kinds, as other countries do. But you have one great advantage: You have been approaching democracy uninterruptedly for more than two hundred years, and your journey toward the horizon has never been disrupted by a totalitarian system."

Nations and foreign aid (which already represents a minuscule portion of the federal budget). He has mindlessly enforced across-the-board hiring freezes at the State Department and threatened to cut its budget by a third. He has committed the United States to withdraw from a climate accord signed by every other country in the world, including North Korea.

Through his second year in office, President Trump seemed committed to outdo each previous diplomatic misstep with one that earned even more disregard at home and abroad. In June, he turned the G7 meeting, an annual economic planning summit with our strongest allies, into a Trump-against-the-world showdown. Little less than a month later, at the conclusion of extraordinary head-to-head talks with Vladimir Putin, he gave the benefit of the doubt to President Putin's claim that there was no Russian interference in the 2016 elections while disputing unambiguous American intelligence findings to the contrary. In September 2018, when he appeared before the United Nations General Assembly, he boasted that his administration "has accomplished more than almost any administration in the history of our country." The delegates laughed at him.

And then, shortly afterward, Saudi Arabian agents with close ties to Crown Prince Mohammed bin Salman brutally assassinated the *Washington Post* opinion writer Jamal Khashoggi. President Trump went on a spree of diplomatic botch work that captures his approach to diplomacy. First he said nothing, hoping the crime against press freedom, one of America's founding principles, would blow over. When the news storm persisted, he turned to tough talk. "We're going to find out what happened." When pressed on American consequences for Saudi Arabia, he said, "Well, it'll have to be very severe. I mean, it's bad, bad stuff."

Journalists found holes in one Saudi alibi after another. American intelligence, like that of other countries, produced nothing to let the Saudis off the hook. Nevertheless, as the evidence mounted, Trump backpedaled in order to show continued support for the kingdom and its rulers. When the *Washington Post* reported that the CIA had high confidence that the killing was ordered by the crown prince, the president said, "I hope that the king and the crown prince didn't know about it." He then staked out his position with a statement that American intelligence would continue assessing the situation and that we "may never know all the facts surrounding the murder." In this statement, which was littered with exclamation points, he went on to note about the crown prince, "Maybe he did or maybe he didn't!" (This elliptical observation about the crown prince presaged Trump's subsequent exoneration of Kim Jong-un for the murder in North Korea of an American college student, Otto Warmbier.) The next day, when reporters asked him about possible sanctions in response to the murder, the president invoked national economic interests: "They have been a great ally . . . the United States intends to remain a steadfast partner." He cited sales of arms and military technology to the Saudis worth $110 billion, a number inflated by promised future sales, not reflecting committed contracts. Washington had been whispering since the spring that the Trump administration was looking to tie up a nuclear deal with the Saudis. Heading to Mar-a-Lago for the Thanksgiving holiday, he said to reporters, "I'm not going to destroy our economy by being foolish with Saudi Arabia," as if jeopardizing an arms deal with an autocratic regime in the Middle East would put our nation's economic future at risk.[21]

---

21 To this, Senator Bob Corker (R-TN) reacted on Twitter: "I never thought I'd see the day a White House would moonlight as a public relations firm for the Crown Prince of Saudi Arabia."

If these events were not so cruel and tragic, we might mistake them for farce. Every gesture the president of the United States makes sends signals to the world. Secretary Mattis, in his letter of resignation at the end of 2018, made it clear that he believed the president's values and outlook stood in utter contradiction to America's values, its honor, its tradition, and its historic approach to alliances and to international affairs. Any citizens witnessing our current president in action would be right to wonder what he is up to. They might be right if they concluded that he wasn't always sure himself.

President Trump's disdain for diplomacy extends to trade. He has adopted the most protectionist trade policies in a century. Instead of doing the tough work of building coalitions to set the rules of the road and counter unfair practices, he has attacked not only China, but our closest allies and trading partners.[22] Taken together, his actions risk provoking a trade war with the entire world at once. The president's claim that "trade wars are good and easy to win" echoes the Bush administration's false claim that a war with Iraq would be over quickly and pay for itself.

The twenty-first century's international order is still forming, struggling to align a post–Cold War reality with the emergence of stateless terrorism. President Trump may want to erect a wall around the United States, but we cannot wish away the global nature of the threats we face. Terrorism, nuclear and conventional weapons proliferation, cybercrime, predatory trade practices by the Chinese, the potential for attacks in space, pandemics, and environmental degradation demand solutions that transcend national borders and

---

22 He imposed tariffs on France, the UK, and Germany in the name of protecting national security while advocating for Russia to rejoin the G7 after the group expelled it for violating the principle of state sovereignty. Instead of working with our NAFTA partners to make North America more competitive against China, he imposed harsh tariffs on Mexico and Canada.

ideologies. To respond to these challenges and to the crises that
will come, we will need the support of other nations—particularly
our allies. President Trump's disdain for international cooperation
puts that future support at risk. The United States has the greatest
capacity for self-defense in human history. We must maintain it.
But we also require a foreign policy that recognizes, even embraces,
the shared interests of other nations and peoples.

And we would do well to reacquaint ourselves with our founding republican values. Russia, China, Iran, and terrorist groups such
as al-Qaeda and ISIS have no use for pluralism, the rule of law,
and respect for individual freedoms and rights. If we, along with
our closest allies, fail to reject that dim view of humanity, no one
else in the world will. The world has never had greater need for
an example of a pluralist society committed to the rule of law. The
founders, close readers of Montesquieu and other Enlightenment
writers, knew that republics were rare and that other nations needed
instructive examples if their citizens were to enjoy the liberty of self-
government. Jefferson, perhaps the most internationally minded of
the founders, stressed this very point in his first inaugural address,
when he called the United States "the world's best hope." Although
he was often disillusioned by our partisan politics, he held on to his
optimism on this point to the end. In his last letter, he wrote this
of the American example:

> May it be to the world what I believe it will be, (to some parts
> sooner, to others later, but finally to all) the Signal of arousing
> men to burst the chains, under which monkish ignorance and
> superstition had persuaded them to bind themselves, and to
> assume the blessings and security of self-government.

We cannot rely solely on the imperfect examples set by our forefathers. We have to use our principles to set a course of action that suits our time, just as their actions attempted to suit their own time. When President Trump calls a free press "the enemy of the people," when he calls for his political opponents to be imprisoned, when his words and actions corrode our standards of truth and honor and decency, he not only weakens American democracy but also muzzles the hope of people around the world struggling to win freedom, democracy, and equality.

Most people on this planet live in societies ungoverned by the rule of law and without the benefits of democracy. Corruption, lawlessness, violence, and sectarian strife strip the future from billions of human beings. Across the world, more people are refugees than at any time since the end of World War II. South of our border, families pay a year's wages to send their young daughters on dangerous journeys northward. They weigh the very real risk of abuse and rape alongside the near certainty that their daughters' lives will be cut short by gangs in Mexico, El Salvador, Honduras, and Guatemala.

In 1965, my grandparents sent me a note on the occasion of my first birthday. It was fifteen years after they and my mother arrived in this country after surviving the horrors of the Holocaust. They wrote:

> The ancient Greeks gave the world the high ideals of democracy, in search of which your dear mother and we came to the hospitable shores of beautiful America in 1950. We have been happy here ever since, beyond our greatest dreams and expectations, with democracy, freedom, and love, and humanity's greatest treasure. We hope that when you grow up, you

will help to develop in other parts of the world a greater understanding of these American values.

Aware as we must be of our own failings, my grandparents' experience has always underscored to me how important the American example has been. If we falter at this critical moment, America's ability to secure our future and defend our values will be set back, and humanity will suffer.

THE TEST OF
A FREE PEOPLE

*The story behind a rare and improbable
bipartisan agreement on immigration—and how
a minority in Congress destroyed it.*

I. Rabbit Hole

You don't need to know me very well or for very long to know two
things. One is that whenever Congress can't seem to fight its way out
of a paper bag, I turn for comfort to the story of the Constitutional
Convention in Philadelphia, which brought the United States into
being. Two hundred thirty years after the fact, the Convention's
outcome has the aura of inevitability. It didn't seem so at the time;
it could have gone off the rails in so many ways. That it didn't was
the result of a particular conception of politics, a particular notion
of political respect, and a particular idea of what a citizen is and
what the duties of a citizen entail. If the Convention was going to
succeed, the overwhelming majority of delegates would have to
agree, and for that to happen, there would have to be compromise.
The story of the Constitutional Convention embodies what ought
to be our political standards.

The second thing you learn about me quickly is that a poem by
Walt Whitman, "Crossing Brooklyn Ferry," lies close to my heart.

If the "miracle at Philadelphia" set the political bar, Whitman set a different kind of bar, explaining how he saw all of us—and how we should see ourselves—as a people. As one people.

Our politics, our people: they're related but not the same thing. The relationship is sometimes simple, sometimes complicated. A republic like ours requires that both—including our perception of both—enjoy a condition of good health. And it's hard to think of an issue where both are subjected to greater challenge and strain than the issue of immigration. We call ourselves a nation of immigrants—as to a great extent we are—and yet the prospect of future immigration, legal and illegal, fills many with ambivalence. If we're honest, we have to acknowledge that many Americans harbor fears about what immigration will do to us as a people. Which in turn creates a political problem: how do we craft a set of policies that accommodates those who feel they have a dog in this fight—which, in this case, is just about everyone?

I've already written of my own background: on one side postwar Jewish refugees from Poland, on the other a line that goes back to the *Mayflower*. These days, the very name of that ship bestows on some an imprimatur of age-old legitimacy, although if Fox News existed at the time (as Jay Parini, among others, has observed) it would probably have called the disembarking men and women— desperate, dirty, and diseased—a caravan of asylum seekers. I was deeply engaged with immigration as a school superintendent in Denver and then again when I came to the US Senate and was part of a group known as the Gang of Eight. We hammered out a comprehensive package of immigration reforms that passed in my own chamber of Congress but was derailed by partisan obduracy and ugly nativism in the House. The history of that effort illustrates what politics can accomplish when the majority of Americans, and the politicians who represent them, have the will to overcome the factions standing in our way—and also what politics can destroy when a small minority sees politics as a "winner take all or no one takes anything" proposition.

Through all these years, immigration has been at the center of my concerns. I've flown along the US-Mexico border in a Black Hawk helicopter with Senator John McCain, one of my Gang of Eight colleagues, and visited detention centers where undocumented people were being held—in one case, parents who had been forcibly separated from their children. Many of the victims of the Colorado floods I described earlier were people of uncertain status—reluctant to reach out for assistance because they feared being sucked into a bottomless legal rabbit hole. I have attended many naturalization ceremonies and will never forget the one at Fort Carson, Colorado, in 2014, when thirteen young members of the army in their camouflage fatigues took the oath of citizenship. They came from eleven different countries. For years I kept a list of their names on a piece of paper in my wallet—reciting it to anyone who would listen—until it disintegrated from overuse.

And I remember the day in January 2018 when my senatorial colleagues Dick Durbin and Lindsey Graham returned from a meeting in the Oval Office, both visibly shaken after hearing President Trump complain that the United States was taking too many immigrants—legally—from what he referred to as "shithole countries," meaning ones whose people have skin that is black or brown. In the same meeting, the president reneged on his vow to support a bipartisan plan to revive the Deferred Action for Childhood Arrivals (DACA) policy, an Obama-era effort that allowed people brought by their parents into the United States as children, without proper identification, to remain in the country and apply for citizenship. Trump had unilaterally ended the program, throwing seven hundred thousand young men and women, who called themselves Dreamers—some of whom were active-service military personnel or veterans and all of whom had known themselves as Americans for virtually their entire lives—down their own legal rabbit hole.

Although a bipartisan agreement was there for the taking, Stephen Miller, one of the president's vociferous anti-immigration aides, stepped in at the eleventh hour and apparently produced bone spurs in the president's resolve.[1] Before long the administration would be pursuing a policy of wresting the children of detainees—thousands of them—from their parents, while at the same time failing to keep track of which children belonged to which mothers and fathers.

I will come back to all this. But first a detour to another era and a reminder about a different way politics can be conducted—and in some places, at some times, still is.

II. The Colorado Compact

On the morning of September 17, 1787, when delegates gathered one last time to decide whether to affix their signatures of support to the final draft of the Constitution, Benjamin Franklin offered the opening remarks. He was eighty-one and frail, so he asked his Pennsylvania colleague, James Wilson, to read the remarks for

---

1 Stephen Miller by his own account helped write President Trump's inaugural address (which included the first use of the word "carnage" in such an address and, even more remarkable, the modifier "American" before it), took a primary role crafting the president's failed early attempts at travel and immigration bans aimed at Muslim-majority countries, and assisted former attorney general Jeff Sessions on immigration matters, including the horrific child-separation policy.

him. Addressing the Convention president, George Washington, Franklin began with humble irony:

> I doubt too whether any other Convention we can obtain, may be able to make a better Constitution: For when you assemble a Number of Men to have the Advantage of their joint Wisdom, you inevitably assemble with those Men all their Prejudices, their Passions, their Errors of Opinion, their local Interests, and their selfish Views. From such an Assembly can a perfect Production be expected? It therefore astonishes me, Sir, to find this System approaching so near to Perfection as it does; and I think it will astonish our Enemies, who are waiting with Confidence to hear that our Councils are confounded, like those of the Builders of Babel, and that our States are on the Point of Separation, only to meet hereafter for the Purpose of cutting one another's throats. Thus I consent, Sir, to this Constitution because I expect no better, and because I am not sure that it is not the best.

Franklin's warm and humorous words defy the norms of today's political talk. Where is the outrage and indignation? The melodrama of polarization and animosity? The dog whistles to special interests and intemperate voting blocs? Anyone who has glanced at eighteenth-century political oratory knows it can get harsh fast. Franklin's speech could not be further from what we tolerate in most of today's politicians and serves as a reminder that we ought to demand better.

The Convention had come to order nearly four months earlier. It gathered delegates from twelve of the thirteen colonies. By today's reckoning, the group was nearly homogeneous. All were white men, wealthy by the standards of the time. Some, but not all, had been revolutionaries. Most enslaved others, and in the end every one of them could live with that. They expressed their fear of direct democracy routinely and designed a government in which voters, all of them male, directly elected the members of only one chamber, the House of Representatives. (Senators were originally elected by state legislatures.) No one in the room would have argued that there was a place for women or men without considerable property among the delegates, let alone for Native Americans or slaves. We can never pass by this moment in our history without remembering how the legacy of these tyrannies persists to this day, tarnishing all aspects of our heritage, even those liberties the framers helped construct and that we today prize the most.

In his remarks, however, Franklin paid attention to the diversity of his fellow delegates' views, not their like-mindedness. In so doing, he reminds us that during those months of deliberation, there was no guarantee they would leave the meeting with anything to take back to the people. Certainly by the Convention's end, after months in close confinement, those in the room had a deeper appreciation of one another's prejudices, passions, errors of opinion, local interests, and selfish views. These are the inevitable qualities of any group of people dedicated to completing a political task. Somehow, out of many points of view, they found a single political direction. Out of many, one. These are the kinds of differences that every minute today in Washington undermine efforts that are far less momentous.

Franklin did not come right out and say it, but one meaning of his remarks is this: only those who never undertake to accomplish a political task get to keep their personal views utterly intact and uninfluenced by someone else's. More than two centuries after Franklin spoke and sixteen hundred miles west of Philadelphia, I saw this reality firsthand as I entered public life in Colorado. What struck me then is how close the practice of politics in the state sometimes came to embodying the country's founding spirit (as politics there still does). What strikes me now is how vast the difference has become between politics as it is conducted in Washington and politics as it is conducted at other levels of government. The issue of immigration offers a case in point.

Colorado is a Spanish word. My state is named for the river that bisects it, whose own name came from its red-colored waters. Colorado abounds in Spanish names: Las Animas, Trinidad, Alamosa, Durango. In the San Luis Valley, Spanish land-grant ranches still exist from a time when that part of the state lay within Spain's Mexican territory. There, just outside the state's oldest town, San Luis, you will find a stone marker identifying the families entitled to draw water from Colorado's first irrigation ditch, the People's Ditch. The name Salazar stands among them, and my predecessor in the Senate, Ken Salazar, comes from that family.

As the schools superintendent in Denver, I ran a district that was 57 percent Latino, 20 percent African American, and 20 percent Anglo. Our Latino students, like their families, were diverse. Some came from families that had been in Colorado for generations—centuries before any English-speaker. Others were new to the United States, brought across our southern border as children. I often met high schoolers who realized for the first time that they were not American citizens and therefore were prohibited from attending Colorado public universities for the price of in-state tuition—a flaw we eventually remedied.

It was not the only flaw. When I became a senator, I followed Ken Salazar's advice and began traveling in the state from the outer edges inward. Again and again I encountered disappointment with the immigration system overseen by the federal government. At ski resorts, I heard about how hard it was to hire bilingual foreign students as seasonal workers (they're essential in helping with international tourists who want to take skiing lessons in their native tongue); at bioscience companies around Boulder, I heard about promising university graduates forced to return home to China or India because they had been tripped up by an administrative hurdle in the visa process. Immigrant advocates shared concerns about people who had lived in the United States for decades in the uncertain shadows of a cash economy.[2]

Although a wide range of Coloradans from differing perspectives found our immigration system broken and ineffective, I came to realize that they were not talking to one another and were largely unaware of one another's concerns. I also realized that the way they spoke about their concerns didn't sound much like the political debate in Washington or on cable news, which favored argument over agreement. In an effort to bring Coloradans together around immigration, in early 2012 I asked Hank Brown, a former Republican senator, to join me as a cochair of what we called the Colorado Compact.[3] My staff and I fanned out across the state to meet with hundreds of Coloradans on their home turf, and with them we hammered out a set of principles that reflected a statewide consensus on immigration. By doing the work together, we established relationships across significant political differences, relationships that endure to this day.

---

2 It was not until the Trump era that I would meet farmers with flyers advertising their own equipment for sale. There is no longer sufficient labor for their operations.

3 The Colorado Compact followed a similar example developed in Utah in 2010. Though substantially different in its content, the Utah Compact was developed as a result of a bipartisan effort to "address the complex challenges associated with a broken national immigration system" and establish a more civil tone in state policy discussions. Colorado was not the only state to follow Utah's example. In all there were seven others: Indiana, Iowa, Maine, Nebraska, Arizona, Texas, and Washington.

The Colorado Compact recognized that immigrants are an inseparable part of Colorado's communities, history, and economy. It also recognized that immigration policy is a federal matter, one of the responsibilities delegated to Congress by the Constitution. The Compact called on Colorado's congressional delegation to pursue an immigration policy at the federal level "that protects our borders, keeps our communities safe, and improves our immigration system." It then described a set of policy priorities that included the following.

- Ensuring our national security: the immigration system must protect our citizens, communities, and national borders.

- Strengthening our economy: acknowledging that immigrants make beneficial economic contributions as workers, taxpayers, and consumers, the immigration system should address the needs of businesses and the interests of workers. It must include a responsive visa system that meets the demands of Colorado's economy.

- Family: immigration policies should prioritize keeping close families together in order to ensure the most supportive home environments for children.

- Effective enforcement: enforcement strategy must improve public safety and target criminal activity. At the same time, it must provide a reasonable and predictable regulatory environment that considers the interests of and unintended consequences to businesses, workers, and consumers. Furthermore, as part of a broader reform effort, the government must provide businesses with an accurate, reliable, and low-cost way to determine who is permitted to work.

- Common sense: immigration policies must provide a sensible path forward for immigrants who are here without legal status, are of good character, and are committed to becoming fully participating members of our society and culture.

It took work, but the first group to endorse the Colorado Compact was Club 20, the "voice" of Colorado's Western Slope—a conservative coalition of businesses, governments, and tribes in the state's twenty westernmost counties. Around Club 20, we assembled a group of supporters as diverse as the state itself, including the Colorado Cattlemen's Association, chambers of commerce, county sheriffs, labor leaders, and immigrant advocates. These groups had their differences, but when we invited them to the University of Denver in December 2012 to announce that we had finalized the Compact, what captured their imagination was their combined size and diverse nature.

III. The "Autopsy"

By the time we advanced the Colorado Compact, reform at the federal level was long overdue. A quarter of a century had elapsed since Congress last addressed America's immigration system. In 1986, Senator Alan Simpson (R-WY) and Congressman Romano Mazzoli (D-KY), sponsored landmark legislation aimed at dealing with illegal immigration. The law placed new burdens on employers to determine the immigration status of their workers, regulated migratory agricultural labor, and offered a pathway to citizenship (at the time called amnesty) for millions of workers who had entered the country before 1982. When President Ronald Reagan signed the bill, he recognized its significance, saying, "Future generations of Americans will be thankful for our efforts to humanely regain control of our borders and thereby preserve the value of one of the most sacred possessions of our people, American citizenship." The bill was the first of its kind but left important work undone. Its main purpose was to deal with undocumented immigrants. It did little to bring up to date the other pathways to citizenship, especially our system of quotas and visas, which was better designed for the flood of refugees from Europe after World War II than it was for America in the era of Carter and Reagan.

Four years later, in 1990, Senator Ted Kennedy (D-MA) picked up where Simpson-Mazzoli left off. He led an effort to reform how workers, students, families, and refugees gained admission to the United States, some on a temporary basis and others en route to naturalized citizenship. The provisions of his bill included an increase in the cap on the total number of immigrants per year from 270,000 to 700,000; new visa categories that specified priorities for education, job skills, family members, and refugees; and funding for one thousand additional Border Patrol agents.[4] Like Simpson-Mazzoli, Kennedy's bill had bipartisan support, including backing from President George H. W. Bush. Michael Boskin, who chaired the President's Council of Economic Advisers, went on the record for the administration:

> Numerous studies suggest that the long-run benefits of immigration greatly exceed any short-run costs. With projections of a rising demand for skilled workers in coming years, the nation can achieve even greater benefits from immigration by augmenting the traditional emphasis on family reunification with policies designed to increase the number of skilled immigrants.

---

4 The bill was not above the harsh political realities and irrational fears of the day. It made special provision for refugees from the then raging Salvadoran civil war. Near the peak of the AIDS crisis, it also made a "health-based exclusion" to keep out "suspected homosexuals."

George H. W. Bush signed the Kennedy bill into law in 1990. But in the decades that followed, finding a coherent strategic approach to immigration reform eluded Congress. The sheer scope of the task would certainly have been daunting. To take in the entire policy landscape, writing immigration legislation meant addressing border security, verification of employee immigration status, demand for skilled and unskilled labor, visas, refugees, and the multiple possible pathways to citizenship.[5] Consensus was also hampered by the competing interests involved. Organized labor—historically worried that guest-worker programs could undermine job security and working conditions—often found itself at odds with immigrant advocates. Hard lines were drawn between those who supported and those who opposed a pathway to citizenship for undocumented workers and their families. Unlikely allies on the left and right were wary of updating the methods for verifying citizenship status: they would be either too cumbersome or too intrusive. Employers and employees from relatively small labor markets—regional agriculture, hospitality and hotels, ski resorts and cruise ships—wanted appropriately parochial solutions tailored just for them.

Subsequent legislation either made narrow adjustments or failed to pass. Bills that did pass tinkered with special visa categories or set national standards for driver's licenses. More ambitious bills proved polarizing and went down to defeat. After President Obama's election in 2008, his administration and Congress were preoccupied with stabilizing the economy and passing the Affordable Care Act. They put off immigration reform.

---

5 Verifying an employee's immigration status is no simple task. Is it the employer's responsibility or the government's? How do you verify the immigration status of a migrant agricultural worker? Is that the same process as verifying the immigration status of a college student? Or of a physicist working in a nuclear plant in Tennessee?

Democrats took a political beating in 2010, especially in the House of Representatives, where, fueled in part by the insurgent Tea Party movement, Republicans added sixty-three seats and gained control of the chamber. In the Senate, Patty Murray, of Washington; Harry Reid, of Nevada; and I all survived the election and preserved the Senate's Democratic majority. Many political observers credited our wins to the Latino vote. After the election, pressure mounted on Democrats to address immigration. Two years later, running for reelection himself, President Obama took executive action and instituted a policy called Deferred Action for Childhood Arrivals, or DACA. The action allowed "Dreamers," children who through no fault of their own were brought illegally to the United States by their parents, to work and attend school without threat of deportation.[6]

During the 2012 presidential election, Republican candidates pushed and pulled one another into positions ever more hostile to illegal immigrants. At one uniformly shrill debate in Tampa, Florida, former Massachusetts governor Mitt Romney, the eventual nominee, managed to stand out by arguing that the Republican Party stood for "self-deportation" as a solution to illegal immigration.[7] His hard-line stance proved understandably unpopular

---

6 As a technical matter, DACA was an action taken by Janet Napolitano in her role as secretary of the Department of Homeland Security: the department, according to a statement, would henceforward "exercise prosecutorial discretion." In practice, as the *New York Times* repoted, this meant that the department would forgo "the deportation of illegal immigrants who came to the United States before age 16, have lived here for at least five years, and are in school, are high school graduates or are military veterans in good standing."

7 The September 12, 2011, Republican presidential primary debate in Tampa included eight of the candidates. When asked what they would do to win the support of Latino voters, debaters jumped on Texas governor Rick Perry for having granted students access to the state college scholarship fund regardless of citizenship status. After Perry defended himself, former Utah governor Jon Huntsman reacted, saying that it was "treasonous" for Perry to suggest he "could not secure the border." Huntsman, in turn, took a licking for having granted driving privileges to Utahans regardless of their status.

with Latino voters. President Obama went on to defeat Romney that November, in the process changing the map so that swing states such as New Mexico, Nevada, Colorado, and Virginia—all with significant Latino populations—became somewhat bluer.

Following the election, for a brief moment, the obvious and continuing demographic shift created pressure on both parties. Not only was the number of Latino voters steadily increasing, but their votes were making a difference. Whereas President George W. Bush had won 44 percent of the Latino vote in his 2004 victory over John Kerry, Mitt Romney had won only 27 percent. Republicans momentarily seemed to recognize the political harm they'd done themselves by harsh rhetoric. The day after the election, Rupert Murdoch tweeted: "Must have sweeping, generous immigration reform, make existing law-abiding Hispanics welcome. Most are hardworking family people." The next day, Speaker John Boehner announced that he was "confident" that Congress could quickly pass comprehensive immigration legislation. On the same day, Sean Hannity, the influential Fox commentator, announced that his position had "evolved"; he now favored a "pathway to citizenship."

The Republican National Committee, led by Reince Priebus, eventually issued an election "autopsy" report. It made the point—indisputable and yet preposterously overdue—that "America looks different" and that the party was alienating voters of color. The report identified voters of color as the party's "demographic partners" and stated that they deserved respect. It especially stressed the opportunity of winning back Latino voters:

> If Hispanic Americans perceive that a GOP nominee or candidate does not want them in the United States (i.e., self-deportation), they will not pay attention to our next sentence.

> It does not matter what we say about education, jobs or the
> economy; if Hispanics think we do not want them here, they
> will close their ears to our policies.[8]

One thing was clear: ignoring the immigration issue had not
solved any problems. By the time of the 2012 election, 11 million
people without a path to legal status were living in the United
States. Depending on the region, as much as 16 percent of our
construction workforce and 18 percent of our hospitality workforce
was undocumented. Our southern border was permeable. Some 40
percent of the undocumented population had overstayed lawful
visas, but the government had no way to identify them. Employers relied on an error-prone system to hire, which led to pervasive
violations of the law.

All in all, it seemed like a propitious time to act—the most
propitious time in years.

IV. The Gang of Eight

Although both parties seemed ready, it was clear from the outset
that any serious effort would have to begin in the Senate. In spite of
his immediate post–Election Day ambitions, Speaker John Boehner
would be tangled up in what Republicans called the Hastert Rule,
named after Illinois representative and former Speaker of the
House Dennis Hastert. That self-imposed gesture of Republican
solidarity prohibits the Speaker from bringing legislation forward
unless it has the support of a majority of the House Republican

---

8 Dick Armey, the former Texas representative turned political consultant, made the same
point more bluntly: "You can't call someone ugly and expect them to go to the prom with
you. We've chased the Hispanic voter out of his natural home."

Conference. In the 113th Congress, when the Republicans had a majority of 234 seats, the rule required Speaker Boehner to have the support of 117 Republicans before a bill could be advanced to the floor for debate—even though a bill could pass with the support of as few as 16 Republicans if all 201 Democrats supported it. The Hastert Rule, by its nature, inhibits bipartisanship and vests enormous power in a minority of members of the House.[9] Although there was Washington chatter about how, in the case of immigration legislation, Boehner might be willing to break that rule, it was also clear he could not get a majority of the House Republican Conference to initiate legislation providing a pathway to citizenship for 11 million undocumented individuals. From the beginning of his tenure as Speaker, Boehner was vulnerable to attack from within his caucus. For an immigration bill to pass the Republican House—without support from a majority of the conference and without costing Boehner his speakership—it needed a strong bipartisan endorsement from the Senate.

With these dynamics in mind, Senate Majority Leader Harry Reid drew the starting line shortly after the election. He asked Senator Chuck Schumer to assemble a bipartisan group of senators to begin work on a bill. Schumer, who had worked on immigration since the Simpson-Mazzoli days, brought on board two Democratic veterans: Bob Menendez, of New Jersey; and Dick Durbin, of Illinois. Latino groups across the country regarded Bob Menendez highly. They trusted him, and his presence among the Gang of Eight would do much to validate its work. For his part,

---

9 Some say the rule dates back to when Newt Gingrich was Speaker. Hastert himself has said that it "was kind of a misnomer" and that "it never really existed" (because, technically, it was never officially entered into the chamber's rulebook). Although occasionally violated, the rule has remained basically in force.

Durbin had been the primary drafter of the Dream Act, legislation that would have granted provisional or permanent resident status to undocumented residents who had come to America with their parents and who had earned a high school diploma (or better) and had no criminal record. It didn't pass and has been reintroduced frequently thereafter—and, shamefully, still has not become law. Melendez's and Durbin's support would carry weight. Schumer brought me on board to round out the Democratic side.[10] The role of Latino voters in my reelection was certainly factored into his choice. So was the Colorado Compact.

On the Republican side, Lindsey Graham, of South Carolina, was Schumer's first choice. Graham had worked on immigration reform since he was first elected to the Senate in 2002. In 2010, he and Schumer had developed a broad outline for reform that President Obama had endorsed (but that, again, went nowhere). He was living evidence that a Republican in a deeply red state could support immigration reform and win reelection.

Just as important was Senator John McCain. Like his friend from South Carolina, McCain had a track record on immigration reform that went back to the days of George W. Bush. His role in crafting the 2005 Secure America and Orderly Immigration Act, often called the McCain-Kennedy bill, made him the most senior Republican immigration leader. He was from Arizona—a red state but also a border state with a large Latino population. These cross-currents posed difficult political challenges, but it was McCain's nature to take them on directly.

Although he had less Senate experience than Graham or McCain, Senator Jeff Flake, also from Arizona, was a natural candidate for the

---

10 The minute I caught wind of the Gang of Eight's formation, I was in Chuck Schumer's and Harry Reid's offices pestering them to let me participate.

Gang of Eight. Like Graham, he was a member of the Judiciary Committee and would bring another vote for that decisive hurdle. His understanding of immigration was also deeply personal. As a young man he had worked side by side with immigrants on his family farm. As a former executive director of the Goldwater Institute, he also brought sterling conservative credentials to the group.

The final question was who would represent the most conservative wing of the Senate, which had swelled in the wake of several Tea Party victories in 2010. The other seven members had agreed that one condition for joining the Gang of Eight was a commitment that citizenship—somehow—for the 11 million undocumented residents had to be a final part of any deal. To fill this role, Senator Durbin worked intently to encourage Florida's Marco Rubio to sign on.

Rubio was a darling of the Tea Party, having defeated Florida governor Charlie Crist in the 2010 Senate Republican primary. Rubio had also worked on versions of the Dream Act. When Durbin approached Rubio, the junior senator had just as many confidants telling him not to join the group as telling him to join it. In the end, he decided that it was better to lead than to criticize from the sidelines.

Without great fanfare, *Politico* reported on the Gang of Eight in December 2012, the first time its existence became public knowledge. We kept up a ferocious schedule of meetings. Unlike many other congressional working groups I have participated in, we routinely started on time, often ran on for extra hours, and never canceled our work sessions. This may seem like a low bar—it *is* a low bar—but it was a pace unlike any other effort I have witnessed in the Senate.

We developed confidence in a collaborative way of doing business. Graham set an example. Early in negotiations, we gathered at the Capitol in Senator Reid's spacious meeting room, with its long westerly view down the National Mall to the Washington

Monument and Lincoln Memorial. Laying out one of the major issues before the group, someone explained that we needed a pathway to "legalization" for the undocumented people living in America. Graham reset the expectations for everyone in the room. "No," he said. "You mean citizenship." In so saying, he established the right aspirational tenor for our work.

The Gang of Eight's set of working principles, as they ultimately emerged, made a point of taking on directly the complexity of the issues that needed to be addressed:

- Create a tough but fair path to citizenship for unauthorized immigrants currently living in the United States that is contingent on securing our borders and tracking whether immigrants have left the country when required.
- Reform our legal immigration system to better recognize the importance of characteristics that will help build the American economy and strengthen American families.
- Create an effective employment-verification system that will prevent identity theft and end the hiring of future unauthorized workers.
- Establish an improved process for admitting future workers to serve our nation's workforce needs while simultaneously protecting all workers.

The antithesis of soaring rhetoric, the principles avoided both fighting words and pacifying euphemisms. They struck a balance, calling for both a secure border and a fair path to citizenship. They recognized the rights of workers and the need for a strong business economy. Ours was a rare legislative effort to push all the deal points to the middle of the table to make it more likely to achieve a good result. When I set these principles alongside the Colorado Compact, I was struck by their basic consistency.

On Sunday, January 27, 2013, we brought the principles forward to a national audience. McCain and Menendez appeared on *This Week* with George Stephanopoulos. Schumer gave interviews to New York reporters. Rubio made himself available. Two days later, President Obama gave his support at a rally at a high school in Las Vegas. Although there remained skepticism that we could actually go on to write and pass a bill, the principles were greeted warmly by both parties. Intense partisan criticism was limited to the usual Tea Party legislators in the House. Ultimately the principles were embodied in an 844-page bill unveiled in April 2013.

Writing the bill was more balancing act than compromise. We built it out of three interlocking reforms: securing the border, charting a path to citizenship for undocumented people, and defining a set of assurances, or "triggers," to determine whether the border was secure. Our principles made activating the path to citizenship contingent on securing the border. There was both policy and political logic in this. We knew that unless we secured the border, we would never stem future flows of unauthorized immigration. Although this was good policy on its own, it was also a particular sore point with Republican members of the Gang, who believed that Reagan's 1986 reform had granted "amnesty" but failed to stem unlawful immigration. The Gang held together by respecting both rationales. All of us knew that creating a path to citizenship, however fair and rigorous, depended on public confidence that we had addressed the underlying problem of illegal immigration.

By the end, the bill featured a bipartisan commitment to extensive security resources, including: more than 19,000 additional Border Patrol agents stationed along the southern border, more than doubling the current force; complete electronic surveillance of the entire border; 350 additional miles of fencing; and full implementation of an electronic visa entry/exit system, called E-verify, which would make it virtually impossible to work in the United States illegally. This amounted to a $46.3 billion investment in border security, far more than the Trump administration has demanded for its "beautiful wall."

As we strengthened provisions for border security, we began creating the pathway to citizenship for undocumented immigrants. We simplified the green card system, replacing our outdated visa mechanism with its quotas, caps, and complicated categories. In its place, immigrants would earn a green card through a new merit-based system open to any foreigner. Those with the most points (allocated by education level, English-language level, family ties, and work experience) in any given year would become permanent residents. The bill also provided that any persons living in the United States without documentation could apply for provisional status. After ten years of provisional status—and after paying a fine, while maintaining employment and a clean criminal record—they could apply for a green card. Three years after that, they could apply for citizenship. There were special provisions that sped up the process for the Dreamers and agricultural workers.[11]

Throughout the drafting process, the Gang committed to a bill that could win support from a bipartisan majority in both the Senate Judiciary Committee and the Senate as a whole. Along the

---

11 The jargon we used for an undocumented person was Registered Provisional Immigrant (RPI). The Gang of Eight principles called for the pathway to legalization and citizenship to be "tough but fair." To be approved as an RPI, an applicant needed to register and, among other things, to have lived in the United States since December 31, 2011; have had no conviction for a felony or for more than two misdemeanors; have paid assessed taxes; and have passed a background check.

way, staff and senators kept the press and Beltway influence groups apprised of progress. This transparency was not some sort of special privilege. It served as a feedback loop that helped us work out the bugs and improve the bill. It also shaped how we would present the bill. As we described the bill before growing audiences, we would face inevitable mischaracterization by opponents. While working with so many prospective audiences, we drafted and revised detailed summaries and talking points—storytelling tools that helped focus the debate on the bill itself rather than on the demagogic fictions spun by talk radio hosts and other nativist zealots.[12]

In April, the Gang of Eight held a press conference and introduced the proposed Border Security, Economic Opportunity, and Immigration Modernization Act of 2013. The bill's supporters formed a broad base, including many who could agree on little else: for instance, the US Chamber of Commerce, a newly formed coalition of evangelical leaders, and the AFL-CIO. Karl Rove appeared on weekend political shows, including *Fox News Sunday*, to rally support for it.[13] Unwavering Republicans like the antitax zealot Grover Norquist stood side by side with equally unwavering liberals like AFL-CIO president Richard Trumka on the podium, joined by business, faith, and police and community leaders.

Inevitably, opposition began to mobilize. On the Sunday program *This Week*, Senator Jeff Sessions, of Alabama, trotted out two arguments successfully used against previous immigration bills: it

---

12 This was no imaginary threat. In 2005, despite support from President Bush, the Corwyn-Kyl immigration reform bill was brought to defeat when Sean Hannity and Rush Limbaugh (among others) drummed up their listeners to join a call-in campaign targeting the bill's supporters. (This tactic was to reappear in an even more vicious way in 2018.) Republicans in Congress were scared away.

13 Imagine anyone appearing on *Fox News* making a credible case in favor of immigration reform after 2016, let alone Karl Rove.

would "give amnesty now" and "bring in a massive supply of low-wage workers." Both arguments were demonstrably false. On that same show, conservative commentator George Will took Sessions on, observing that "conservatism begins with facing facts." He went on to list some of them.

> The facts are that of the 11 million people who are here illegally, two-thirds have been a decade or more, 30 per-cent, fifteen years or more. They're woven into our society. They're not leaving. And the American people would not tolerate the police measures necessary to extract them from our community.

Marco Rubio faced perhaps the greatest political challenge as the Tea Party and its affiliates attacked the bill. Rubio defended himself by noting that the bill gave no special privileges to the undocumented—indeed, they would be required to go to "the back of the line." It was rough duty for Rubio, and no amount of gratitude from Democrats could be comfort enough.

When we introduced our bill, there were fifty-four Democrats and forty-six Republicans in the Senate. We could count on the four Republicans in the Gang to vote yes, but not all Democrats immediately supported the legislation. To reach the sixty votes required to pass a bill in the Senate, we had to increase the yes votes among Republicans without losing support from Democrats. One way to do that was with amendments. Today's Senate is so frozen that months can drag by without the consideration of a single amendment on the Senate floor. Major legislation like the Gang of Eight bill presented a rare opportunity for a proper legislative process. We welcomed this opportunity, believing that no first take, even our own, couldn't benefit from revision. Patching holes left over from the drafting process would also introduce fresh thinking across the country.

The amendment process is not without risks. Congressional history has more than its share of bipartisan legislation that would float as drafted, only to sink under the weight of divisive amendments—to defund Planned Parenthood or ban semiautomatic weapons, for instance. The Gang of Eight anticipated that we would see scores of amendments, some with merit and others designed to be toxic. We would have to sort them out and deal with them quickly.

As a general matter, we understood that if some senators had concerns about substantive policy, we might be able to address them to gain a yes vote (while not losing other senators). We knew it was highly unlikely that we could gain the vote of senators who believed supporting the bill was catastrophic for them politically. But we also thought there was room to win some votes by addressing specific issues for certain senators—for instance, by further strengthening border security and enforcement to give conservative senators a win to point to. This was the most likely end point of a settlement. At the same time, we had to defend our measure from amendments intended to paralyze it by breaking its bipartisan backbone.[14]

I have left out many steps in the legislative process. No sane reader would have the patience for all the arduous negotiation and procedural minutiae. The bottom line is this: on June 27, fourteen Republican senators joined all fifty-four Democrats to pass the

---

14 The bill's opponents brought many kinds of amendments. The meanest were intended to deny rights to aspiring citizens even after they had crossed the threshold for citizenship. Ted Cruz brought an amendment that would have relegated all of them to second-class status for their entire lives and in so doing deprive them of benefits that you, your neighbors, and I take for granted, including services purchased by the taxes they paid or contributed toward. Jeff Sessions brought an amendment to eliminate use-of-force standards for arresting officers in detaining suspected illegal immigrants, on the ground that such suspects were not yet covered by the Constitution.

Gang of Eight's bill by a vote of 68–32. It was a resounding bipartisan victory. It was also the last vote the bill would face.

V. The Worm Turns

In hindsight, we wrongly assumed that a strong bipartisan vote in the Senate would give Speaker Boehner the momentum to advance the bill despite opposition within his caucus. As it happened, the Senate bill never saw the light of markup or debate, let alone a vote, in the House. Had Speaker Boehner allowed a vote, the Gang of Eight bill would have passed with unanimous support from Democrats and support from as much as a third of the House Republican Conference. But after meeting with the conference to discuss its position on immigration, Boehner said:

> I also suggested to our members today that any immigration reform bill that is going to go into law ought to have a majority of both parties' support if we're really serious about making that happen, and so I don't see any way of bringing an immigration bill to the floor that doesn't have a majority support of Republicans.

Two factors forced the Speaker into this position. The first was the threat by a small number of members, most affiliated with the Tea Party movement, to challenge him for the speakership, a threat that had existed since the fiscal fights of 2011. House members like Steve King, of Iowa; Tim Huelskamp, of Kansas; Raúl Labrador, of Idaho; and Kevin McCarthy, of California, were outspoken opponents of immigration reform and had participated in previous efforts to challenge the Speaker. They used the Hastert Rule like a shiv, killing the bill in the closed room of the House Republican Conference. The second factor was the threat of a primary challenge that was hanging over the heads of many members of the House Republican caucus—a challenge from the right, engineered by Tea Party activists and their big-money allies. Every House Republican would recognize the reality of this threat when, in June 2014, Representative Eric Cantor suffered an astounding loss in a primary fight largely because he had been perceived as soft on immigration.[15] It became obvious that the most extreme minority faction of the Republican Party was preventing the House from even voting on legislation that most Americans supported.

My colleagues and I have puzzled over when we knew that the Gang of Eight bill was done for good. Certainly by the time of Eric Cantor's defeat, we knew it was all over: the fear among Republicans that they could be taken down by a challenger—and the fear on the part of the Speaker that he could be taken down by his conference—was real and unassuageable. But there had been other troubling signs. The initial failure of HealthCare.gov—the public face of President Obama's signature Affordable Care Act—combined with Ted Cruz's cynical and narcissistic government shutdown had further sapped the public's faith in government.[16] The

---

15 Cantor's defeat caught people by surprise. He was rising in the party leadership. According to *Politico*, he had more than $6 million in campaign funds while his challenger, David Brat, had less than $1.5 million. Cantor opposed the Gang of Eight legislation but not harshly enough for some tastes. The *New York Times* observed: "Regardless of the exact reason for Mr. Cantor's defeat, the news media's focus on immigration is likely to deter Republicans from supporting comprehensive immigration reform."

16 The HealthCare.gov website, which now works well, is the portal to the Obamacare insurance marketplace. The launch was a disaster; the site didn't work. As chair of the Democratic Senatorial Campaign Committee in 2014, I was able to talk directly with President Obama about that debacle. Shortly after a meeting where I told him that our odds of retaining a majority in the Senate were low, we traveled together by helicopter from the White House to Joint Base Andrews, outside Washington. I asked him about the website. President Obama had a lot to say. One of his aides observed: "It's even worse because he won't yell at us."

circumstances made it harder to convince people that the United States could competently perform a difficult task, like securing its borders or developing a working biometric visa-monitoring program.

Some say the outcome was evident in June 2013 if one considered the map of House districts. There was too much red in the House, they contended, and it was filled with districts that were carefully gerrymandered not only to secure victory but also to deter diversity of any kind. The representatives elected from these districts could plausibly argue that their constituents had no interest in reforming the immigration system.

By choosing not to act, House Republicans allowed problems the bill would have solved to persist. This is not speculation. Eleven million undocumented people continue to live and work in the shadows. Our northern and southern borders are still not secure. Our visa system remains an operation from deep in the last century.[17] I believe that some of the bill's most ardent detractors actually like it this way: they can keep the pot boiling, nurturing the nativist grievances that elected them.

Certainly the results of the 2016 election cast critical light on the Republican National Committee's idea that to prevail in elections, Republicans needed to improve their appeal to Hispanic voters. Donald Trump clearly had not read the RNC election autopsy when he announced his presidential campaign. From day one, he defined himself in opposition to its advice. Here's what he said when he descended the escalator at Trump Tower and announced his candidacy:

---

17 On the plus side, an antique system of hand-filled forms, pencils, and rubber-stamped approvals might protect visa holders' personal information from Russian and Chinese hacking.

When Mexico sends its people, they're not sending their best ... They're sending people that have lots of problems, and they're bringing those problems with us. They're bringing drugs. They're bringing crime. They're rapists. And some, I assume, are good people. But I speak to border guards and they tell us what we're getting. And it only makes common sense. It only makes common sense. They're sending us not the right people. It's coming from more than Mexico. It's coming from all over South and Latin America, and it's coming probably—probably—from the Middle East. But we don't know. Because we have no protection and we have no competence, we don't know what's happening. And it's got to stop and it's got to stop fast ... I would build a great wall, and nobody builds walls better than me, believe me, and I'll build them very inexpensively, I will build a great, great wall on our southern border. And I will have Mexico pay for that wall.

At the time, Trump's immigration rhetoric seemed as preposterous as it was offensive. His election proved conclusively that the power of nativism in American politics was not a thing of the past. The bigotry and hatred that fueled the Know-Nothings in the 1850s, the Chinese Exclusion Act later that century, and Japanese internment camps in the 1940s—not to mention the literacy tests and English-only ballot initiatives that came back time and again in the twentieth century—also lived in his campaign. We will never know how many Trump supporters truly agreed with him, but enough stomached his rhetoric to deliver him a victory in the Electoral College.

As president, Donald Trump has kept nurturing this ugly nativism. When Representative Paul Ryan took over from Speaker John Boehner, he seemed content to leave immigration reform unmentioned and unaddressed.[18] President Trump kept the issue alive. He ordered a series of bans on Muslims coming into the country, dashed the hopes of the Dreamers, kept insisting that the government build a "big, beautiful wall," and continued to indulge his habit of hateful name-calling, ethnic and racial stereotyping, and disregard for the truth.[19]

Evidently, the president enjoys the charge he gets from a crowd when he indulges in this ugliness. In May 2018, the *Washington Post* reported:

> The night before Trump delivered his first speech to Congress in February 2017, he huddled with senior adviser Jared Kushner and [Stephen] Miller in the Oval Office to talk immigration. The president reluctantly agreed with suggestions that he strike a gentler tone on immigration in the speech.
>
> Trump reminded them the crowds loved his rhetoric on immigrants along the campaign trail. Acting as if he were at a rally, he recited a few made-up Hispanic names and described

18 I always sort of liked John Boehner. I invited myself over to his office one day, and he kindly pointed to where I should sit to avoid smoke from his cigarette. Since he retired, he has found time to cut his own grass, play golf, and reflect on his erstwhile colleagues. He took the opportunity at Stanford to call Ted Cruz "Lucifer in the flesh." He said, "I have never worked with a more miserable son of a bitch in my life." Of the Freedom Caucus, the former Speaker told *Politico*, "They can't tell you what they're for. They can tell you everything they're against. They're anarchists. They want total chaos. Tear it all down and start over. That's where their mind-set is." He has criticized the Freedom Caucus's cofounders, calling Congressman Mark Meadows "an idiot," and Congressman Jim Jordan "a terrorist as a legislator." More recently, Boehner has been the face of the National Institute for Cannabis Investing, saying, "Cannabis is here to stay, the industry is only getting bigger, and I am all in."

19 President Trump is not one to cling tightly to facts, and he throws them completely to the wind when stoking fears in order to generate support for his border wall. According to the Department of Homeland Security, undetected unlawful border crossings have dropped from 851,000 in 2006 to approximately 62,000 in 2016. Customs and Border Protection statistics report a similar decrease in the number of arrests, falling from more than 1.5 million in 2000 to under 500,000 per year since 2009. What has increased is the number of families requesting asylum—a legal pathway to entry for people seeking safety in the United States.

potential crimes they could have committed, such as rape or murder. Then, he said, the crowds would roar when the criminals were thrown out of the country—as they did when he highlighted crimes by illegal immigrants at his rallies, according to a person present for the exchange and another briefed on it later. Miller and Kushner laughed.

The president's approach drove a wedge deeper into the Republican Party. When Speaker Ryan announced that he would not seek reelection, he also promised that he would "run through the tape," finishing his last term as Speaker of the House.[20] But by the summer of 2018, Ryan's finishing sprint was being tripped up by both moderates and extremists in his party. On one side, members led by Jeff Denham, of California, and Carlos Curbelo, of Florida, began organizing to demand a vote on immigration reform. Whether it passed or not, they would be able to go on the record before Election Day as having supported something better tempered than the president's angriest outbursts. On the other side, sensing that this upstart movement could be a threat to conservative hegemony over immigration policy, Kevin McCarthy and other members of the House Freedom Caucus leveled a threat: if Ryan brought these bills to the floor of the House, they might well challenge him as Speaker even before he left office. The closer Election Day drew, the hotter the rhetoric became. Exhibit A was the fearmongering by President Trump, his allies in Congress, and the right-wing media over the infamous "caravan" of asylum seekers from Central America trying to make its way to the United States—an "invasion," the president

---

20 In the event, Ryan left in the midst of a government shutdown over the wall and never returned. His final legislative act as Speaker, at the command of Donald Trump, was to pass a bill (containing funding for a border wall) that he knew could never pass the Senate.

falsely maintained, as he made a wasteful show of deploying troops to the border.[21] Ultimately, the president's campaign organization ran an issue ad in targeted districts that was so ugly that every outlet, including Fox News, decided to take it off the air.[22]

There are no rewrites of history, but it is hard not to wonder how things would have turned out had the House taken up immigration reform in 2013—or anytime afterward, for that matter. If reform had reached the floor, there are any number of ways a coalition of 218 votes could have been cobbled together. There are plenty of Republicans who would have benefited if they supported the bill or at least not been harmed, despite threats of tough primary opposition. And even if a handful of Democrats could not support the bill, it is easy to imagine that 185 others would. My guess is that the Gang of Eight legislation would have passed. Instead, a minority of the majority strangled it with the Hastert Rule.

VI. "Yearning to Breathe Free"

And where are we now? No single political issue preoccupied the 115th Congress and the Trump Administration more than

---

21 My friend Senator Jon Tester, a Democrat from Montana, told me about the first time Donald Trump came to campaign against him in the fall of 2018. Jon was riding his tractor on his farm in Big Sandy, listening to the rally on the radio, when President Trump started talking about the gang MS-13. Jon wondered why he was focused on a gang no one in Montana had ever seen or heard of. Why wasn't the President talking about things that mattered to rural communities—things like access to broadband, roads, small business? By the end of the campaign, after President Trump, the Fox News anchors, and Republican campaign committees had done their work, immigration had become a top issue in Montana, as it was for the same reasons in the Senate races in North Dakota, Indiana, and Missouri—all places where there is little evidence of MS-13 gang activity.

22 According to PolitiFact, the video in the ad showing people pouring unchecked over a fence—presumed to be migrants from Mexico and elsewhere in Central America spilling across the US border—was news footage from events in Morocco.

immigration—not the Affordable Care Act (also known as Obama-care, which Trump had promised to repeal), not the opioid crisis, not climate change, not wage stagnation, not taxes, not even the budget. In December, as the lame-duck Congress tried to pass a budget that lacked funding for the president's wall on the southern border, the usual nativist zealots, including Ann Coulter, Sean Hannity, and Rush Limbaugh, turned up the heat on President Trump.[23] Heeding their call, President Trump forced a record-breaking thirty-five-day shutdown of the federal government in order to jam a $5.7 billion appropriation for a border wall down the throat of a lame-duck Congress controlled in both houses by his own party. (In his campaign, as most Americans remember, Trump had promised that Mexico, not the US taxpayer, would pay for such a wall.) By failing to deliver for the president, Speaker Ryan and Majority Leader McConnell guaranteed that immigration, which had dogged the 115th Congress, would continue its domination into the 116th. The folly of Trump's medieval approach to border security aside, the meanness of spirit demonstrated by the administration and its allies is stomach-turning and violates America's most honorable traditions while recalling our worst. In the end, Trump capitulated and allowed the government to reopen without funding for a wall. In the waning hours of the shutdown the Senate floor staff had begun referring to the chamber as a "Hope Free Zone."

---

23 Coulter, a virtuoso troll, was especially scathing. She titled a December column, "Gutless President in a Wall-less Country" and warned Trump in a podcast that same day that he was on the verge of being remembered for a "joke presidency that scammed the American people." Trump blocked her Twitter account but went on to do his part in the shutdown anyway. In the new year, as the shutdown dragged on to become the longest in American history, Coulter continued her attack. "He is dead in the water if he doesn't build that wall. Dead, dead, dead," she tweeted. After Trump agreed to reopen the government with no funding for his wall, Coulter told *Vice News Tonight*, "Good news for George Herbert Walker Bush: As of today, he is no longer the biggest wimp ever to serve as President of the United States."

During our work together on the Gang of Eight, Lindsey Graham would sometimes say, "America is an idea." I would take that thought further. The idea of America changes over time. It is not stuck in the eighteenth century like a bee trapped in amber. It is our duty as citizens to tend to this idea and make sure it grows into something we would wish for our children and our neighbors' children. In this sense, all of us play a role as founders.

The original founders imagined a republic, not a despotism. According to their idea of America, we were not dependent on a tyrant or boss or party strongman to resolve our differences. We were a free people and had to resolve our differences ourselves. As we settled our differences along the way, we had to recommit ourselves to start the process again as free people engaged in the work of the republic. Central to the founders' idea was legislative effectiveness.[24] Citizens would elect representatives who would assemble to make and remake law. The founders did not expect elected officials to do nothing until they received exactly what they wanted. They expected elected officials to compromise. In my time in office, opportunities to participate in effective legislative debates have been few and far between. The Gang of Eight process was a rare exception.

Effective legislating involves some basic hard work. Assembling good thinkers, hearing from experts and advocates, choosing among imperfect options, grinding out the language of the bill—this is where it starts. Holding markups, making revisions, building

---

24 *The Federalist*, for example, was in no small part an argument for Americans to abandon the weak government of the Articles of Confederation and to adopt the more "vigorous" or "energetic" government of the new Constitution. Political theorist Martin Diamond writes that for Hamilton and Madison, "the end of union is palpably inconsistent with the 'imbecility' (i.e., weakness) of the Confederation and requires an 'energetic' government." There are positive references to vigorous or energetic government, or criticisms of weak, unstable, or imbecilic government, in almost every essay of *The Federalist*. Obviously, our government is weak if Congress refuses to govern on the major issues of our time.

coalitions, handling amendments—this is how legislation comes across the finish line. This is the stuff of high school government classes. As citizens, we think this is what should take place in every city council meeting room, in every state legislative chamber, and certainly in the halls of Congress. In Washington, we rarely meet this basic expectation.

Each member of the Gang of Eight shared a basic understanding of what makes American citizenship attractive to those who want to become Americans. There are countless ways to picture it. Think of the parents who want their children to enjoy opportunities unimaginable in their home country. Think of the student who wants to learn at one of our great universities and intends to call America home. Think of someone displaced by war or terror or hatred—and the sanctuary he or she seeks. Think of anyone who, in Emma Lazarus's great words, is "yearning to breathe free." We worked together because we understood that immigration has been a defining characteristic of American history and will help define our future. We knew that no good comes from hoarding citizenship and that we should grant it in a manner that respects and upholds the rule of law. When we take the opposite view, we act against our traditions. As a nation, we will never flourish if we choose to depend on a permanent underclass, deprived of some or all of the freedoms others enjoy. Free people do not remain free by denying freedom to others.

In the end, the Gang of Eight also understood that immigration gives America a continual infusion of people with talent, energy, and ambition—people who eagerly embrace our democratic values. The gift of citizenship to someone who dreams of becoming an American is also a gift to ourselves.

ACTING LIKE
FOUNDERS

When campaigning never ends, governing never begins.
How can we break the cycle?

I. Reconciliation

We are, as we have been many times before, at political loggerheads
and rightly wondering what we can do to emerge as a stronger
union—and maybe wondering if, indeed, that is even possible.

On March 4, 1801, after a protracted fight against John Adams for
the presidency, Thomas Jefferson, the victor, took the oath of office.
Americans had every reason to be gravely worried. The government
was scarcely a decade old. During those years, disagreements over
everything from trade and taxes to the role of the central government
had resulted in the formation of America's first political parties, the
Federalists and the Democratic-Republicans. Newspapers had lined
up behind the parties. Partly in response, the Federalist-controlled
Congress, in 1798, passed the Alien and Sedition Acts, which made it
a criminal offense to "write, print, utter or publish" any "false, scan-
dalous, and malicious writing or writings against the Government of
the United States." After this legislation passed, the administration
of President John Adams prosecuted fourteen journalists and editors,

all from newspapers favoring Democratic-Republican causes.[1] State legislatures in Kentucky and Virginia declared the Alien and Sedition Acts, along with a companion measure known as the Naturalization Act, unconstitutional. There was talk of secession.

Then, when Jefferson defeated Adams, it was still unclear that Jefferson would hold the office. I won't recount all the constitutional peculiarities—they have since been fixed—but although Jefferson had clearly defeated the Federalists, he and his own running mate, Aaron Burr, found themselves in an Electoral College tie. The election was thrown into the House of Representatives. Partly owing to Burr's ambition but also as a result of mischief by the Federalists, Jefferson did not emerge as the winner of the race until the thirty-sixth vote to break the stalemate.

Even after that—at the end of February, with only nineteen days before Jefferson was to take office—the Federalist-controlled Congress expanded the federal judiciary, adding thirteen federal circuit court seats and packing them with Federalist judges. The last two of these "midnight judges" were confirmed the day before Jefferson took the oath of office. John Adams signed the necessary documents on his last night in the White House.

At his inauguration, President Jefferson would have had every reason to excoriate his opponents. His partisans would have shared with him a sense that the Federalists had done all they could to thwart the will of the people. Jefferson himself was no paragon. Like many of the founders, Jefferson was a slaveholder. In his own lifetime he was taken to task for many things: he mismanaged his

---

1 The number varies from one historian's account to another's. I drew mine from Dumas Malone's *Jefferson and His Time*. I used to think there was a present-day consensus of outrage at the Alien and Sedition Acts, despite the times when we as a nation have slid back to the repressive tendencies they embodied. The rise of Donald Trump and his administration's relentless scapegoating of immigrants and journalists have put my trust in that consensus at risk.

finances, nurtured grudges, and stoked intrigue. He left office disillusioned. But Jefferson was also one of liberty's great visionaries. On the day of his inauguration, he had this to say:

> Let us then, fellow-citizens, unite with one heart and one mind. Let us restore to social intercourse that harmony and affection without which liberty, and even life itself, are but dreary things. And let us reflect that having banished from our land that religious intolerance under which mankind so long bled and suffered, we have yet gained little if we countenance a political intolerance, as despotic, as wicked, and capable of as bitter and bloody persecutions . . . We have called by different names brethren of the same principle. We are all republicans: we are all federalists.

Speaking as a citizen among his peers and not from above as their ruler, Jefferson called for unity—but not for unanimity. America is sturdy enough to contain disagreements. More precisely, even in a republic where citizens have the liberty to compete on behalf of their passions and interests, there are and must be limits to our disagreements. Jefferson warned against "political intolerance." Free citizens, entrusted with their own government, have a responsibility to understand that not every disagreement is one of principle. We must try to understand one another's perspectives and come to resolution when we can. We should expect, and even embrace, vigorous disagreement in our democracy, but we cannot allow it to disable, as it has now disabled, our ability to make decisions. In the end, someone, and it doesn't have to be everyone, must be there after the argument to do the work of governing.

After the brutal election of 1800, a reasonable citizen might justifiably have questioned how much any republic could endure. Jefferson's words at the inauguration are pertinent today:

> I know indeed that some honest men fear that a republican government cannot be strong; that this government is not strong enough. But would the honest patriot, in the full tide of successful experiment, abandon a government which has so far kept us free and firm, on the theoretic and visionary fear, that this government, the world's best hope, may, by possibility, want energy to preserve itself? I trust not. I believe this, on the contrary, the strongest government on earth. I believe it the only one, where every man, at the call of the law, would fly to the standard of the law, and would meet invasions of the public order as his own personal concern.

Jefferson placed high expectations on Americans as citizens. The "call of the law" still speaks to each and every one of us. And it is no vague duty.

What is that duty? Part of the answer is to rise to the occasion—as Abraham Lincoln put it, to disenthrall ourselves from old ways of thinking and resolve to act. That can mean removing by election those who reject our republican values, whether because their impulses are by nature tyrannical or because they believe themselves to possess a monopoly on wisdom. It is as much a part of the American tradition to peacefully eject a charlatan as it is to elect a champion.[2]

---

2 Teddy Roosevelt warned: "Of one man in especial, beyond anyone else, the citizens of a republic should beware, and that is of the man who appeals to them to support him on the ground that he is hostile to other citizens of the republic, that he will secure for those who elect him, in one shape or another, profit at the expense of other citizens of the republic."

But victory is not enough. There is also the hard work of governing—enabling the republic, in Montesquieu's observation, to "correct its faults by its own laws." This means electing candidates willing to work with those who are not of like mind.

Writing in 1865 at the end of the Civil War, Walt Whitman sought to define what he believed to be our patriotic duty to see the humanity in one another. The word "reconciliation," also the title of his poem, seems to rise off the page in front of us:

RECONCILIATION

WORD over all, beautiful as the sky,
Beautiful that war, and all its deeds of carnage, must in time
    be utterly lost,
That the hands of the sisters Death and Night, incessantly
    softly wash again, and ever again, this soil'd world;
For my enemy is dead, a man divine as myself is dead;
I look where he lies, white-faced and still, in the coffin—I
    draw near;
Bend down and touch lightly with my lips the white face in
    the coffin.

No challenge before us today compares to the one that faced the nation of Lincoln in 1860 or Whitman in 1865. Hopefully no future challenge ever will. To make good on what we owe posterity, we must hand over a republic in better repair than the one we inherited. Those to whom we give it must do the same. Neither we nor they need to make this up from scratch. We have more than two centuries of examples from which to draw.

II. "What Is It Then Between Us?"

No one participating in the debate over the Constitution could foresee the republic we have now. Today, the United States has a population of 330 million—eighty-five times greater than in 1790. The framers, the small number of leaders who assembled in Philadelphia to create a new Constitution, would likely be astonished that the nation has endured this long. Even as they looked to the future to guide their hopes, they were aware that most nations were short-lived. Certainly they would never have pictured a nation of this size, wealth, and strength; a nation that spans a continent; an economy that drives the productivity and wealth of the rest of the world; a military that can overwhelm all others.

Likewise, the framers could not have imagined the extent of our democracy. Their government guarded against—even more than it empowered—direct participation of the people. Under the Constitution, voters—almost entirely composed of white male property holders—directly chose only one-half of one branch of the government.[3] The framers would never have conceived that we would directly elect senators or that states would ever yield to voters the power to elect the president. They particularly would never have imagined the extent to which the franchise is now shared by so many citizens, not just white men with property. Some would be astonished that we have abolished the inhuman cruelty of slavery, although others would be profoundly disappointed at how slow our progress has been in addressing racism and injustice. In

---

3　The Constitution granted the states the power to set their own voting requirements. A few states—New Hampshire, Massachusetts, New York, New Jersey, and North Carolina—offered the vote to free men of color. Maryland excluded Jews, despite the prohibition of religious tests in Article VI. New Jersey permitted women to vote. Kentucky permitted women to vote if they were the head of a household.

this moment, the framers would be captivated by our continuing struggle to live up to the aspiration enshrined in the Declaration of Independence: that all people are created equal.

The framers shared a simple, revolutionary idea of what it meant to be citizens of the United States—an understanding that we can never take for granted and that suffers when we neglect or distort it. In other nations, citizens were subjects of a king, but the framers saw the citizens of the United States, through their vote, as the sovereign rulers.

Those who fought the Revolution and ratified the Constitution we properly call founders. But others who came afterward, who shaped our republic and through their enormous sacrifice and patriotism made it more democratic and fair, should also be called founders, along with everyone who has done the work of shaping these ideals—in our neighborhoods, workplaces, and union halls; our pulpits and congregations; our armed forces and emergency services; our classrooms, dinner tables, school boards, city councils, and state legislatures.

In moments of reflection, I often think of Thoreau's defiant individualism in "Resistance to Civil Government." He summons citizens to demand a morally accountable government:

> But, to speak practically and as a citizen, unlike those who call themselves no-government men, I ask for, not at once no government, but at once a better government. Let every man make known what kind of government would command his respect, and that will be one step toward obtaining it.

More often I think of Zora Neale Hurston's chiding sense of humor in *How It Feels to Be Colored Me*:

I have no separate feeling about being an American citizen
and colored. I am merely a fragment of the Great Soul that
surges within the boundaries. My country, right or wrong.

Hurston shares with Thoreau an urgency for telling the truth,
for feeling out the gap between what we wish for and what we tolerate.
Her nuanced inflection on the patriot's cliché—"My country right or
wrong"—takes subtle ownership of even the most egregious forms of
injustice as something to be made right. Every one of us must own
our country's wrongs, just as we take pride in what the country gets
right. Ultimately, Hurston refuses to grant herself the privilege of
withdrawing allegiance, no matter how wrong her country might be.

Above all, I return to Walt Whitman's mind-clearing poem
"Crossing Brooklyn Ferry." His visionary description of his relationship with his fellow travelers reminds us how we as citizens should
comport ourselves in a pluralist republic. Whitman, heading across the
East River, surveys the crowd of men and women around him on the
boat and asks, "What is it then between us?" Like him, they are all in
motion, and that motion is not random and scattering. As they travel,
they share the same experience, and they share it with countless others.

> Others will enter the gates of the ferry and cross from
>   shore to shore,
> Others will watch the run of the flood-tide,
> Others will see the shipping of Manhattan north and west,
>   and the heights of Brooklyn to the south and east,
> Others will see the islands large and small;
> Fifty years hence, others will see them as they cross, the
>   sun half an hour high,

A hundred years hence, or ever so many hundred years
    hence, others will see them,
Will enjoy the sunset, the pouring-in of the flood-tide, the
    falling-back to the sea of the ebb-tide.

It is a shared experience that reaches beyond distance, beyond the present moment. However different, as travelers they are united with all others like them. And in this Whitman finds faith, not in a world greater than the one he shares with his fellow travelers, but in them, as people.

What gods can exceed these that clasp me by the hand, and
    with voices I love call me promptly and loudly by my
    nighest name as I approach?
What is more subtle than this which ties me to the woman
    or man that looks in my face?
Which fuses me into you now, and pours my meaning into
    you?
We understand then do we not?
What I promis'd without mentioning it, have you not
    accepted?
What the study could not teach—what the preaching could
    not accomplish is accomplish'd, is it not?

Whitman offers us, as people all on the same journey, now and in the future, a faith in one another to which we must aspire as citizens if we are to thrive together. When American citizenship is understood this way—which is to say when it is understood properly—we should have no difficulty grasping its powerful

attraction. It unites us in spite of our vast geography, our myriad
differences, and our tumultuous history.

> It avails not, time nor place—distance avails not,
> I am with you, you men and women of a generation, or
>   ever so many generations hence,
> Just as you feel when you look on the river and sky, so I felt,
> Just as any of you is one of a living crowd, I was one of a
>   crowd,
> Just as you are refresh'd by the gladness of the river and the
>   bright flow, I was refresh'd,
> Just as you stand and lean on the rail, yet hurry with the
>   swift current, I stood yet was hurried,
> Just as you look on the numberless masts of ships and the
>   thick-stemm'd pipes of steamboats, I look'd.

Citizenship becomes a generous and welcoming invitation to
share a world bigger than any one of us.

> . . . we plant you permanently within us,
> We fathom you not—we love you—there is perfection in
>   you also,
> You furnish your parts toward eternity,
> Great or small, you furnish your parts toward the soul.

Anyone who doubts the allure of full American citizenship
should think upon the words of—or, as Whitman would prefer, look
face-to-face at—someone who is denied that fullness. There you will
encounter another founder. The list of these other founders is long

and honorable. It includes those who sought the vote; those who expected the freedom of rule by law and safety from the vigilante justice of lynch mobs; those who knew they should share the same working conditions granted as rights to others; those who were the first to graduate from high school and college; those who were the first to be seated on a city council, school board, or legislative assembly; those who strove to see the lives of their children exceed the expectations and opportunities they themselves were afforded by their parents and grandparents. Their demand is fundamentally the same as that made by the hundred signers of the "Declaration of Sentiments" adopted at the 1848 Seneca Falls Convention—mainly but not entirely women seeking the same civil rights and liberties as men: "Because women do feel themselves aggrieved, oppressed, and fraudulently deprived of their most sacred rights, we insist that they have immediate admission to all the rights and privileges which belong to them as citizens of these United States."

Should you ever question the urgency of a vigilant citizen's demands, you should weigh the hard words that Frederick Douglass spoke to so many comfortable patriots celebrating the Fourth of July in Rochester, New York, in 1852.[4] He addressed his audience as equals while asking them to consider a past they did not yet fully share with him:

> Fellow Citizens, I am not wanting in respect for the fathers of
> this republic. The signers of the Declaration of Independence

---

4 Actually, Douglass addressed the audience on July 5, at his own request and in keeping with the traditions of the New York African American community. Historian and biographer David Blight is among many who speculate that this practice was due in part to African American's awareness that July 4 was a day for slave sales in the antebellum South.

were brave men. They were great men too—great enough to give fame to a great age. It does not often happen to a nation to raise, at one time, such a number of truly great men. The point from which I am compelled to view them is not, certainly, the most favorable; and yet I cannot contemplate their great deeds with less than admiration. They were states-men, patriots and heroes, and for the good they did, and the principles they contended for, I will unite with you to honor their memory.

They loved their country better than their own private interests; and, though this is not the highest form of human excellence, all will concede that it is a rare virtue, and that when it is exhibited, it ought to command respect. He who will, intelligently, lay down his life for his country, is a man whom it is not in human nature to despise. Your fathers staked their lives, their fortunes, and their sacred honor, on the cause of their country. In their admiration of liberty, they lost sight of all other interests.

They were peace men; but they preferred revolution to peaceful submission to bondage. They were quiet men; but they did not shrink from agitating against oppression. They showed forbearance; but that they knew its limits. They believed in order; but not in the order of tyranny.

Then Douglass turned the tables. At the moment when his audience would be happy to rest on history's accomplishments, he warned them to beware complacency: Americans, who "are remark-ably familiar with all facts which make in their own favor," cannot let the liberty earned by their forefathers be their excuse to ignore present tyrannies:

Your fathers have lived, died, and have done their work, and have done much of it well. You live and must die, and you must do your work. You have no right to enjoy a child's share in the labor of your fathers, unless your children are to be blest by your labors. You have no right to wear out and waste the hard-earned fame of your fathers to cover your indolence.

Having refused to let them off the hook by virtue of their history, he laid into their hypocrisy.

The existence of slavery in this country brands your republicanism as a sham, your humanity as a base pretence, and your Christianity as a lie. It destroys your moral power abroad; it corrupts your politicians at home. It saps the foundation of religion; it makes your name a hissing, and a by word to a mocking earth. It is the antagonistic force in your government, the only thing that seriously disturbs and endangers your Union. It fetters your progress; it is the enemy of improvement, the deadly foe of education; it fosters pride; it breeds insolence; it promotes vice; it shelters crime; it is a curse to the earth that supports it; and yet, you cling to it, as if it were the sheet anchor of all your hopes.

His criticism is a ferocious reminder, to us as much as to the people he addressed so long ago, that we will always be culpable for the injustices of our era, regardless of any justice that precedes it. That is why he told them, "My business if I have any here to-day, is with the present."

So too is ours.

In 1958, Martin Luther King declared that "the arc of the moral universe is long, but it bends toward justice." Although we find it a comfort to believe so, we should remember that in the whirlwind of national agitation, we are all too likely to look back on our past for unearned permission to let wrongdoing pass now—as something that will surely be resolved sooner or later. This delusion is fatal.

In early 1942, shortly after the bombing of Pearl Harbor, President Franklin Roosevelt issued Executive Order 9066, calling for the newly formed War Relocation Authority to wrest Japanese American citizens from their homes and exile them to prison-like camps. Some were located in rural Colorado. Some Coloradans in communities near the camps voiced a groundless and shameful fear of their fellow citizens and objected to their presence. The response of the Republican governor of Colorado, Ralph Carr—who opposed the internment policy—helps demonstrate what "our business with the present" actually looks like when people of principle take it in hand. Speaking to an audience of angry citizens, Carr explained first:

> I am talking to . . . all American people whether their status be white, brown or black and regardless of the birthplaces of their grandfathers when I say that if a majority may deprive a minority of its freedom, contrary to the terms of the Constitution today, then you as a minority may be subjected to the same ill will of the majority tomorrow.

He went on to say of the Japanese Americans wrongfully held in captivity:

> They are not going to take over the vegetable business of this state, and they are not going to take over the Arkansas Valley.

But the Japanese are protected by the same Constitution that protects us. An American citizen of Japanese descent has the same rights as any other citizen . . . If you harm them, you must first harm me. I was brought up in small towns where I knew the shame and dishonor of race hatred. I grew to despise it because it threatened [pointing to various audience members] the happiness of you and you and you.

At this moment the moral arc of the universe bent toward justice only because Ralph Carr chose to pull it in that direction. His example should also make us wonder what would have happened had he not been there.

Carr reminds us that one duty of citizens is to be strong when others are vulnerable. Another Coloradan, Rodolfo "Corky" Gonzales, in his bilingual poem "I Am Joaquin/Yo Soy Joaquin," conveys the same message. Speaking back to us from the future, in the voice of his son Joaquin, Gonzales asserts that one way to live life as a founder is to persevere in the cause of justice:[5]

I have endured in the rugged mountains
Of our country
I have survived the toils and slavery of the fields.
I have existed
In the barrios of the city
In the suburbs of bigotry
In the mines of social snobbery
In the prisons of dejection
In the muck of exploitation

---

5 Joaquin Gonzales is not a creation of his father's famous poem. He is a resident of northwest Denver.

And
In the fierce heat of racial hatred.
And now the trumpet sounds,
The music of the people stirs the
Revolution.
Like a sleeping giant it slowly
Rears its head
To the sound of
Tramping feet
Clamoring voices
Mariachi strains
Fiery tequila explosions
The smell of chile verde and
Soft brown eyes of expectation for a
Better life.

I SHALL ENDURE!
I WILL ENDURE!

Joaquin's final exclamation—shouting to us, his forebearers—can be understood as a rallying cry for young Dreamers, who, like him, want nothing more than to be citizens of the United States. In many ways, Joaquin's demand is no different from the revolutionary call of America's founders in 1776.

The ties of citizenship are as demanding as they are lovely. Citizenship always balances between a generous approach to our aspirations and the temptation to keep the benefits for ourselves. The necessary give-and-take of citizenship is enacted now, not later. It is enacted now, on this passage of the ferry. It is not something that happened once upon a time, and it is not a burden that we can simply ask the future to bear. Citizenship in a republic always occurs in the present.

III. Opposite Day

In his book on the fall of Rome, Montesquieu describes the obligation of republican governments to repair themselves. "In a word, a free government, that is, one always in a state of agitation, cannot survive if it cannot correct its faults by its own laws." For most of our history, because we are a republic, the United States has been in "a state of agitation." Over the past decade, our central failure has been our inability to correct our faults by our own laws.[6]

As I look back on a decade in the Senate, I can't help being haunted by a profound sense of lost opportunity. Instead of figuring out a bipartisan way to pay our bills—the only way we will pay them—we posted record deficits during years of economic growth and yet at the same time we underinvested in the next generation. Instead of perpetuating a bipartisan tradition of confirming nominees to the Supreme Court, we chose to adopt a purely partisan process, risking that the court will become just another partisan institution. Instead of adopting policies that would ensure America's leadership in the new energy economy while playing our part in diminishing the threat of climate change, we championed the benefits of coal and other fossil fuels—and stood alone in the world,

---

6 Even Edmund Burke, a political hero of Mitch McConnell's and often quoted by the majority leader's fellow conservatives, recognized the need to make progress in our governing institutions. Burke wrote, "A state without the means of some change is without the means of its own conservation."

denying that climate change is real. Instead of preserving Americans' faith that they have a means to influence their government's agenda, we created a campaign finance system that transformed money into speech and allowed those with the most money to pursue the power to call the shots in our democracy. Instead of passing a bipartisan bill that secured our border, gave us the ability to detect who was here illegally and who was not, and provided a tough but fair pathway to citizenship for millions of people—almost all of whom are contributing in one way or another to our economy and our country—we elected a president who demonized immigrants and called for reducing legal immigration by half. Finally, instead of upholding our end of a negotiated arms control agreement which involved many of our allies and with which an enemy was largely complying, we overrode the advice of our own intelligence agencies and scuttled the deal. At the same time, the administration heralded an illusory nuclear deal with the North Korean dictator and denied that Russia relentlessly interfered with our 2016 elections.

This record reminds me of a game my children played with my wife and me when they were young—"opposite day." It was a way to have pancakes for dinner, stay home from school in the middle of the week, and generally try to persuade us they should get anything they wanted. It was fun, but Susan and I were sharp enough not to be fooled all the time—no dessert before pancakes. My daughter Anne points out that truly embracing opposite day means acknowledging a never-ending sequence of opposites, much like facing mirrors in a barbershop. One opposite begets another in an endless series—not unlike the ruinous political dynamics we're in the throes of now.

This is no way to run a government. None of the decisions we made—or failed to make—in the episodes recounted above brought our country more security. None of them made our communities or our institutions more robust. Meanwhile, we failed to address in any way the central economic challenges facing our country. Indeed, with Donald Trump's tax cut, we made income inequality even worse. Set this record against the mission laid out in the preamble of the Constitution and we would all have to admit our abject failure. To take this state of affairs in stride—as just another night of gambling at Rick's Café—misjudges the degree of Washington's political degradation and profoundly underestimates the stakes.

Looking ahead, we have only three possible courses of action. We can continue to do nothing and hope that the problems facing the American people will work themselves out on their own. We can treat problem solving as a winner-take-all game and wait for moments of one-party rule to push through a partisan agenda (or reverse one). Or we can return to the pluralist mechanisms that were created by the framers of the Constitution and have been periodically revived and reinvigorated by subsequent founders.

Recent history offers ample evidence of the effects of doing nothing. In the years 2010 through 2016, the legislative pace in both chambers of Congress wound down to a sluggishness not seen in the past hundred years. We came to accept politics that substituted small disputes for legislative action. Many politicians perfected the craft of accomplishing nothing while casting the blame for inaction on their opponents. With every year, it seemed we moved closer to a system where members created controversy to raise money in order to win elections—all for the privilege of creating further controversy to raise money in order to win further elections. In Congress, as on cable television, we accepted a level of debate that has little to do with anything of importance. Meanwhile, the roughly 90 percent of Americans on the wrong side of the wealth and opportunity divide saw that divide only widen. It's hard to imagine how another decade of doing nothing will help.

That's why many Americans are tempted by the second course—one-party rule. Republicans finally achieved that in the last Congress, and they used their power to reshape the Supreme Court and the judicial branch for a generation. They reversed decades of environmental legislation. And they passed a tax cut that will exacerbate inequality, curb upward mobility, and create more national debt. But even if all these policies had been wise, the one-party course would still be wrong—wrong on grounds of both principle and expediency. It's reasonable to assume that if Democrats gain control of both houses of Congress and the presidency, they will do everything they can to throw the policies of recent years into reverse. But sound, stable government can't be a perpetual game of shirts and skins.[7] That aside, most of the time there isn't one-party rule: power is shared, with a presidency of one party and a House or Senate of another. And even at those moments when one-party rule exists in theory, the power of faction within the party often makes doing business impossible—as the Tea Party and the Freedom Caucus, displaying an arrogance of righteousness that would have drawn contempt from the founders, have done in recent years.

The third course requires us to sail waters first charted by our founders and then to do more than replace one version of single-party rule with the version you or I find more acceptable. Electoral victory is not an end in itself. It is intended to set in motion a

---

7 As George Washington recognized, factionalism "serves always to distract the public councils and enfeeble the public administration. It agitates the community with ill-founded jealousies and false alarms, kindles the animosity of one part against another, foments occasionally riot and insurrection. It opens the door to foreign influence and corruption, which finds a facilitated access to the government itself through the channels of party passions. Thus the policy and the will of one country are subjected to the policy and will of another."

pluralist process to resolve disputes and move the country forward. It is a process that Americans live out in almost every other aspect of their lives: when parents decide where to send a child to school, when city council members balance a municipal budget, when local commissions draw the line between commercial and residential zones, when universities chart their way forward, when nonprofit organizations spend money. In all of these venues the principles of respect and compromise are shared by everyone. To argue that somehow our national government deserves a waiver from pluralist dynamics is absurd.

It is commonplace now in America that campaigns never end. The corollary is that governance never begins. We have forgotten how to manage the country and forgotten as well the important role politics plays in providing guidance to our decision making. Decoupled from governance, politics has lost its purpose. It has degraded into endless fund-raising and dishonest promises rendered in a vocabulary sometimes indistinguishable from Russian propaganda.[8] Returning to Montesquieu, a republic that fails to correct itself by its laws slides into tyranny. There are many points of view in this country, and rediscovering our will to reconcile, navigate, and negotiate them is the way we correct our course.

This is not a call for lazy moderation or lame bipartisan agreements that split the difference between obsolete ideas. It is a call for the difficult, imaginative give-and-take that can produce enduring results. It is the kind of work the founders did when they laboriously

---

8 Compare the following two statements: "Immigrants! They are all criminals!" "Democrats are the problem. They don't care about crime and want illegal immigrants, no matter how bad they may be, to pour into and infest our Country, like MS-13." The first was slipped into American social media feeds in 2016 by Russian agents, trying to tamper with our elections. The second was tweeted in 2018 by President Trump, trying to animate his base.

picked their way through what seemed like intractable issues: how to treat big and small states equally and yet not equally at the same time, whether states or the federal government had the right to levy duties on imports, and whether the Constitution should or should not include a bill of rights. They didn't get all of the answers right, and none of what we face will be easy to solve in the context of a national government that is awash in special-interest money and in which elected officials quake at the first sign of a social media storm. But that's the reality. The Depression wasn't easy. World War II wasn't easy. The civil rights movement wasn't easy. We've shown the necessary mettle before.

IV. At the Center of the Arc

As I was finishing this book, I had the opportunity to visit Americans in two very different communities. One visit was with a group of young men who lived in West Garfield Park on the West Side of Chicago. The second was with a group gathered in the River Rock Café, a breakfast and lunch spot on Colorado State Highway 125 (which also serves as Main Street), in the county seat of Jackson County, Walden (population 1,385). In my meeting there, someone pointed out that I had won 275 votes in the county or 28 percent of all votes cast. When I said I was sorry I lost the county, the local reporter congratulated me for outperforming the county's Democratic registration of 9.98 percent by 177 votes.[9]

The meeting in Chicago was unlike any I had ever had as the Denver Public Schools superintendent. In that job, I spent many hours visiting with children living in poverty, with their moms and

---

9 Someone else leaned over and whispered, "It was the school people."

dads, and with the teachers and principals who were determined to give the kids a better future. I had never met American children as hard hit by violent crime, especially gun-related murders, as the ones in West Garfield Park.

The conversation had been made possible by Arne Duncan, President Obama's secretary of education. Now back in Chicago, Arne has devoted himself to the cause of preventing young men from killing each other. While I was there, he explained to me that to reach the per capita level of handgun homicides in New York City last year, Chicago would have to reduce the number of murders from 650 to 97.

Several months into their work with Arne and his colleagues, the young men were making progress, partly through their own efforts and partly because of a nurturing environment they had not previously experienced. One said he had never known what love was before joining the group. Another said that learning about the Bible had changed his life. Still another talked about the satisfaction of learning a skill and being paid for it. That was good news.

West Garfield has the highest homicide rate and the lowest life expectancy of any neighborhood in Chicago. The young men told me that in grammar school they were first made to choose "sides"—sides in gang warfare. They talked about how they grew up on their blocks just hoping to survive until the end of each day. They described a world in which escalating provocations and signs of disrespect—some known and some unknowable—created crushing stress and tension.[10] As the young men introduced themselves,

---

10 In his remarkable recent book *There Will Be No Miracles Here*, Casey Gerald describes his childhood in the South Oak Cliff neighborhood of Dallas, a place "where boys had nothing but the pride of a few blocks they had inherited—blocks that, absent any other cause to believe in, were worth dying for, I suppose."

each told me about friends he had lost to guns and other violent crime. Every young man knew more than one. Some said they had lost count. Almost all had been incarcerated.

It was as if they had come from a neighborhood in Iraq or Afghanistan, but this neighborhood is in America. It is a place with no jobs. There are no schools where any members of the Senate would send their children. There is no peace. The Americans living in Garfield Park have no place on Washington's do-nothing calendar.

Walden, Colorado, is a long way from the West Side of Chicago. There, a dozen or so citizens talked about the joys of raising children in a small community where if your kid looks sideways in school or on the way home, you get three calls from neighbors before the child gets home. They talked about how at every sporting event, even if it is hundreds of miles from town, the stands are filled with blue and white, the North Park Junior-Senior High School's colors.

But the school is down to under 200 kids, from prekindergarten through twelfth grade. And there are few jobs that pay a salary that allows people to own a house in a market where out-of-towners pay top dollar for second homes—a bargain compared with prices in Colorado's resort communities. Virtually no one at our meeting had health insurance except for the county commissioner and the school principal, who had it through their jobs. The owner of a local restaurant and pool hall explained that he had job openings but that he could not hire anybody, because potential applicants would lose their Medicaid if they went to work. He had to cut back the days his business operated because of the labor shortage; his wife was working fifty hours a week. Neither of them had health insurance. These Americans also have no place on Washington's do-nothing calendar.

If we were truly pursuing the interests of the republic and the next generation of Americans, we would be asking ourselves how we could generate greater economic mobility in our society and how we could better mitigate the effects when there is none. We would consider why our health care system creates such misery for so many and how we might fix it; we would take seriously the challenges faced by rural and urban communities where the word "economy" is a joke. We would ask what we could do differently so that more children had high-quality early childhood education, more college students could pursue their studies without incurring debt, more people seeking an alternative to college could undertake high-quality apprenticeships, and more Americans throughout their lives could advance their careers by improving their existing job skills or learning new ones. I ask these questions not to generate some worthy checklist but to emphasize a point made earlier: the health of society and the health of republican government cannot be separated. We do not get to pick. The erosion of the quality of life for most Americans erodes our politics. The erosion of our politics erodes the quality of life for most Americans.

Thomas Paine, one of the founders, understood the urgent necessity of the long time horizon, of looking at the present from the point of view of a more distant future. (A cantankerous and difficult man, he himself looks better in retrospect.) In his book *Common Sense* he wrote:

> As parents, we can have no joy, knowing that this government is not sufficiently lasting to ensure anything which we may bequeath to posterity; and by a plain method of argument, as we are running the next generation into debt, we ought to do

the work of it, otherwise we use them meanly and pitifully. In order to discover the line of our duty rightly, we should take our children in our hand, and fix our station a few years farther into life; that eminence will present a prospect which a few present fears and prejudices conceal from our sight.

He was writing about the government of Great Britain, and the debt of which he speaks is figurative, but in our present context these words should be clear enough to stun us into attention.

It is an American cliché to believe that any child could one day grow up to be president of the United States. But it is a belief proved by everyone from Abraham Lincoln to Barack Obama. It is a belief that parents whisper to their children and kindergarten teachers proclaim to their students on the first day of school.

As superintendent of Denver's public schools, I had many occasions to ponder what this aspiration actually meant when it came to thinking about the future of tens of thousands of students in our schools. It occurred to me that perhaps their future (as well as our own) would be more secure if we thought of each of these young Americans as someone our country requires to become a founder in the same sense that Hurston followed Thoreau, that Douglass followed Franklin, and that King followed Carr.

Unfortunately we are a long way from that.

Tonight, as I bring this book to a close, I sit near the marble chambers of the United States Senate with their paintings, statues, and other lavish furnishings that tie us to our past, but I am thinking of our future. I am thinking of the millions of children our founders could not have imagined heading home after a long day at school, shifting their backpacks of books to find a more comfortable position, sharpening pencils for math and pastels for art, clearing a space on a crowded dinner table for homework. I'm thinking about children teaching other children, older brothers and sisters teaching younger siblings, expecting they will all have more opportunity than their parents. And, as I think about our children, I know that each of them has a job to do as well. That job is to learn what creates the powerful force of a volcano or what Janie knows at the end of *Their Eyes Were Watching God* that she didn't know at the beginning or why to invert the second fraction when they divide. They are up to those tasks, but they are right to expect that we, their elders, will also fulfill our responsibilities.

I come back to James Baldwin's words, as I began with them. At the end of his essay "Letter from a Region in My Mind," written deep in the crisis years of the American civil rights movement, he said:

> And here we arc, at the center of the arc, trapped in the gaudiest, most valuable, and most improbable water wheel the world has ever seen. Everything now, we must assume, is in our hands; we have no right to assume otherwise. If we—and now I mean the relatively conscious whites and the relatively conscious blacks, who must, like lovers, insist on, or create, the consciousness of the others—do not falter in our duty now, we may be able, handful that we are, to end the racial nightmare, and achieve our country, and change the history of the world.

I wish I could tell those children doing their homework that we have settled the long-enduring problems that Baldwin confronted in his essay. I cannot. They are among the problems we must and can still solve today. But Baldwin's creed must be ours today. *Everything now is in our hands; we have no right to assume otherwise.*

FOUR FREEDOMS

The path ahead.

To achieve perspective, an artist puts a dot on a sheet of paper—it's called the vanishing point. With this single act an entire composition comes into focus: angles, sizes, depth, proportions. This trick is an essential tool for comprehending—and conveying—reality.

When we think about our society, similar methods can be used to gain perspective. If only we used them. Imagine, for instance, that we face momentous decisions about the future. What if instead of making those decisions as partisans, we made them from the perspective of parents and grandparents? Or, to frame it another way: what if we asked ourselves what the impact of our decisions would be not in a year or two but in a decade or two? What if we took our own personal benefit out of the calculation and asked: what are the benefits we desire but might not live to see?

And as we think about such questions, what if we took a philosopher's famous thought experiment and applied it to our society? Imagine, the experiment goes, that you are about to be reborn into the society you currently inhabit. You have no choice in the outcome. Parents, race, gender, health, geography, income, schools: it's all up for grabs. Where you end up is a throw of the dice. As you think about that possibility, are you filled with confidence? Do you believe you'll get a fair shake, an open path to progress, or a helping hand when you need it? Would you confidently entrust your children to this possibility, no matter where they landed? If you entertain any worries at all, as I certainly would, then your worry is something profound. Your worry is a measure of how far our society lies from justice.

There is ample cause for worry. As Americans we may disagree about how to address certain problems, but the problems themselves are matters of fact. They are not open to dispute. In terms of income and wealth, inequality is growing. Social mobility has sputtered to a standstill. Proper health care is beyond the reach of tens of millions. So is a good education. So is a life lived in safety. So is the sense that you have a say in your own destiny, because your voice is heard in the councils where decisions are made. But we are stuck. We are stuck because we are too often fighting yesterday's battles instead of seeking to anticipate, as our founders did, how we might change things for the better in the future.

This isn't a matter of liberals versus conservatives. To one degree or another, all of us are conservative. If being conservative means wanting to protect our nation's principles and ideals, I am a conservative. If being conservative means wanting to preserve a culture of tolerance, justice, and equality, I am a conservative. If being conservative means respecting the cultural and natural heritage of America, I am a conservative. But while we protect and preserve the best of what makes us who we are, we must adapt to meet the future. We do not live in a stagnant world. We are living in revolutionary times. The twenty-first century will be as different from the twentieth as the twentieth century was from the sixteenth or seventeenth century. Fortunes are being made—and economies and society upended—because of technologies that did not exist five years or five months ago. The national government, for its part, is desperately out of sync. To give but one example: the government has cut taxes, but the underlying tax code has not been revised since 1986. What are the chances that this creaky instrument, patched and rumbling, is still helping to drive job and wage growth three decades later? And yet today, the inheritors of the Tea Party banner, including President Trump, resist all change. Indeed, they want to go back, to a past that never existed or to one that has no relation to the era in which we live.

We have been here before. I think of the America of my parents' generation: in the grip of economic despair, Jim Crow racism, fervent isolationism, and a populist anger that took ugly forms. In 1941, as America was just emerging from under the weight of the Great Depression and the world plunged ever more deeply into global war, Franklin D. Roosevelt gave what has come to be called his Four Freedoms speech, crystallizing American ideals before the eyes of the world. Freedom of speech. Freedom of worship. Freedom from want. Freedom from fear. These, Roosevelt maintained, were the irreducible building blocks of a more just society and a more just global order.

If we are again at one of history's turning points, as I believe we are, then we have a choice to make.

One road leads to the depths of the American past. In times of uncertainty, it has always been tempting for some to try to capitalize on our darkest fears. Anytime Americans have become anxious or worried, there have been those who saw advantage in fanning the flames. Theirs are not among the names inscribed on history's honor roll. Yet sowing division can be all too easy.

It is precisely at moments of crisis when the confidence of a people is at the lowest ebb. These are the moments when we are most tempted to abandon our democratic traditions. They are also the moments when confidence in oneself and confidence in one another are needed most. This is especially true in a republic, where only the citizens can answer the fire bells in the night. If we are to remain a republic, no one alone can fix it.

When we hold on to our values through tough times, we forge them anew, as Roosevelt did in his time, and burnish them for future generations. These values are made stronger and more useful to those who will face challenges in days far ahead. At times of deepest crisis in our past, we have ultimately overcome malign forces wishing to hoard the promise of democracy for themselves. When we succeed, we recast our freedoms for the trials of our own times, consistent with our ideals. Freedoms to be won not simply through government action but, more important, by what all of us do in our homes and our communities. We treasure the freedoms embodied in the first ten amendments to the Constitution. But, like Roosevelt, we must think more ambitiously. And as we do we should remember the lesson of that throw of the dice. What does a just society look like?

Freedom to rise. Upward mobility is an engine of prosperity and justice. Rigid, generational inequality is the enemy of both. For decades, consciously or not, America has moved in a direction that suppresses mobility and enhances inequality. Our policies need to value workers and working families—and they need to enable workers who wish to organize on their own behalf, not impede them. They need to treat immigrants with the respect all human beings deserve—and to recognize that newcomers to our shores are part of the future of our country. Mobility in our society is impossible without decent health care, which should be available to every American, and at costs comparable to those in other rich democracies. Tax policies should support working-class families—not poke a thumb in their eye while swelling the portfolios of those whose great-grandchildren couldn't possibly spend the money they already have. For generations, Americans struck an implied deal with one another: if the system is fair and there's a safety net for the most vulnerable among us, we'll compete and take our chances. This deal has been the source of America's political and economic resilience. We must restore it.

Freedom to learn. "Education" is a broad term. It includes the nation's schools but it also includes the training and coursework that keep adults up to speed in a dynamic economy. And it includes promoting the knowledge and values that underlie civic life in a republic. Our public schools were once America's glory; today, too many short-change their students. By their very nature, traditional funding mechanisms—based heavily on local property taxes—harm schools in poor communities and bolster schools in rich ones. We must break that link—and we must find new ways to make higher education available to anyone who seeks it. That means supporting budgets and supporting students—not cutting financial aid and coddling predatory lenders. At the highest levels of public life, meanwhile, voices stir ignorance into voracious life by questioning the very idea of objectivity, of accepted facts, of truth itself. All Americans have a responsibility to call these people out. Without education—education that lasts a lifetime, education that extends to the way we advance our most cherished ideals—mobility and justice are beyond reach. The impulse to unceasing self-improvement is a profoundly American trait, inherent in the founders' creed. We need to nurture it.

Freedom from violence. We're all aware of the images, maybe even immune to them by now: the shootings, whether by criminals or those who are supposed to protect us, the widespread family trauma, the angry mobs, the acts of outright terrorism. A less visible violence affects our everyday lives. In many neighborhoods a walk to school is a journey undertaken in a shadow of menace. A quieter, more insidious violence flourishes in social media, feeding adolescent despair. The inner violence of addiction hits communities everywhere. Meanwhile, the criminal justice system is broken; our long history of unequal treatment of poor and minority criminal offenders has in recent times evolved into a system of mass incarceration unlike that of any other developed democracy. A network of dystopian privatized prisons spreads across the land to house people who in many cases should not be behind bars. Attitudes and opinions on every one of these issues have long since hardened. And every one of them needs to be reexamined—informed not by ideology but by pragmatism and the moral dictates of a just society.

Freedom to govern ourselves. Sovereign power belongs to all of the people, not just a vocal or wealthy few, or the most partisan. In recent decades the exercise of that power has been undermined in many ways. We need to confront voter suppression in all its forms, gerrymandering, the influx of dark money into politics, and the rules in Congress that reward partisanship. We need to resist a culture that sees reasonable disagreement as existential antagonism—a culture that not only erodes but disdains respect in the way citizens speak to and behave toward one another. The loss of faith in our governing institutions, and in one another, is a death spiral. We can counter it only by recapturing the idea of ourselves as citizens.

*   *   *

Citizens! How I wish we would start using that word again. The concept is old, and implies much more than rights. It comes with obligations. The founders set out to create a republic of a scope and scale never before attempted. They set out to create a republic that others expanded as the country grew. They believed in putting the common interest above personal or narrow interests. And, because of the work of subsequent Americans who did their patriotic duty, they succeeded in their ambitions to an extent they could never have fathomed. The United States today is the world's oldest and greatest democracy. It has grown in prosperity and power even as it has matured in its understanding of the rights its founders first articulated, as subsequent generations of founders sharpened those rights and extended them to people long denied them.

There is so much more to be done. Each of us, with individual talent and spirit and hard work, is called upon to be a founder. Each of us—in obligation to others—is called upon to rebuild the republic. What if each of us were to answer that call?

THE AMERICAN DREAM

Our predicament—a capsule summary in eight charts.

I n 1831 the French aristocrat Alexis de Tocqueville started out on the famous journey through the United States that resulted in his book *Democracy in America*, an indispensable source of description and analysis. At one point he writes: "Amongst the novel objects that attracted my attention during my stay in the United States, nothing struck me more forcibly than the general equality of conditions." The situation was a far cry from the one that existed in much of Europe, where the chasm between impoverished masses and a gilded upper class was vast and seemingly unbridgeable.

Exactly a century later, the American writer and historian James Truslow Adams coined the term "American dream," which he defined as "not a dream of motor cars and high wages merely, but a dream of a social order in which each man and each woman shall be able to attain to the fullest stature of which they are innately capable, and be recognized by others for what they are, regardless of the fortuitous circumstances of birth or position."

What follows is a short sequence of eight charts that you might want to discuss with your neighbors and your representatives in Congress.

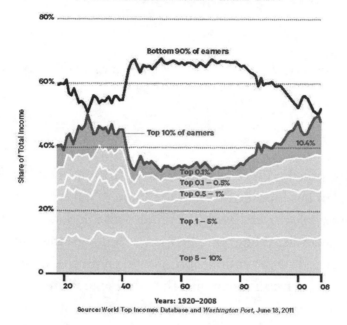

Growing Share of Income for the Top

Inequality in the US has grown for the past 40 years

Years: 1920–2008
Source: World Top Incomes Database and *Washington Post*, June 18, 2011

1. Fewer Have More

Nearly two centuries after Tocqueville and nearly a century after Adams, the American dream is faring poorly. In the middle decades of the twentieth century, the share of income claimed by the top 10 percent of all earners held fairly steady at around 35 percent. But beginning in the Reagan era, the share has gone up and up—to about 50 percent. The situation has only grown worse in recent years.

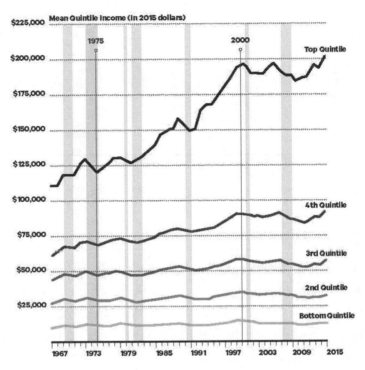

Income Growth by Quintile

Income growth has been concentrated where it's needed least

Source: http://www.crs.gov/reports/pdf/R44705

2. Winners and Losers

We can break the numbers down further, each one showing a "quintile" of American households—that is, a 20 percent slice. During the past fifty years, income growth for the bottom four quintiles has been pretty much flat whereas income growth for the top quintile has accelerated.

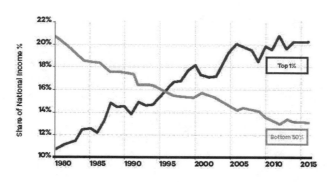

Income Shares

The top 1% in the US takes home 20% of the income vs. 13% for the bottom 50%

Source: https://wir2018.wid.world/files/download/wir2018-summary-english.pdf

3. Opposite Directions

Looking at it another way, you can see the fortunes of the top 1 percent of households and the bottom 50 percent crossing paths in the mid-1990s. The United States had been heading in that direction for years, and since the moment of intersection the divergence has continued to widen.

Absolute Mobility

Children now have only a 50% chance of earning more than their parents

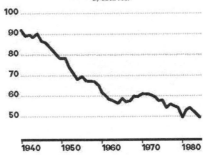

**Percent of Children Earning More
at Age 30 Than Their Parents**
By Birth Year

Source: "The Fading American Dream: Trends in Absolute Income Mobility
Since 1940," by Raj Chetty, David Grusky, Maxim Hell, Nathaniel Hendren, Robert
Manduca, and Jimmy Narang (NBER Working Paper 22910, December 2016),
https://www.brookings.edu/essay/senator-booker-american-dream-deferred/

4. Not Far from the Tree

One key element of the American dream has been the hope—and the expectation—that each generation will do better than the previous one did: "I just want my kids to have a better life." The possibility has been diminishing, especially in the last forty years. If you were an American born in 1940, you had about a 90 percent chance of earning more than your parents did, regardless of where on the income ladder your family stood. If you were born in 1980—which means that you have entered your prime earning years—your chances are only about 50 percent.

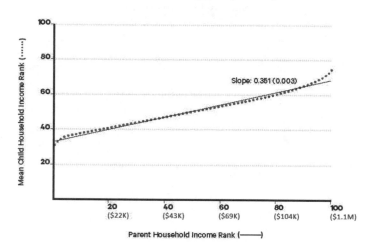

Intergenerational Mobility

An individual's income is driven in large part by his or her parents' income

Source: http://www.equality-of-opportunity.org/assets/documents/race_slides.pdf

5. A Parent's Paycheck—and Yours

Economists use the technical term "intergenerational income elasticity" to describe how much a child's income varies from a parent's. Greater variance means more room for the next generation to move up or down. The authors of the study from which the next chart comes put their sobering conclusion in the dry language of economics: "The conditional expectation of a child's rank given his parents' rank is almost perfectly linear." What they mean is that in America today the best predictor of a child's income is that of his or her parents.

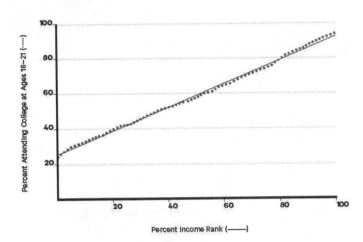

Effect of Income on College Attendance

Whether or not a student goes to college depends on family income

Source: https://www.brookings.edu/blog/social-mobility-memos/2018/01/11/raj-chetty
-in-14-charts-big-findings-on-opportunity-and-mobility-we-should-know/

6. Game Changer—for a Few

The same holds true for college attendance. An individual's access to higher education has historically been one of the most significant determinants of future economic well-being in America—and it still is. Children from families in the bottom half of American earners who attain four-year college degrees are likely to reach much higher levels of income than their parents did (or than their peers who don't go to college will reach). College propels upward mobility. But who gets to college in the first place? As the next chart demonstrates, your chances depend on the family income you're born into—less income, less opportunity.

MICHAEL BENNET

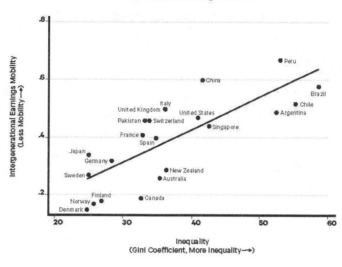

Source: https://milescorak.com/2012/01/12/

7. Getting It Wrong

For perspective, it's often useful to step back and look at America in the context of other nations. The graph here correlates two factors: the degree of income inequality in a country and the degree of intergenerational mobility in a country. The farther to the right a country appears on the horizontal axis, the more inequality it has. The higher it appears on the vertical axis, the less intergenerational mobility it has. Compared with those of the United States, the circumstances of Canada, Japan, and Spain seem enviable. One conclusion: if you want a formula for rising inequality and falling mobility, America seems to have found it.

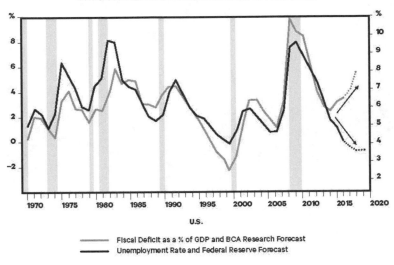

Fiscal Stimulus over Time

Current deficit spending is out of sync with economic conditions

Fiscal Deficit as a % of GDP and BCA Research Forecast
Unemployment Rate and Federal Reserve Forecast

Source: BCA Research; Fed Summary of Economic Projections

8. Lost Opportunity

A different kind of perspective is provided by this chart, which correlates deficit spending and the unemployment rate. For the most part, the two numbers rise and fall together, as they should; historically, the federal government spends more in times of economic distress, then tightens up when conditions improve. That is, until now. Thanks in large measure to tax cuts for the wealthy, the federal deficit is soaring at a time when the economy is stable and unemployment is as low as it has ever been.

Not only does this diminish our capacity to respond to crises in the future, it also represents a huge opportunity cost: as much as $2 trillion poured into the sand at a time when our society urgently needs investment in education, infrastructure, housing, health care, and nutrition.

FOR FURTHER READING

Some books that have helped me along.

"What are you reading these days?" It is a question that quietly waits in line at my town hall meetings, usually making an appearance toward the end. It is one of my favorites, because it kindles a warm and open-ended dialogue with the questioner. And it's a reminder of the humbler ties that hold us together as a republic. We are a nation of readers, and readers invariably end up comparing notes with one another—whether the conversation is about books, about essays, about speeches, or about diaries and letters.

Here's how I would answer the question if I were asked today to look back over the last twenty-four months or so, the period during which I was working on this book.

American Founders

- Thomas Paine, *Common Sense*. A case could be made that this brief pamphlet was almost as important to the American Revolution as the Declaration of Independence. In it, the English expatriate urged his fellow American colonial citizens to throw off the yoke of tyranny in the name of republican self-government.

- George Washington, speeches and writings, but especially his Farewell Address. A Senate tradition originally intended to honor these words has degenerated into an annual ritual where one of us is chosen to read them on the floor to an empty Senate chamber. The hall is empty because in the era of televised coverage we are not compelled to be on the floor unless there is a vote. Maybe some of us are watching in the privacy of our offices.

- *The Federalist*. Somewhere between AP American history and law school, my best teachers taught me to appreciate these fascinating commentaries for what they are—high-potency campaign literature arguing for ratification of the Constitution and written by future political rivals James Madison and Alexander Hamilton, along with John Jay. As *Hamilton*'s Lin-Manuel Miranda has reminded us, these essays are not sacred scrolls recording our original constitutional thought. At their best, they offer insight into our republican aspirations; at their worst, they quibble over long-forgotten points of debate. Nonetheless, their distinction between the "energetic" government they propose and the "imbecilic" government they want to put behind them remains relevant today. I find myself frequently returning to "Federalist No. 1," where Hamilton convincingly makes the case that the American experiment in self-government is an example from which the world could learn; to "No. 10" for its insight into the "mischief of faction"; to "No. 14" when I need to be reminded of the radical defiance of conventional political wisdom that informed our political system; to "No. 62" and "No. 63" on the nature of the Senate; to "No. 51" on the role of checks and balances in our government; and to "No. 78" for its explanation of the necessity of an impartial judiciary.

- Thomas Jefferson, speeches and writings. Although he is rightly remembered for his state papers, especially the Declaration of Independence and his first inaugural address, his letters offer an even more rewarding glimpse into his sometimes brilliant, sometimes contrarian, and nearly always restless intelligence. Jefferson's writings are numerous enough to encompass many of our nation's founding contradictions— not in a heroic consensus, but in a way that should nag at our latter-day conscience. When we read him with what Ta-Nehisi Coates calls "a hard memory," we cannot imagine "a Monticello without slavery."

- Seneca Falls Convention, "Declaration of Sentiments." Aside from Lincoln's Gettysburg Address, there may be no finer reworking of the best ideas expressed in the Declaration of Independence, in part because "Sentiments" calls attention to the most egregious omissions.

- Abraham Lincoln, speeches and writings, including "Remarks to Congress, December 1, 1862." Lincoln stands with Jefferson and Frederick Douglass as the trinity of our greatest political writers. I am always struck that both Lincoln and Douglass were entirely self-taught, and in this way less caught up in the tangled net of conventional wisdom. At almost any point in his life as a writer, Lincoln was capable of a deeply thought passage, a brilliant argument, a perceptive turn of phrase. Nonetheless, it is what he wrote as president that I find most compelling. His words should be the model for all holding elected office: he is always searching, certain only when he knows he must act, and keenly aware of our place together as Americans.

- Frederick Douglass, speeches and writings, including "What to the Slave Is the Fourth of July?" "We Have Decided to Stay," and "Oration in the Memory of Abraham Lincoln." As noted, I think of Douglass and Lincoln as a pair, two stars pointing the way forward in one of our darkest moments. Douglass plays the part of the citizen who knows the republic can offer more. Lincoln is the official who must respond to those demands. In this regard it is all the more fitting that Douglass outlasted Lincoln by decades: we live our lives as citizens; as elected officials we take our turn. The story of their four meetings and the story of how Douglass's appraisal of Lincoln changed throughout his life is told and told again. Those retellings teach us of our obligations to one another.

- Walt Whitman, *Leaves of Grass*. I can't remember when I didn't turn to Whitman to prod my thinking. He combines his expansive understanding of America with a dynamic sense of individual and collective potential that should serve as an aspiration for all of us. I keep an 1884 reprint of the 1881–82 edition in my office. It's an antique; I suspect I should leave it alone.

- Emma Lazarus, "The New Colossus." In an age when we've shut down the government over a border wall, we should pick up her poem, read it again, and remember that we once saw ourselves as a welcoming nation.

- Ida B. Wells, "Lynch Law in All of Its Phases." No one makes the case for the importance of a free press in an imperfect republic better than she.

- Zora Neale Hurston, "How It Feels to Be Colored Me." Her place among the American founders is established with every word she wrote, although public recognition of her stature was long overdue. This short and very subtle essay alone earns her this place.

- Susan B. Anthony, "Is It a Crime for a Citizen of the United States to Vote?" The right to vote is easily taken for granted until we remember how long and hard the fight has been to earn it and how much longer and harder the fight has been to protect it.

- Margaret Chase Smith, "Declaration of Conscience." Smith was a Republican senator from Maine. Anyone looking for an example of telling an uncomfortable truth to her own political party need look for no better one.

- Martin Luther King Jr., speeches and writings, including "Letter from Birmingham Jail." King's letter to the city's white clergymen explains why they, through their tolerance of injustice, are doing violence to our founding principles.

- James Baldwin, "A Letter from a Region in My Mind" (sometimes called "The Fire Next Time," which is actually the name of the collection it is part of). In my view, this is simply the best magazine piece ever written.

- Rodolfo "Corky" Gonzales, "I Am Joaquin /Yo Soy Joaquin." His family still leads the civil rights work he started in Colorado.

- Cesar Chavez, "On Democracy" and "On Public Schools." Chavez's successor at the United Farm Workers of America was Roberto Rodriguez, a great ally in the Gang of Eight negotiations.

American History and Contemporary Affairs

- Ta-Nehisi Coates, the books *Between the World and Me* and *We Were Eight Years in Power* and the essays "The Case for Reparations" and "I'm Not Black, I'm Kanye." Coates offers a fundamentally different understanding of our history, demanding that we face up to those systematically excluded from the way we shaped our republic. He places on all of us the burden of answering the hard questions he persistently asks. We may not always agree, but he gives us nowhere to hide.

- Jill Lepore, *These Truths*. Maybe the most important thing about this American history is its considered ambivalence. This is better than can be said of nostalgic consensus narratives or relentlessly disenchanting ones. She gives us the full promise of American history—promises made, broken, and patched together again.

- Matthew Desmond, *Evicted*. Among many other contributions of this extraordinary piece of reporting, Desmond shows how hard we make it for the poor to work their way out of poverty in America.

- George Packer, *The Unwinding: An Inner History of the New America*. Packer's relentless reporting, combined with John Dos Passos–style storytelling, reveals how economic immobility tears at American families.

- Matthew Stewart, "The 9.9 Percent Is the New American Aristocracy," published in *The Atlantic*. Stewart assembles the factual case that our economy no longer offers opportunity to most families, a case critical to understanding why the stories told by Desmond and Packer persist in our country.

- David Frankel, *Thank You for Your Service*. An ironic title that reflects America's careless treatment of our returning veterans.

- Michelle Alexander, *The New Jim Crow*; and James Forman Jr., *Locking Up Our Own*. Their full critique of our system of mass incarceration reminds us that inequality in the United States is a matter not only of economics but also of race. Alexander describes an epidemic of cruelty that has reinforced a system of American racial castes. Forman's careful research and beautiful writing recount a history that resulted in a brutal erosion of rights.

- Adam Serwer, "The Nationalist's Delusion," published in *The Atlantic*. His reminder that "history has a way of altering villains so that we can no longer see ourselves in them" is vital to understanding the American story. But his later advice is equally important: "Nothing is inevitable, people can change. No one is irredeemable. But recognition precedes enlightenment."

- Sam Quinones, *Dreamland*. A former *Los Angeles Times* reporter, Quinones tracks how, almost in plain sight, many Americans became addicted first to legal opioids and then to black-tar heroin.

- Nancy Isenberg, *White Trash: The 400-Year Untold History of Class in America*. Isenberg's rarely told story of white poverty would never have been found in my university's course catalog.

- Edward Luce, *The Retreat of Western Liberalism*. This was my favorite of many books in the post-Trump-election wave. They all serve us well in their reminder of the risks facing our republic. Few, however, offer as much insight as Luce does into how our present problem is at least partly one of our own making. Others in this genre include Timothy Snyder's *On Tyranny*, Steven Levitsky and Daniel Ziblatt's *How Democracies Die*, and Yascha Mounk's *The People vs. Democracy*.

- Casey Gerald, *There Will Be No Miracles Here*. I read this thirty-one-year-old's astonishing memoir as I was finishing this book and bought copy after copy for family and friends. His book reminds me of what it would mean if we treated every American child as a future founder and what it looks like when we don't.

- Katherine Boo, *Behind the Beautiful Forevers: Life, Death, and Hope in a Mumbai Undercity*. I cherish this book, which is still the best book I have ever read about people living in poverty.

- David Fromkin, *A Peace to End All Peace*. My brother James was the Jerusalem bureau chief for the *New York Times*. I once asked him what was the best book he had ever read about the history of the Middle East. This was his answer.

- Dexter Filkins, *The Forever War*; Lawrence Wright, *The Looming Tower: Al-Qaeda and the Road to 9/11*; and Marc Lynch, *The New Arab Wars: Uprisings and Anarchy in the Middle East*. These exemplary books are part of a rich literature that should make us cautious about our intervention in the Middle East and aware of unintended consequences of both action and inaction.

The Bigger Picture

- Plutarch, *Roman Lives*. There may be no better proof that as far as politics goes, there is nothing new under the sun. His biographical sketches illustrate stories of political failings and, less frequently, successes. If we changed the names and places, the tales could easily have been torn from the headlines.

- Marcus Aurelius, *Meditations*. When I am in the Capitol I often see statues of people, unremembered today, who died at the right time to generate such sculptures of themselves. Ironically (since his book actually survived), Marcus Aurelius reminds us over and over that even Roman emperors eventually will be forgotten. This perspective, he writes, should lead us to do our best in the present.

- Mary Beard, *SPQR: A History of Ancient Rome*. I picked up this volume to help deepen my understanding of a period of history our eighteenth-century founders knew as well as their own.

- Montesquieu, *Considerations on the Causes of the Greatness of the Romans and Their Decline* and *The Spirit of the Laws*. Although Montesquieu offers much to readers, including insight into what our eighteenth-century founders were arguing over when they began our republican experiment in government, his most important lesson may be that republics, always fragile, are obliged to repair themselves through their own political processes if they are to stand strong.

- Isaiah Berlin, "Two Concepts of Liberty." Berlin's formulation of positive liberty and negative liberty and their importance to the citizens living in a pluralist society strikes a balance that would be very familiar to Coloradans.

ACKNOWLEDGMENTS

I first want to thank the people of Colorado for the privilege of representing them in the United States Senate. Whether you voted for me or not, the give-and-take we have shared over the past decade in town halls and less formal settings formed the basis for this book and my service in the Senate. Those conversations—in schools, small businesses, and county courthouses; on farms and ranches; on our public lands and in our wilderness—instill me with confidence about the future of our democracy. I am indebted to Governor Bill Ritter for appointing me to the Senate in the first place. It is said that someone who makes such an appointment creates one ingrate and a thousand enemies. Conscious of that conventional wisdom, I have tried to prove it wrong.

Throughout my career, I have had the chance to work with extraordinary colleagues every step of the way. I want to thank them for their patience, allowing me to learn from them and integrate a view of the world informed by their work in business and in local, state, and federal government. I particularly wish to thank the students, families, teachers, and other employees of the Denver Public Schools. I continue to draw inspiration from your example.

Sometimes people drop by my office to ask for career advice. I usually tell them that my secret is hiring people who are much better at doing their job than I ever would be, and then letting them do that job. This has never been more evident than in the Senate, where the quality of my staff has often compensated for my shortcomings. In particular, I would like to thank Riki Parikh, Candace Vahlsing, Brian Appel, Vivek Chilukuri, Maria Mahler-Haug, Charlie Anderson, and Jack Turnage for volunteering their deep knowledge to this project. Jonathon Davidson, Kristin Mollet, and Sarah and Craig Hughes made it all possible.

I am indebted to my agent, Rafe Sagalyn for selling this book. But, much more than that, for introducing me to Cullen Murphy, my editor. Upon hearing Cullen's name from Rafe, I called my brother, James, himself a distinguished editor and newspaperman. Not having read any of these pages yet, he told me, "There is no one in this country that I would have edit your book before Cullen Murphy." He was right. After reading my manuscript, Cullen observed, "There is a lot of good writing here, a lot of good information, but if you want anyone to read this outside a proctored examination there is more work to do." If you are reading this outside a proctored examination, you have Cullen Murphy to thank.

I didn't come to Washington looking for the dysfunction described in these pages, and wish the reality I found was other than it is. I also didn't want to write a who's-up, who's-down, backroom political book—the challenges of our times, and the inspiration provided by our history, provoked a different ambition. George Gibson and Morgan Entrekin at Grove Atlantic saw the possibilities, and I am grateful for their confidence and for their team's professionalism.

Before I accepted the offer to become superintendent of the Denver Public Schools I placed a call to Brad Jupp, explaining that I would only take the job if he would work with me. Brad is a middle school language arts teacher, a leader of the 1994 teacher strike in Denver, and a deep believer in the urgent need to confront the profound inequities in our public education system. He agreed to come on board, and, with that contingency resolved, I went to work in the school system. As I once said to Arne Duncan, the secretary of education in the Obama administration, "There is only one Brad Jupp." Arne agreed—and he, too, hired Brad.

Over the last two years, Brad compiled binders filled with some of the best-known and most obscure American writing, much of it by founders of one kind or another. We read this material together and discussed its implications for many months. At the same time, he patiently sat at his computer at home in Washington, as I sat in front of mine in my study in Denver, working and reworking together one Google doc after another. He shares none of the blame for any faulty conclusions that I may have reached, but this book simply would not exist without Brad Jupp.

Finally, my wife, Susan; and our daughters Caroline, Halina, and Anne have sustained me in and out of politics and allowed me the time to pursue this additional project. I am grateful for their love, as well as their suggestions and advice. I am glad to have had the chance to put in one place what I have learned about the republic our daughters, along with the rest of their generation, will soon inherit. In that context, I also want to thank my brother, James; my sister, Holly; and their families for sharing so well the legacy conferred by our parents, Doug and Susie Bennet.